DRIVING TOURS
SCANDINAVIA

Macmillan • **USA**

Written by Kim Naylor

Original photography by Kim Naylor

Edited, designed and produced by AA Publishing.

Published by AA Publishing.

Published in the United States by Macmillan Travel
A Prentice Hall Macmillan Company
15 Columbus Circle
New York, NY 10023

Macmillan is a registered trademark of Macmillan, Inc.

ISBN 0-02-860072-X

Cataloging-in-Publication Data is available from the Library of Congress.

Color separation: Daylight Colour Art Pte, Singapore

Printed and bound in Italy by Printers SRL, Trento

Title page: *Halleviksstrand, Orust (Sweden)*

Opposite: *Lappish silverwork*

CONTENTS

INTRODUCTION

This book is not only a practical touring guide for the independent traveller, but is also invaluable for those who would like to know more about Scandinavia.

It is divided into the four main constituent countries, Denmark, Sweden, Norway and Finland, and excludes Iceland; each country contains between five and eleven tours. Where towns and villages have been described elsewhere in the book, the appropriate tour number is mentioned in brackets in the route directions. The tours start and finish in major towns and cities which we consider to be the best centres for exploration. Each tour has details of the most interesting places to visit *en route*. Side panels cater for special interests and requirements and cover a range of categories for those whose interest is in history, wildlife or walking, and those who have children. There are also panels which highlight scenic stretches of road along the routes and which give details of special events, gastronomic specialities, crafts and customs. The numbers link them to the appropriate main text.

The simple route directions are accompanied by an easy-to-use map of the tour and there are addresses of local tourist information centres in some of the towns *en route*, as well as in the start town.

Simple charts show how far it is from one town to the next in kilometres and miles. These can help you to decide where to take a break and stop overnight, for example. (All distances quoted are approximate.)

Before setting off it is advisable to check with the information centre at the start of the tour for recommendations on where to break your journey and for additional information on what to see and when to visit.

BANKS

Denmark: 09.30 to 16.00, Monday to Friday; Thursday, open until 18.00.

Sweden: 09.30 to 15.00, Monday to Friday; in larger towns banks may be open until 17.30, while in smaller places they may close earlier. Hours may be shortened on the eve of a bank holiday.

Norway: 08.15 to 15.30 (15.00 from June to September), Monday to Friday; Thursday, open until 17.00.

Finland: 09.00 to 16.15, Monday to Friday.

CREDIT CARDS

All principal credit cards (eg Access, American Express, Diners Card, Visa, Eurocard) are fairly widely accepted.

CURRENCY

Denmark: The unit of currency is the Danish crown (krone; abbreviated kr or DKK), divided into 100 øre. Notes are issued in denominations of 50, 100, 500, and 1,000 kr. Coins are issued in denominations of 25 and 50 øre and 1, 5, 10 and 20 kr.

Sweden: The unit of currency is the Swedish crown (krona; abbreviated kr or SEK), divided into 100 øre. Notes are issued in denominations of 10, 50, 100, 500 and 1,000 kr. Coins are issued in denominations of 10 and 50 øre and 1 and 5 kr.

Norway: The unit of currency is the Norwegian crown (krone; abbreviated kr or NOK), divided into 100 øre. Notes are issued for 50, 100 and 1,000 kr. Coins are issued in denominations of 50 øre and 1, 5 and 10 kr.

Finland: The unit of currency is the Finnish mark (markka, plural markkaa; abbreviated mk or Fmk), divided into 100 penniä (singular penni; abbreviated p). Notes are 10, 50, 100, 500 and 1,000 mk. Coins are issued in denominations of 10 and 50p and 1 and 5 mk.

CUSTOMS

Personal effects and travelling equipment may be taken into the Scandinavian countries without payment of duty. The import of hunting weapons and walkie-talkies and the export of certain works of art are subject to special regulations; further information can be obtained from the tourist offices.

Duty Free Allowances:

Denmark: 2 litres of wine and 1 litre of spirits; 200 cigarettes or 100 cigarillos or 50 cigars or 250g of tobacco. Travellers must be over 17 years old. The EU regulations apply to the import and export of alcohol and tobacco; the latest rules are posted on the ferries.

Sweden: 1 litre wine, 1 litre spirits

Maritime hardware for sale, Finland

Geiranger Fjord provides ocean liners deep access into Norway

ELECTRICITY

The current is generally 220 volts AC throughout Scandinavia, with plugs of the two round-pin type (an adaptor will therefore be needed). British, Australian or New Zealand appliances normally requiring a slightly higher voltage will work. Visitors from the US and Canada with appliances requiring 100/120 volts, and not fitted for dual voltage, will require a voltage transformer.

and 2 litres beer, or 2 litres wine and 2 litres beer (over 20 years old); 200 cigarettes or 100 cigarillos or 50 cigars or 250g tobacco (over 15 years old).
Norway: 1 litre wine, 1 litre spirits and 2 litres beer, or 2 litres wine and 2 litres beer (over 20 years old); 200 cigarettes or 250g of other tobacco goods (over 16 years old).
Finland: 2 litres of wine and 2 litres of beer, or 1 litre of wine, 1 litre of spirits and 2 litres of beer (over 20 years old – 18 year olds can import 2 litres of wine and 2 litres of beer); 200 cigarettes or 100 cigarillos or 50 cigars or 250g of tobacco (over 16 years old).

EMERGENCY NUMBERS

Denmark: tel: 112 for fire, police or ambulance
Sweden: tel: 9 00 00
Norway: look under SOS in the phone book for the local number.
Finland: tel: 112 for fire, police or ambulance

ENTRY REGULATIONS

UK, Irish, Australian, US and Canadian citizens require a valid passport (or a British Visitor's Passport) for entry into the Scandinavian countries.

HEALTH

There are no special health requirements or regulations. The Scandinavian countries have reciprocal health agreements with Britain under which British citizens can get certain services free and can obtain reimbursement of part of the cost of other services (retain all bills). Even so it is worth while taking out comprehensive insurance cover before leaving home; and citizens of countries which have no reciprocal health agreement should certainly do so.

MOTORING

Accidents

In the event of an accident, a report must be made to the insurance company. If the accident involves personal injury, medical assistance must be sought for the injured party and the incident reported to the police. There are special bureaux which deal with accidents involving foreign motor vehicles; local police will advise. Elks are numerous in parts of Sweden, Norway and Finland and they often cross the roads (the same applies to reindeer in Lappland). Warning signs showing the approximate lengths of the danger zones are posted in these areas. These animals weigh anything up to 500–600kg and collisions involving them are usually serious. Elks are most active at dusk but may also be encountered at other times. If you are involved in a reindeer or elk collision, report this without delay to the local police.

Breakdowns

In case of breakdown: in Denmark ask for the services of Dansk Autohjalp (tel: 31 31 21 44) or Falck (tel: 44 66 22 22); in Sweden contact Alarm Centres (020) 91 00 40 (free phone); in Norway contact Norges Automobil-Forbund (NAF) – Oslo, tel: (02) 34 16 00, Bergen, tel: (05) 29 24 62, Trondheim, tel: (07) 96 62 88, Tromso, tel: (083) 7 07 00. In Finland contact Autolitto, tel: (97) 00 80 80.

Car Hire

Car hire is available in most cities, resorts and main airports throughout Scandinavia. Many international firms operate this

FERRIES

The ferries to and around Scandinavia are excellent and are rather like mini-cruises on the longer services.

Denmark to Norway
Copenhagen–Oslo (16 hours): Scandinavian Seaways
Hirtshals–Oslo (10–13 hours): Color Line
Hirtshals–Kristiansand (4–7 hours): Color Line
Frederikshavn–Larvik (6–10 hours): Larvik Line
Frederikshavn–Oslo (9–12 hours): Stena Line
Frederikshavn–Moss (7 hours): Stena Line
Hanstholm–Egersund (7 hours): Fjord Line

Denmark to Sweden
Helsingør–Helsingborg (25 minutes): Scand Lines
Dragør–Limhamn (55 minutes): Limhamn–Dragør Line
Frederikshavn–Göteborg (4 hours): Stena Line
Grenå–Varberg (5 hours): Lion Ferry
Grenå–Halmstad (5 hours): Lion Ferry
Frederikshavn–Göteborg (2 hours): Seacatamaran
Rønne–Ystad (3 hours): Bornholmstrafikken

Sweden to Finland
Stockholm–Helsinki (15 hours): Silja Line, Viking Line, Birka Line
Stockholm–Turku (12 hours): Silja Line, Viking Line
Sundsvall–Vaasa (7 hours): Silja Line
Ornsköldsvik–Vaasa (5 hours): Skellefteå–Jakobstad (5 hours): Jakob Lines
Skellefteå–Karleby (4 hours): Jakob Lines
Umeå–Vaasa (3 hours): Wasa Line

PUBLIC HOLIDAYS

Denmark
1 January New Year's Day
Maundy Thursday
Good Friday
Easter Monday
Store Bededag (Prayer Day)
sometime in April or May
Ascension Day
Whit Monday
5 June Constitution Day
24–6 December Christmas

Sweden
1 January New Year's Day
6 January Epiphany
Good Friday
Easter Monday
1 May Labour Day
Ascension
Whit Monday
6 June National Day
All Saints (last Saturday in
October or first Saturday in
November)
24–6 December Christmas
31 December New Year's
Eve

Norway
1 January New Year's Day
Maundy Thursday
Good Friday
Easter Monday
1 May Labour Day
17 May National Day
Ascension
Whit Monday
25–6 December Christmas

Finland
1 January New Year's Day
6 January (or following
Saturday) Epiphany
Good Friday
Easter Monday
30 April–1 May May Day
Ascension Day
30 May Whitsun
All Saints (last Saturday in
October or first Saturday in
November)
24–6 December Christmas

Midsummer Day is celebrated
in Sweden, Norway and
Finland on the second-last
Friday/Saturday in June

TOURIST OFFICES

The Scandinavian Tourist
Boards are represented in
certain countries abroad,
including:
UK
Danish Tourist Board, Royal
Danish Embassy, 55 Sloane
Street, London SW1X 9SR
(0171 259 5959)
Swedish Travel and Tourism
Council, 73 Welbeck Street,
London W1M 8AN (tel: 0171
935 9784)
Norwegian Tourist Board,
5–11 Lower Regent Street,
London SW1Y 4IX (tel: 0171
839 2650)
Finnish Tourist Board, 66-8
Haymarket, London SW1Y
4RF (tel: 0171 839 4048)

US
The Danish Tourist Board, the
Swedish Travel and Tourism
Council and the Finnish and
Norwegian Tourist Boards
share the following address:
655 Third Avenue (18th floor),
New York NY 10017 (tel: 212-
286 0896)

*Clusters of wooden houses dot
Sweden's beautiful west coast*

service; local rivals – see the
Yellow Pages – often offer better
deals. Rates sometimes include
breakdown services, maintenance
and oil, but not petrol. Basic insurance is also included and additional cover can be bought. Costs
fluctuate according to type of car,
duration of rental and time of
year. The minimum age of the hir-
er varies from 18 to 25 years; they
should be in possession of an
international driving licence.
People travelling by air or rail can
take advantage of special inclu-
sive arrangements.

Documents
Tourists taking their own (therefore foreign-registered) car to
Scandinavia must be at least 18
years of age, and in possession of
the vehicle's registration docu-
ment, an international green card
or other insurance, and a valid,
full driving licence; it is also advisable to be in possession of an
international licence. There
should be a clearly visible sign
attached to the vehicle showing
the nationality.

Driving conditions
Vehicles must keep to the right-
hand side of the road and close to
the nearside kerb, even when the
road is clear. Side mirrors should
be fitted on the left-hand side of
the car. The wearing of seat belts
is compulsory in the front and
rear of the car. Dipped headlights
should be used at all times.

Route directions
Roads, except for the minor ones,
are numbered. A road prefixed by
an E denotes a main Europa road;
other roads are not prefixed by a
letter.

Speed limits
Denmark: In built-up areas 50kph
(30mph), outside built-up areas
80kph (50mph); on motorways
110kph (66mph).
Sweden: In built-up areas 50kph
(30mph), outside built-up areas
90kph (56mph); on motorways
110kph (66mph).

Norway: In built-up areas 50kph
(30mph), outside built-up areas
80kph (50mph); on motorways
generally 90kph (56mph).
Finland: In built up areas 50kph
(30mph), outside built-up areas
80kph (50mph); on motorways
120kph (75mph).

POST OFFICES

Denmark: mostly 09.00 to 17.00,
Monday to Friday; 09.00 to 12.00,
Saturday.
Sweden: 09.00 to 18.00, Monday
to Friday; 09.00 to 12.00, Saturday.
Norway: 08.00 or 08.30 to 16.00 or
17.00, Monday to Friday; 08.00 to
13.00 Saturday.
Finland: 09.00 to 17.00, Monday to
Friday.

TELEPHONES

The use of telephone cards (from
tobacconists and various other
outlets) is becoming increasingly
common in Scandinavia; for the
time being there are also coin
boxes in most towns, using 1, 5
and 10 kr/mk coins.

To call abroad use the following
international dialling codes:
Denmark to UK: 00 44
Denmark to US or Canada: 00 1
Sweden to UK: 009 44
Sweden to US or Canada: 009 1
Norway to UK: 095 44
Norway to US or Canada: 095 1
Finland to UK: 990 44
Finland to US or Canada: 990 1

TIME

Denmark, Sweden and Norway
follow Central European Time,
which is one hour ahead of
Greenwich Mean Time, while
Finland follows Eastern European
Time (two hours ahead of GMT).
Summer time – one hour ahead of
normal time – is observed from
the end of March to the end of
September.

Right: a Jutland mill at dusk

DENMARK

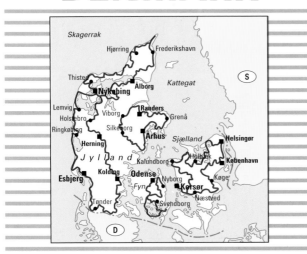

Denmark's long westernmost region of Jylland (Jutland) protrudes as a peninsula northwards from Germany, its west coast exposed to the winds and waves of the North Sea. The west coast is Denmark's wild quarter where trees are bent eastwards by the constant force of the winds and countless ships have been wrecked through the ages. It is a thinly populated region, traditionally inhabited by herring fishermen and farmers who scratched a living from the poor soils. However, this coast is blessed with one of the finest sand beaches in Europe, which stretches virtually unbroken from the Skallingen peninsula to the tip of the Prong (Grenen) at Skagen, Denmark's northernmost point. In summer the Danes flock here to stretch out and bask in the long warm hours of sunshine.

Push on eastwards and the land becomes increasingly populated and more intensely farmed. Home of Legoland, the flat potato and arable regions of central Jutland give way to the Lake Highland District, where hills up to 171m (561 feet) are the highest in Denmark. Beyond is the east coast; gentler, more sheltered and richer than the wild open west, there are many more towns here, the largest and most impressive being Århus. The southbound road from Århus forks near Fredericia for Fyn (Funen), the island stepping-stone between Jutland and Sjælland (Sealand), where Hans Christian Andersen was born. In Funen, crooked country lanes lead to castles and villages where narrow cobbled streets are lined by colourfully painted half-timbered cottages, with roses creeping around their doorways. The Danes delight in such places; they would call them *hygge*, a word which implies a sort of enchanting cosiness. Ferries leave Funen for the western ports of Sealand from where you are drawn irresistibly through a land scattered with royal and noble estates to the northeast corner of the country. Here Roskilde, København (Copenhagen), Helsingør and their surrounds provide a splendid climax to a journey through Denmark.

The Danish Council of Tourist Trade have devised the excellent 3,540km (2,325 mile) Marguerite Route which winds through Denmark's most picturesque countryside, linking the main attractions and sights. The tours outlined in this book trace selected sections of the Marguerite Route, a trail well signposted by a daisy symbol on a brown background.

København (Copenhagen)

With a population of 1.5 million, Copenhagen is Scandinavia's largest city. It was founded in the 12th century by Bishop Absalon, who built a fortification on the site of the present Christiansborg Palace. Despite this early beginning, it was not until 1416 that it became the capital of Denmark. King Christian IV (1588–1648) initiated an extravagant building programme which included the Rosenborg Palace, the Round Tower and the Old Stock Exchange; Christian V (1670–99) added his regal touch with Kongens Nytorv and Charlottenborg.

Esbjerg

Esbjerg lies on the west coast of Jutland, relatively sheltered from the winds of the North Sea behind the Skallingen peninsula and Fanø Island. As the port for British ferries from Harwich and Newcastle, Esbjerg is the English traveller's gateway to Denmark. The town evolved after south Jutland was lost to Germany in 1864, growing from a village of 30 souls to become Denmark's fifth largest city, with a population of 83,000. This rapid development is well documented in the Esbjerg Museum. Local seafaring lifestyles are explained at the Fisheries and Maritime Museum, where an aquarium and sealarium display the full range of Denmark's marine species. The Memorial Grove remembers the fishermen of Esbjerg who have lost their lives at sea. Other museums of interest are the Modern Art Museum, with 20th-century Danish art, and the Printing Press Museum, which explains the craft of printing through the ages. Esbjerg's principal landmark since 1897, the restored Water Tower has a museum with changing exhibitions.

Nykøbing

Situated on the island of Mors in Limfjorden, Nykøbing is one of the larger old market and fishing towns of northern Jutland. Local traditions and crafts are on display at the medieval Dueholm Kloster (Dueholm Cloister) and at other more specialised museums, such as the Mor's Tractor Museum. Jesperhus, a short drive west of town, is Scandinavia's largest flower park and lists among its attractions a butterfly house, an aviary, an aquarium, a terrarium and activities for children.

Århus

With its busy port, commercial centre, opera, symphony orchestra, renowned art museum, university and young and vibrant streetlife, Denmark's second largest city is Jutland at its most cosmopolitan, sophisticated and fashionable. Århus was originally a Viking settlement (whose history is told in the Viking Museum) and it flourished during the medieval period, as the huge cathedral stands testament.

Boats depart from Copenhagen's
old harbour of Nyhavn

Århus' modern landmark is the City Hall, built in 1941 with a finish of Norwegian marble and a 60m (200 feet) tower from where there is a panoramic view of the city. But the city's greatest pride is Den Gamle By, a collection of some 70 traditional town buildings which have been gathered from around Denmark and reassembled as the Old Town.

Odense

Odense's star attraction is Hans Christian Andersen, who was born in the city in 1805, the son of a shoemaker. His childhood home is now the H C Andersen Barndomshjem Museum, while the house of his birth, in another quarter of the town centre, is the H C Andersen Museum. Close to the latter is the Carl Nielsen Museum, which commemorates the famous composer who was born in a nearby village. Quaint, traditional Funen is portrayed at the open-air heritage museum, but any fairytale image this medieval cathedral city may have is rather overshadowed by its present size and purpose; it is a modern industrial centre and the third largest city in the country.

Korsør

For the past 1,000 years the small port of Korsør has been the entrance into Sealand for travellers from Funen. The history of this role as ferry terminus is related in the Museum of Korsør, housed in the old cannon hall of the castle. All that remains of the castle's original medieval structure is the 23m (75 feet) -high tower, which is open to visitors.

The Little Mermaid, a mariner's
dream on Copenhagen waterfront

4 days – 796km (495 miles)

JYLLAND (JUTLAND)

Esbjerg • Blåvand to Ringkøbing • Lemvig Salling to Holstebro • Herning to Billund • Kolding to Åbenrå • Løgumkloster to Højer • Ribe • Esbjerg

Jutland's west coast is wild and windy in winter, but come summer the unending stretches of fabulous wide sand beach are bathed in long hours of sunshine. This tour follows the west coast northwards from Esbjerg and then cuts inland, heading southwards through the flat farmlands of central Jutland, via Legoland, to the gentler east coast. Beyond Kolding the route continues into southern Jutland, a region once annexed by Germany. It follows the present German border before turning north through the marshlands to Ribe (Denmark's oldest town) and back to Esbjerg.

BACK TO NATURE

1 The island of **Tipperne** in Ringkøbing Fjord is a sanctuary for ducks, geese and swans.

FOR HISTORY BUFFS

1 A countless number of ships have been wrecked along this wild western coast. The greatest disaster occurred on the night of Christmas Eve, 1811, when two English vessels, the flagship HMS *St George* and HMS *Defence*, were dashed against the rocks off Torsminde with the loss of more than 1,300 men. Objects salvaged or washed ashore from the wrecks off the west coast are on display at the **Strandingsmuseum** in Torsminde.

ⓘ Skolegade 33, Esbjerg

From Esbjerg follow the coast road, via Hjerting, to Billum and Oksbøl. Then take road 431 west for 36km (22 miles) to Blåvand. From Blåvand it is about 91km (55 miles) to Ringkøbing.

Blåvand to Ringkøbing, West Jutland

1 Beyond Blåvand a **lighthouse** marks Denmark's most westerly point; by climbing the tower you get a view of the reef it warns mariners to avoid. The narrow peninsula of sand and marshland which projects south of Blåvand is Skallingen, an empty land rich in birdlife. The West Jutland coast north of Blåvand consists of an unbroken stretch of magnificent wide sand beach backed by high *klitter* (dunes) or *klinter* (cliffs).
Take the road northwards through patchy woodland and continue beyond the resort of Henne Strand to join road 181. This becomes the route along Holmsland Klit, the long,

---

The Danes gave the world the little plastic building brick and from it evolved Legoland

narrow spit of sand which is both the shore and the barrier between the large inland waters of Ringkøbing Fjord and the open North Sea. A view of the sea on the left is obscured by the dunes, but there are parking spots along the way and to reach the beach simply climb over the *klit*. A short waterway at Hvide Sande (White Sand) serves as the mouth between fjord and ocean. There are few settlements on this exposed west coast and the harbour of the small, busy fishing port of Hvide Sande finds shelter on the inner side of the fjord's lip.
Ringkøbing, inland on road 15, flourished during the Middle Ages as a fishing town in the same way as Hvide Sande does today and was without rival along this stretch of coast. However, shifting sands began to reshape the shoreline and eventually closed the gap which had long allowed Ringkøbing easy access to the outer seas, and it literally became a backwater. Nowadays it is a pleasant market town which retains something of its traditional character in its small cobbled streets and 17th-century merchants' and shipowners' houses.

ⓘ Torvet, Ringkøbing

From Ringkøbing continue northwards on road 16, returning to the coast and road 181 via Stadil church. The 181 runs along the narrow strip of Bovling Klit (Nissum Fjord is to the right), through the fishing village of Torsminde and bears inland before the Bovbjerg cliffs at Ferring. Bear right for Lemvig on road 513 (74km/46 miles).

Lemvig, West Jutland

2 The small town of Lemvig is found at the end of a bay in a dip known as the 'Buttonhole of Lemvig'. Its fishing fleet once trawled local waters for herring, but today there are fewer ships and they have to sail far into the North Sea and the Atlantic in search of cod. Lemvig's exhibitions focus on shipwrecks off these western shores and the works of local artist, Niels Bjerre. The 'astral poet' Thøger Larsen was also from this region, and there is a pleasant walk along the 12km (7 mile) **Path of Planets** (Planetstien), following the shore of the bay. Scaled models of the planets are placed at appropriate distances beside the route.

ⓘ Toldbodgade 4

From Lemvig return to the 181 and just before Thyborøn catch the ferry across the mouth of the Nissum Bredning (12 minutes). Continue on the 181, past the fishing village of Agger, and head inland via Vestervig church and Hurup to catch the ferry for the Island of Mors (5 minutes). Cross the island on road 545, via Jesperhus Blomsterpark (flower park), and take the bridge (road 26) over the sound to the Salling peninsula (80km/50 miles).

SPECIAL TO...

1 Located nearer to Kolby than Stadil village, the small medieval parish church of Stadil has a splendid and rare 'golden altar' dating from around 1200.

SPECIAL TO...

2 There are many prehistoric burial sites scattered around Jutland. One is at Ydby Moor, 10km (6 miles) south of Hurup, which has around 200 tumuli.

SCENIC ROUTE

3 The countryside of central Jutland tends to be relatively flat and dull. However, the moorlands between Holstebro and Herning turn rich shades of purple when the heathers flower between July and August. There are peatlands south of Herning and lignite used to be mined around Søby, where the Lignite Museum (Brunkulsmuseet) can be found.

Blåvand lighthouse, on Denmark's westernmost point

Salling Peninsula to Holstebro, Limfjorden Country

3 The tour bears right off road 26 and follows the western shore of the Salling peninsula, which juts into Limfjorden, via Krejbjerg and Rødding, to Spottrup. Dating from around 1500, the splendid medieval fort of Spottrup has two moats separated by a large earth rampart. Seemingly impregnable to attack, it fell into ruin and had to be restored before opening to the public in 1937. The estate includes a medicinal herb garden.

Continue to wend a southward path along country lanes to **Sahl**, where the church has a medieval 'golden altar' (the only other one of this kind being at Stadil church). Near by are the moorlands of **Hjerl Hede** and the **Frilandsmuseum** (open-air museum) where village life from a bygone time has been neatly reconstructed. The scene is all the more lively in July, when craftsmen create their wares in the old-fashioned way, plump oxen pull wooden carts laden high with hay, and hearty peasants in traditional costume go about their business. It is a cosy presentation of the Danes' rural roots.

Follow minor roads via Borbjerg to **Holstebro**, a fairly uninspiring market town which has acquired some excellent art. Sculptures – of which the most talked about piece at present is the laser sculpture by Frithioff Johansen – are scattered around the town.

ⓘ Brostræde 2, Holstebro

From Holstebro continue west on road 16, bearing south cross country (via Vind) to Ørnhøj, and then east to Vildbjerg and Herning (52km/32 miles). From Herning to Billund is 68km (42 miles).

FOR CHILDREN

4 Although Lego was created in the 1930s by Ole Kirk Christiansen, it was to be another 20 years before his son, Godtfred, developed the Lego system we are familiar with today. **Legoland** is in Billund and every year it attracts well over a million visitors. There are miniature monuments and country and townscapes from around the world, thousands of objects using over 42 million Lego bricks, funparks, the magnificent Titania Palace dolls' house and much more for the kids. Legoland is open from the end of April to mid-September. The nearby **Mobilium** incorporates the Aviation, Car and Falck Salvage Corp Museums. Four kilometres (3 miles) away is the **Billund Terrarium** with crocodiles, snakes and other reptiles.

SPECIAL TO...

7 Three islands off this stretch of the west coast are worth noting: **Rømø** – enjoyed for its splendid long sand beach – is linked to the mainland by a causeway and tends to be favoured by German visitors; tiny **Mandø** can be reached at low tide by a tractor-bus, and a colony of seals can sometimes be seen in Koresand to the south; **Fanø** – connected by a ferry service from Esbjerg – has well-preserved fishermen's and captains' houses, and a good beach on the northwest of the island.

Herning to Billund, West Jutland

4 Located in the centre of Jutland, Herning is a conference venue, the capital of Denmark's textile industry and the home of the itinerant *hosekræmmere* (sock salesman). Although these are hardly recommendations for a visitor, the town does have an eclectic selection of interesting art. The **Herning Museum** contains a collection of 57 miniature diaramas recounting 'A Year on Jens Nielsen's Farm'. A further 46 such displays are on show at the 16th-century **Herningsholm manor** and reveal 'A September Day on Jens Nielsen's Farm'; the moorland poet Steen Steensen Blicher, is also remembered. In addition, the **Danish Museum of Photography** is at Herning and the delightful 3,000 sq m (32,100 sq feet) **Japanese Garden** is east of the town at **Hammerum**. But of greatest significance are the collections of modern art at the **Herning Art Gallery**, housed in a converted shirt factory, and the museum devoted to the works of the COBRA artists, Carl-Henning Pedersen and Else Alfelt. Both galleries are found at **Birk**, 3km (2 miles) from Herning and *en route* to Hammerum.

Continue south from Herning, branching left off road 18 at Høgild to take minor roads via Fasterholt to **Brande**, where in the 1960s and '70s the people painted their art as murals on the sides of houses. Continue on the other side of road 18 to Billund and Legoland.

🛈 Bredgade 2, Herning

From Billund take road 28 east, bearing right for Randbøl and Egtved, and then via Jordrup to Kolding (43km/28 miles). It is 94km (58 miles) from Kolding to Åbenrå.

The magnificently restored Kolding Castle

Kolding to Åbenrå, South Jutland

5 The castle of **Koldinghus**, around which the town of Kolding grew, dates from the 13th century and served the Danes as a border defence and gateway to Schleswig-Holstein to the south until 1864. Billeted here in 1808, on their way to Sweden, Spanish soldiers serving Napoleon were horrified by the coldness of the Scandinavian winter and rather over eagerly stoked the fires, burning down much of the castle. This large building on the hill has recently been imaginatively restored and now houses a museum. Kolding's **Geographical Garden** has over 2,000 different species of plants from around the world.

Taking the minor road nearest the coast, continue south to **Christiansfeld**, a pretty town founded in the 18th century by the Moravian Brotherhood and famous today for its sweet honey cakes. Further south is **Haderslev**, a small pleasant cathedral city from where a minor coastal road leads to the old port of Åbenrå.

🛈 Akseltorv 8, Kolding; Sønderbro 3, Haderslev; H P Hanssensgade 5, Åbenrå

From Åbenrå continue south to Kliplev and then westwards parallel to the German border, bearing northwards after Rens to Løgumkloster (77km/48 miles). It is a further 33km (20 miles) from Løgumkloster to Højer .

Løgumkloster to Højer, South Jutland

6 All that has survived from the medieval Cistercian abbey of Løgumkloster is the church, the small town it spawned and a 49-bell carillon which is used for courses in campanology. Further south is **Tønder**; once a busy port, market town and centre for lacemaking, it had significant trade with the

Netherlands. The 17th- and 18th-century **merchants' houses** have been splendidly restored and the local **museum** recounts the town's rich history. Located 4km (3 miles) to the west, the village of **Møgeltønder** is charming with its thatched houses and cobbled streets.

The road continues west then north to **Højer**, an isolated town on the marshlands of southwest Jutland with old buildings and a tall windmill. This area, rich in birdlife, is protected by the Ramsa Convention.

From Højer head north along the minor roads through the flatlands and then via Brøns to Ribe (54km/34 miles).

Ribe, West Jutland

7 Danes – or at least Jutlanders – will say Ribe is the most delightful town in the country. It is certainly the oldest, officially dating from 860 when a charter was granted to construct a church. The present Romanesque **cathedral** of Rhinish rock has been the heart and hub of the city ever since it was built in the early 12th century. Climb the tower for a fine view over the town, country and the sea beyond. Originally a port, Ribe is now 7km (4 miles) inland. The town's influence waned in the 17th century when power and privilege passed to Copenhagen. However, many houses from the prosperous period still stand and around 550 are under preservation order. Happily, the place is not over self-conscious of its precious past and it remains well lived in, with the feel of a bustling small town. Local history and treasures are displayed at **Quedens Gård**, a half-timbered

The cobbled streets of Ribe

merchant's house. The tourist office provides a plan of a suggested walking route around the most interesting quarter of the town.

i Torvet 3–5, Ribe

From Ribe take road 24 north for 29km (18 miles) to Esbjerg.

Esbjerg – Blåvand 36 (22)
Blåvand – Ringkøbing 91 (57)
Ringkøbing – Lemvig 74 (46)
Lemvig – Salling (Harre) 80 (50)
Salling – Holstebro 65 (40)

The black top hat is part of the chimney-sweeps traditional attire

Holstebro – Herning 52 (32)
Herning – Billund 68 (42)
Billund – Kolding 43 (28)
Kolding – Åbenrå 94 (58)
Åbenrå – Løgumkloster 77 (48)
Løgumkloster – Ribe 87 (54)
Ribe – Esbjerg 29 (18)

3 days – 611km (380 miles)

NORTH JYLLAND (NORTH JUTLAND)

Nykøbing • Thisted • Hanstholm to Store Vildemose • Løkken to Hirtshals • Skagen Frederikshavn to Hjallerup • Ålborg Nibe to Nykøbing

The tour takes a pleasant meandering path beside the sea and through the gentle countryside of northern Jutland. Virtually the whole coastline comprises splendid sand beach and is dotted with fishing villages and summer resorts. In this region of small parochial towns, there are two places of international renown: Skagen, at the northern tip of Denmark, which is best known for the turn-of-the-century 'Skagen Painters', and Ålborg, the country's fourth largest city.

SPECIAL TO...

With the large expanse of Limfjorden having outlets on both the east and west coasts, this northern part of Jutland is, in effect, an island.

SPECIAL TO...

3 In 1808 the English frigate *Crescent* foundered in these west coast waters, with the loss of 240 lives. The ship's anchor is kept at Mårup church, just south of Lønstrup, and the bodies of the drowned sailors are buried in three common graves in the churchyard.

SPECIAL TO...

1 The north coast of Jutland is particularly rich in golden amber, the hardened resin from the pines which covered northern Europe 40 million years ago. It is washed on to the beaches, especially after a storm.

The windmill on Boel Hill marks the site of King Canute's camp during the 1086 Jutland campaign

ⓘ Havnen 4, Nykobing

*From Nykøbing take the **581** north for 15km (9 miles). Bear left at Sønder Dråby; drive a further 25km (16 miles) for Sundby to join road **26** for Thisted.*

Thisted, Limfjord Country

1 Situated on a bay on the western shore of Limfjord, Thisted is the main town of Thy, the narrow neck of land between fjord and ocean. The region was well populated during the Bronze Age and finds from that period are displayed at the **local museum**. Also on show is an exhibition of the life of the writer J P Jacobsen who was born in Thisted in 1847 and died here 38 years later; his works include *Marie Grubbe* and *Niels Lyhne*. Other local sons of note are educationalist Kristen Kold, scientist Malthe Conrad Bruun and the Very Reverend H C Sonne, the man who founded Denmark's popular co-op shopping system (of which the Brugsen shops are one of the principal outlets). Thisted's nearest seaside resorts are at **Nørre Vorupør** (22km/13 miles), where fishermen still haul their boats on to the beach, and **Klitmøller** further up the coast.

ⓘ Store Torv

*From Thisted take road **539** west to the coast at Nørre Vorupør. Continue north, parallel to the beach on road **181**, via Klitmøller, to Hanstholm (44km/27 miles). From here it is a further 143km (89 miles) to Store Vildemose.*

The red lodge, Voergård estate

Hanstholm to Store Vildemose, North Jutland

2 Hanstholm is approached through the **Hansted Reservat**, a land of woods, dunes and bogs preserved for their rich local wildlife. The reserve's 50sq km (19 sq miles) is Denmark's largest uninhabited region. The fishing and ferry port of **Hanstholm** was a strategic headland during World War II and visitors are taken to the **museum of local history** in the underground bunkers by an old munitions train. It takes 31 hours by boat from the port to Torshavn on the Faroe Islands.

From Hanstholm cut inland on road 26 and after Ræhr continue on road 29 to Øslos. From here turn north, via Skarup and around Lund Fjord (where a road leads through Torup Plantage to the sea at Bulbjerg, a 47m (154 feet) -high cliff), and then eastwards to Fjerritslev and northeast to Slettestrand. From Slettestrand head east and then south along country roads, past Lerup church. Cross road 11 and turn left to Torslev and Vesterby along the next significant road. Turn north again to Halvrimmen, Rødhus, Blokhus and Saltum, and cut southeast, via Sønder Saltum, to road 559 and the heart of Store Vildemose. Covering 6,500 hectares (1,600 acres) of raised waterlogged bogs, this 'Great Bogland' was Denmark's last wilderness until it, too, was increasingly brought under the plough during this century.

ⓘ Bytorvet 2, Hanstholm

*From the junction of the **559** and **585** in Store Vildemose turn north to Stenum and continue west to Vrensted and Løkken. Lokken to Hirtshals is 58km (36 miles).*

Løkken to Hirtshals, North Jutland

3 Løkken is the most commercial of the resorts along this coast of sand and dune, and should be avoided or embraced according to personal taste. Double back from here to Vrensted and head north into hillier countryside and to **Børglum Kloster**, where King Knud den Hellige (Canute the Holy) set up residence in 1086. The local peasants, however, rose up against Canute after he attempted to levy taxes on them. The king fled from Jutland to Funen where he was killed by a spear hurled through a window while praying in the church of St Alban in Odense. The bishopric of North Jutland was transferred to Børglum in 1135 and the building of the abbey commenced later in the 12th century. Although the plans for a great cathedral never came to fruition, the **abbey** flourished until its closure at the time of the Reformation in 1536. The monastery was painstakingly rebuilt in its present style in the mid-18th century by the architect Laurids de Thurah and remained in his family until 1835, when it passed to the present owners, the Rottbøl family. The monastery's Gothic church has a rococo interior with an impressive 15m (49 feet) -high baroque altarpiece.

From Børglum Kloster continue north to **Lønstrup**, a fishing village and a prettier and more stylish resort than Løkken. Here, a 12km (7 mile) -long stretch of cliff rises above the beach, with Rubjerg Knude reaching a height of 74m (243 feet), just south of Lønstrup. In 1900 a 22m (72 feet) -high lighthouse was erected on the Rubjerg cliff to warn shipping of the danger, but in 1968 its lamp was extinguished for good; a sand dune had built up in front of the tower, virtually obscuring it from the sea. At present the **lighthouse** contains a museum of natural sand movements, but it is only a matter of time before the tower will have to be abandoned, buried by the relentless drifting sands of this western coast.

From Lønstrup turn inland and pick up road 55 for **Hirtshals**, a purpose-built port constructed between 1919 and 1930. It harbours one of Denmark's largest fishing fleets and is a major ferry point for services to Norway. The town's **North Sea Museum** has a sealarium and aquariums of the local marine life.

☐ Møstingvej 3, Løkken; Strandvejen 90, Lønstrup; Nørregade 40, Hirtshals

*From Hirtshals take road **597** eastwards, turning north on road **40** for Skagen (48km/30 miles).*

Skagen, North Jutland

4 During the medieval period Skagen – pronounced 'Skane' – was a busy town with around 2,500 inhabitants. But in the 18th century the drifting sands became ever more destructive, covering town and fields and forcing most of the population to move elsewhere. A dash of life returned to Skagen during the Danish war with England around 1808, when privateers came here for 'rest and recreation'. Skagen was assured a permanent future, however, after the railway was extended here from Frederikshavn in 1890 and the town became a port and a highly fashionable resort.

Skagen is on the east shore while Old Skagen, or Højen, is on the west coast. Artists were drawn here by the dramatic light and came to capture the seascapes and fishermen's lifestyles. In the early 20th century a clique known as the 'Skagen Painters' evolved around artists Michael and Anna Ancher and P S Krøyer; examples of the group's work are displayed at the **Skagen Museum** and **Anchers Hus**.

Skagen remains special: in its streets are the old houses from the 'yellow' and 'red' periods, there is the pervasive smell of fish, the taste of salt air and the artistic atmosphere. Known as **the Grenen** (the Prong), the tip of the peninsula is a short distance beyond the town; a lift can be taken on the tractor-bus for the last stretch. The waters of Skagerrak and Kattegat meet at the end of this sandy point and Danes

come here to stand astride Grenen, with a foot in each sea. Do not venture out too far, however, the currents are very strong here.

☐ Railway Station, Sct Laurentii Vej

*From Skagen take road **40** south, via the fishing village and resort of Ålbæk, to the busy ferry port of Frederikshavn (40km/25 miles). From here to Hjallerup it is a further 56km (35 miles).*

Frederikshavn to Hjallerup, North Jutland

5 Known as the 'cheapest shopping place in Denmark' (and Scandinavia, depending on exchange rates), Frederikshavn is one of the world's busiest ferry ports, with services primarily to Sweden and Norway. From here take the country road (in preference to the E45) via Understed to **Sæby**. The 16th-century manor of Sæby (Sæbygard) was once the 'country' residence of the bishops of Borglum and home of the Arenfeldt family for over 250 years. In 1989 it became a museum with a golf course in the grounds.

From Sæby continue south along the coast and bear right to join the 541 to Lyngså and Voerså. Thereafter turn inland to reach **Præstbro** and **Voergård**, where a manor initially built in 1510 by Niels Stygge Rosenkrantz, Bishop of Borglum, was lavishly added to in the Renaissance style in the 1580s by Ingeborg Steel, the lady of the house, who threw her builder in the moat in order to save on his fees. Continue to **Dorf** and **Dronninglund**, where the castle – originally a medieval abbey – is now a conference centre. Turn west along the 559 to **Hjallerup**. The large annual 'vagabond' market here was traditionally a horse fair attracting dealers from all over Jutland.

☐ Brotorvet 1, Frederikshavn; Krystaltorvet 1, Sæby

From Hjallerup continue to Ravnstrup; then head southwest via Grindsted and Sulsted church to Lindholm Høje and Ålborg (26km/16 miles).

The church to the south of Frederikshavn

SPECIAL TO...

3 The medieval capital of the Vendsyssel (east of Lonstrup), **Hjørring** has three 12th–13th-century churches: St Olai, St Catharinae and St Hans. The **Vendsyssel Historical Museum** provides a sound account of the history of this corner of North Jutland.

SPECIAL TO...

4 At one time, Jutland's northern coast was the ridge between Hirtshals and Frederikshavn, but over the years the sea and westerly winds have shifted the sand to create the present northern tip. The elements continue to shape this landscape, and the most dramatic example of the wind's work is the **Rabjerg Mile** – a huge sand dune, 20km south of Skagen, which migrates eastwards about 8m (26 feet) every year. Visit the 14th-century **church of Saint Laurence** (the sand-buried church), which started to suffer from the sands in 1600. Despite all their efforts, the parishioners were unable to save their church from the drifts, and in 1795 they were allowed by royal decree to give up the struggle and build afresh. Today, only the steeple remains visible.

BACK TO NATURE

4 In spring many migratory birds fly northeast to Norway, Sweden and Finland to rear their young during the long warm days of the northern summer; they return southwestwards in autumn to avoid the dark cold winters. Denmark is on their migratory path and Skagen is one of the stopping points for various birds during their long voyage. At the base of the Skagen peninsula, in the village of **Tuen**, there is the **Ørnens Verden eagle sanctuary**, where white-tailed and golden eagles and other birds of prey are bred; visitors are welcome.

Ålborg, North Jutland

6 Built on the site of a Viking settlement at the narrowest point of Limfjord, Aalborg is the main city of North Jutland. A busy port and commercial centre, it has some very fine Renaissance buildings, notably the **house built for Jens Bang** in 1624 (Østerågade 9). A wealthy shipbuilder, Bang failed to gain election into the municipal council and responded by having one of his window ornaments carved with a man sticking his tongue out at the Town Hall across the road. Other buildings of interest in this downtown quarter are **Jørgen Olufsen's** three-storeyed **house** built in 1616, the 15th-century **St Budolfi Cathedral** and the 16th-century **Ålborghus Castle** beside the harbour; with its many restaurants and bars, Jomfru Ane Gade is one of the liveliest streets in Denmark. On show at the **Maritime Museum** is the 54m (177 feet) -long Danish submarine *Springeren*, while the excellent **Nordjyllands Kunstmuseum** (the modern art museum) displays 20th-century Danish and international works of art.

ℹ Østerågade 8

From Ålborg take the 180 southwards and then bear west on the 187 to Nibe (21km/13 miles). It is a further 135km (84 miles) from Nibe to Nykøbing.

Nibe to Nykøbing, North Jutland

7 Bearing the old word for herring as its name and displaying three herrings on its coat of arms, it comes as no surprise that the pleasant town of Nibe was famous in the Middle Ages for its herrings.

However, the waters of its *bredning* were exhausted of herring by the mid-19th century and today the fishermen of Nibe catch eel, trout and flounder.

Continue on the 567, bearing left at Sebbersund for Borup and then right for Limfjorden and the town of **Løgstør**, another erstwhile herring community. Løgstør became the focus of national attention on 13 July 1861 when King Frederik VII opened the 5km (3 mile) canal, thus by-passing the sandbar which had long hindered easy access from the eastern waters to Limfjorden; an improved channel was dug at the turn of the century and the Frederik VII canal was closed in 1913.

From Løgstør head south on road 533, past the ruined medieval **abbey of Vitskol**. Turn left at Strandby for Farsø and Ålestrup, with its **bicycle museum**. Return to Limfjorden, via Fjelsø and Gedsted, and take the ferry from Hvalpsund to Sundsøre on the Salling peninsula. Continue along the minor road which follows the Salling shore through Grættrup, Selde, Åsted and Glyngøre. Join road 26 and cross Salling Sund to regain Nykøbing.

ℹ Torvet 2, Nibe; Sønderport 2A, Løgstør

Nykøbing – Thisted 40 (25)
Thisted – Hantsholm 44 (27)
Hantsholm – Løkken 143 (89)
Løkken – Hirtshals 58 (36)
Hirtshals – Skagen 48 (30)
Skagen – Frederikshavn 40 (25)
Frederikshavn – Hjallerup 56 (35)
Hjallerup – Aalborg 26 (16)
Aalborg – Nibe 21 (13)
Nibe – Nykøbing 135 (84)

2 days – 435km (271 miles)

The 2,200-year-old Tollund Man has aged well; he rests in peace in his glass coffin in Silkeborg

ℹ Radhuset, Århus

*From Århus follow the **coast road** south through Moesgård, Norsminde, Saksild and Gylling. Continue to Sondrup and turn northwards, via Hundslund, to road **445** and on to Skanderborg (77km/48 miles), southern gateway to the Lake Highlands. Continue through Denmark's Lake Highlands to Silkeborg, via Tåning, Alken, Ry, Gammel Rye and Rødelund (43km/27 miles).*

Lake Highlands, East Jutland

1 To talk of the Danish highlands in the context of Scandinavia as a whole only emphasises the flatness of Denmark in comparison to its Nordic neighbours. The country's highest peak is Ejer Bavnehøj at 171m (561 feet), southwest of the old town of Skanderborg. But the Danes are proud of this little pocket of hills and lakes. They come to the small towns of Ry and Gammel Rye and climb Himmelbjerget (Heaven's Mountain) which, at 147m (482 feet), was long thought of as Denmark's highest point and is still the spiritual summit of the nation. The **Hjejlen**, one of the oldest functioning paddle steamers in the world, has been in operation here since 1861 and provides a passenger service along Lake Julsø, between the 'mountain' and Silkeborg (1 hour 15 minutes), at the northern end of this unique corner of Denmark. **Silkeborg** is a modern town famous for its 2,200-year-old 'bog man'. The well-preserved body of the Tollund Bog Man was unearthed in 1950 and is now enclosed in glass at the town's **museum**. Works by the COBRA (COpenhagen, BRussels and Amsterdam) group of artists are exhibited at the **Art Gallery**. The group was founded by Asger Jorn (1914–73) who lived for a while in Silkeborg.

ℹ Adelgade 105, Skandeborg; Klostervej 3, Ry; Godthabsvej 4, Silkeborg

*From Silkeborg take road **52** northwards, bearing left for Vinderslev, Nørre Knudstrup, Torning and then Kjellerup. Continue on road **52**, bearing left for Vium to allow Viborg to be approached from the heathland hills of Dollerup and Hald Sø (Lake Hald) (55km/34 miles).*

Viborg, East Jutland

2 The twin towers of Viborg's large Romanesque **cathedral** are visible from afar. Dating from the late 19th century, they were constructed after the old cathedral burnt down in the 1860s; however, it was decided to rebuild the new granite church in the original 12th-century style. Inside the building, the frescos of biblical scenes were painted by Joakim Skovgaard at the turn of this century. The **Skovgaard Museum** is near by. 'Genuine' old buildings are found in the quarter around the cathedral square, in St Mogens Gade, Nytorv (New Square), the city's cemetery until 1584, and Hjultorv. Situated in St Mikkels Gade, the fine Gothic brick **church of Sønder Sogns Kirke** (1275) has a magnificent early 16th-century altarpiece.

ℹ Nytorv 9, Viborg

From Viborg head east to Vejrum and pass through Ørum, Tjele, Vammen, Hvornum, Hobro and Mariager to reach Randers (80km/50 miles). From Randers it is 95km (59 miles) to Grenå.

Randers to Grenå, East Jutland

3 Traditionally known as the hub of 13 country roads and the location of three abbeys, the old market town of Randers is the gateway to the pretty Djurland peninsula to the east, a region famous for its manors.
Head east from Randers and cross the fjord at Mellerup, the shortest ferry route in Denmark at 472m (516 yards). Continue through Ørsted and Allingåbro to reach **Gammel Estrup manor**, just before Auning. Surrounded by a moat, this impressive manor castle has its origins in the 14th century, though much of the present red-brick Renaissance building dates from the mid-1700s. The Skeel family owned Gammel Estrup for 10 generations and the rooms remain decorated with their effects. The interesting **Agricultural Museum** is in the outbuildings, exhibiting old farming implements and techniques. A blacksmith is at work at the **Old Smithy** (Den Gamle Smedje).
From Auning head northeast through Gjesing and Fjellerup to pass Mejlgård manor on the way to the beach at Bønnerup Strand.

EAST JYLLAND (EAST JUTLAND)

Århus • Lake Highlands • Viborg • Randers to Grenå • Ebeltoft • Århus

Compared to West Jutland, the lands of East Jutland are richer and more populated, its shores more sheltered and its waters calmer. From Århus, the second largest city in Denmark, the tour follows the coast south and cuts inland through Denmark's modest Lake Highlands and the pretty heather fields of Dollerup to Viborg, the former capital of Jutland. From here the route turns eastwards to the peninsula of Djursland and the delightful town of Ebeltoft. The picturesque path back to Arhus is through Mols and passes the Renaissance castle of the Rosenkrantz family.

SCENIC ROUTE

1 The old steam locomotives DSB Litr F 665 and F 658 provide a service along the scenic 5km (3 mile) stretch of rail between Bryrup and Vrads, on the western edges of the Lake District. The engine runs at the weekends from Easter to November, and for the whole of July.

SCENIC ROUTE

2 The **Hærvejen** (the military road) started from Viborg and ran southwards to Schleswig in Germany. Today hikers and cyclists follow sections of this ancient path which was once the main north–south route through Jutland.

SPECIAL TO...

3 With its cobbled streets and rose-clad, half-timbered houses, quaint **Mariager** is promoted as the prettiest village in Denmark. A vintage steam train operates in summer from here to Handest. Once or twice a day it continues to Randers.

FOR CHILDREN

3 There is a Djurs Sommerland-Aquapark for kids near **Nimtofte**, between Auning and Grenå. The entry fee provides access to all amusements.

SPECIAL TO...

4 The people of this region of Mols are traditionally the butt of Danish jokes. One story recounts how the locals decided to submerge their church bell far out at sea, for fear of it being stolen by marauders; they sank the bell, notching on the side of the boat a groove to mark the exact spot. They rowed back to the shore, supremely confident that they knew the location of their treasure.

FOR HISTORY BUFFS

4 The Swedish resistance fighter, Gustav Vasa, was captured by the Danes and held in the tower of **Kalø fort** near Ronde, between Ebeltoft and Århus. He escaped in 1519 and fled home to raise a force which ousted the Danes from Sweden. He remains Sweden's great national hero.

SPECIAL TO...

4 The Rosenkrantz from Shakespeare's *Hamlet* had a family home at **Rosenholm Castle**, between Ebeltoft and Århus. With its moat and spired towers, this is one of the most spectacular of Djursland's Renaissance manors. It was built by State Counsellor Jørgen Rosenkrantz in the later 1500s and remains the private property of the Rosenkrantz family. Rooms are open to the public and there are over 100 portraits of the famous dynasty on display. Rosenholm is near Hornslet.

Continue to Gjerrild. The nearby **Sostrup Castle** (1600) was also the property of the Skeel family; since 1960 it has been a Cistercian convent, where visitors are welcome and accommodation is available.

Follow the road to **Grenå**, Denmark's geographical centre, which has ferry services to Sealand and ports on the west coast of Sweden. A **toy and fishing museum** can be found in the town, while the Kattegat Centre's **shark aquarium** is at Grenå Strand.

ℹ️ Torvebryggen 12–14, Randers; Torvet 1, Grenå

From Grenå take the road south, branching left at Ålsø to take the route parallel to the coast for Ebeltoft (30km/19 miles).

Ebeltoft, East Jutland

4 Ebeltoft, meaning apple orchard, is a charming old town of cobbled streets and half-timbered houses. The small 18th-century **Town Hall** at its centre is now a museum which includes a collection of forged coins manufactured in the 13th century by that romantic rogue, Marsk Stig. In summer the museum's nightwatchmen sing their evening song. Two other museums of interest are **Farvergården**, where the traditional methods of dyeing are still practised, and the **Glass Museum**, where the art of glassblowing is on show. Saved from the scrapyards, the frigate *Jylland* stands today in full splendour down on Ebeltoft's waterfront. The last Danish naval vessel to be made of oak, the *Jylland* was launched in 1860 and saw service in wars against Austria and Prussia before being refitted as a royal yacht in 1874. During World War I she was used as a radio telegraph school and more recently as a holiday home for children.

ℹ️ Strandvejen 2

*From Ebeltoft follow the **coastal road** around the bay and on to Knebel Vig and the hills at Agri. Continue to Ronde, Morke, Hornslet and finally Arhus (55km/34 miles).*

A Danish kro (inn)

Århus – Skanderborg 77 (48)
Skanderborg – Viborg 98 (61)
Viborg – Randers 80 (50)
Randers – Grenå 95 (59)
Grenå – Ebeltoft 30 (19)
Ebeltoft – Århus 55 (34)

A half-timbered building on the cobbled lanes of Ebeltoft

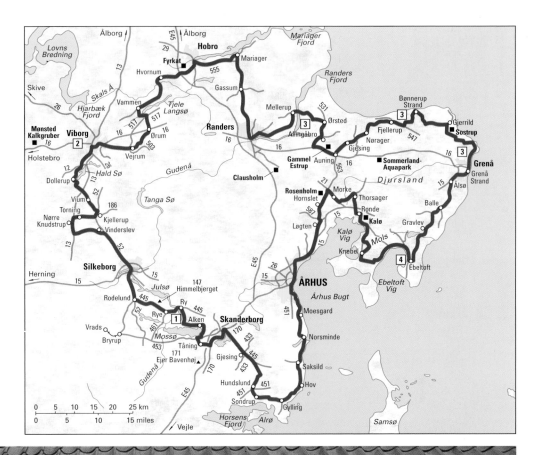

FYN (FUNEN)

Odense • Fåborg • Ærø • Egeskov • Kerteminde
Nyborg • Korsør

A stepping-stone between Jutland and Sealand, the island of Funen was where Hans Christian Andersen, Denmark's most famous son, was born. The mere association of the much-loved writer of fairytales with the island seems to endorse and enhance its charming, *hygge* (cosy, enchanting) qualities. That Andersen is reputed to have said that Funen is 'The Garden of Denmark' makes the small and pretty island all the more alluring.

Starting from the capital of Odense, the tour follows a winding path along country lanes through eastern Funen and crosses by ferry to the mariners' islands of Ærø and Langeland. The final destination is Nyborg, Funen's east-coast port for boats to Sealand.

FOR HISTORY BUFFS

Centuries ago it was declared by royal decree that there should be a *kro* (inn) every 20km (12 miles) along the highways, where travellers could eat and lodge. This tradition survives, and today a variety of old and new *kros*, scattered around the country, are part of the Dansk Kroferie association which provides good hospitality at a reasonable price.

i Rådhuset, Odense

From Odense travel 10km (6 miles) south to Nørre Lyndelse on road 43. Continue to the right off road 43, via Søby Søgård and Allested, to Brobyværk. Turn east, crossing the 43 for Hillerslev and Espe, and thereafter southwards to road 8, turning right to Korinth and then left for Diernaes and Fåborg (55km/33 miles).

Fåborg, Funen

1 With its cobbled streets, old houses and medieval gate, the delightful town of Fåborg sits beside the sea at the foot of the gentle Svanninge Bakker (hills). The imposing yellow-painted **belfry tower** has the largest carillon in Europe; the bells are chimed several times a day to the tunes of well-known hymns. Fåborg's **art museum** shows the works of the 'Funen Painters', a group of turn-of-the-century artists such as Fritz Syberg, Poul

The former mariners' homes on the lovely island of Ærø

Christiansen, Peter Hansen and Johannes Larsen who were greatly influenced by Funen.

From Fåborg take the ferry to Søby on the island of Ærø (1 hour). Continue to the islands of Langeland and Tåsinge, returning to the Funen mainland at Svendborg.

Ærø, Langeland and Tåsinge

2 Ærø is an island with a gentle landscape of meadows which lead down to the sea. The island is only 31km (19 miles) in length, so if you are returning to Fåborg consider leaving the car there and renting a bike. From Søby, in the northwest, there is only one road through the middle of the island to **Ærøskøbing**, halfway along Ærø.

This is one of the prettiest small towns in Denmark. Once occupied by merchants and mariners, the 18th-century half-timbered houses and cottages are colourfully painted in yellows, pinks, blues and greens; the main street leads down to the harbour from where there is a ferry to Vindeby. Ærøskøbing has several small **museums** which recount the island's past; one in particular houses an unusual collection of 750 model ships and ships in bottles.

From Ærøskøbing take the road to Marstal at the eastern tip of the island. **Marstal** was known as a 'captains' town', for this is where the skippers had their residences. It was a busy port during the days of sail and there were times during the 18th and 19th centuries when up to 300 ships docked in the harbour. Something of the strong maritime past can still be sensed when wandering the town – even street names have seafaring references. Worth a visit is the **Jens Hansen ship museum**, which also has a collection of model ships.

From Marstal it is a 1-hour ferry crossing to Rudkøbing on the island of Langeland. Here the tour cuts northwards through pretty countryside to the large 19th-century **manor of Tranekær**, which was built on the site of one of King Valdemar's medieval castles. This is home of TICKON – Tranekær International Art and Nature Centre – set up to make people aware of nature through works of art; hence the many sculptures scattered around the manor's parklands.

Return to Rudkøbing via the parallel country road and cross the bridge to the island of Tåsinge. Pass through the estate of the 17th-century Valdemars Slot (castle), well known for its church, and continue to **Troense**, another delightful 18th-century sea-captains' village with a small maritime museum. A bridge links Tasinge to Svendborg, Funen's second largest city.

From Svendborg follow the country roads west through Ballen to Vester Åby, and then turn northwards to road 8 and turn right to Krarup and Egeskov (45km/28 miles).

Forests of beech border the fertile farmlands of north Funen

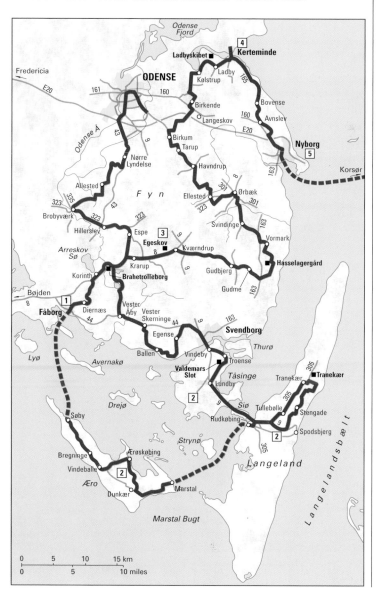

SPECIAL TO...

Composer Carl Nielsen, Funen's other son of international fame, was born in Nørre Lyndelse in 1865, where he is remembered in a few rooms of his old home. Nielsen also wrote the following lines for *Song of Funen*:

'Everything in Funen is different from the rest of the world, and whoever takes the trouble to listen will know. The bees hum in a way of their own with a special Funen accent, and when the horse whinnies and the red cows low, why anybody can hear that it's quite different from anywhere else. It is a lilting Funen that the throstle flutes, and the laughter of the blackbird as it slips under the lilac bushes is an imitation of the starling's whims, themselves an echo of the enchanting chuckle of the Funen girls when they jest and laugh in the gardens behind the clipped hedges. The bells ring and the cocks crow in Funen dialect, and a joyous symphony issues from all the birds' nests every time the mother bird feeds her young. The stillness sings the same tune, too, and even the trees dream and talk in their sleep with a Funen lilt. '

SPECIAL TO...

4 Denmark's only Viking burial ship was discovered at **Ladby**, 4km (2 miles) from Kerteminde. The dead man, plus his horse, dogs and various treasures, was placed inside the 22m (72 feet) -long boat which was then buried under a mound of peat. Dating from around the 10th century, the burial site was excavated in 1935 and is now on display under the mound. The wood of the boat has rotted away but the impression it left gives a graphic idea of the Viking burial customs.

Egeskov, Funen

3 Sixteenth-century Egeskov is the most splendid of Funen's many castles and manors. It was built in a lake on a foundation of oak piles (its name means oak forest) and is credited as the best-preserved island castle in Europe. The interior has been restored and one room displays the weapons and heads of game brought home from hunting expeditions by a former lord of the manor. Within the well-groomed gardens is a magnificent maze with a watchtower in the middle that serves to locate lost friends and family. The old maze was restored by the architect and designer, Piet Hein. The gardens themselves incorporate a range of landscape designs, from Renaissance and baroque to English and French. The castle's **Veteran Museum** specialises in old cars and motorbikes.

From Egeskov continue eastwards, via Gudbjerg, to the impressive 16th-century *Hesselagergård manor. Head northwards, via Svindinge, Ørbæk and Birkende, to Kerteminde (95km/59 miles).*

Kerteminde, Funen

4 The attractive north-coast fishing port of Kerteminde was home of artist Johannes Larsen, one of the 'Funen Painters'. He died in 1961. His house and elegant **gallery** are set in a lovely garden on a hill above the town, with displays of his and other artists' works. The museum of local history is housed in **Farvergården**, an early 17th-century timbered house.

From Kerteminde take road 165 southwards along the coast for 23km (14 miles) to Nyborg.

Egeskov, every bit the romantic castle on the fairytale island of Funen

*The home of artist Johannes
Larsen in Kerteminde*

Nyborg, Funen

5 Nyborg's castle is one of Scandinavia's oldest royal forts and was erected in the 1170s as a defence against barbaric German tribes. It was here in 1282 that King Erik Klipping accepted Denmark's first constitution; thereafter, however, this 'royal castle' saw little of royalty. Much of the original stronghold was later dismantled to provide stone to build Odense Castle, and most of the present structure was commissioned in 1550 by Christian III.

*From Nyborg take the ferry
across to Korsør (50 minutes).*

Odense – Fåborg 65 (40)
Søby – Marstal 31 (19)
Rudkøbing – Svendberg 50 (31)
Svendborg – Egeskov 45 (28)
Egeskov – Kerteminde 95 (59)
Kerteminde – Nyborg 23 (14)

4 days – 757km (456 miles)

SJÆLLAND (SEALAND)

Korsør • Borreby and Holsteinborg • Næstved
Gisselfeld and Bregentved • Højerup • Køge
Roskilde • Helsingør • Hillerød • Jægerspris
Holbæk • Dragsholm • Kalundborg • Sorø • Korsør

The journey through Denmark has progressed eastwards to the island of Sealand, the last region before Sweden. Continue through rural Sealand to the northeast quarter to explore the ancient cathedral city of Roskilde, the capital Copenhagen, the richest royal palaces, the smartest coastline (along Strandvejen) and Helsingør, the setting for Shakespeare's *Hamlet*, from where it is just a short hop to Sweden and the vast world of the Nordic countries. The tour traces almost precisely the Marguerite Route's course around Sealand. Follow the signs bearing the Marguerite symbol (a daisy on a brown background) and they will lead you along the scenic backroads between Sealand's manors and other main sights.

A cherub adorns the brass door knocker on Helsingør's Carmelite monastery

From Korsør follow road 265 through Skælskør to Borreby (19 km/12 miles). From here it is a further 11km (7 miles) to Holsteinborg.

Borreby and Holsteinborg, Sealand

1 Chancellor Johan Friis, the man responsible for Hesselagergård Manor on Funen, built on a grander and stronger scale at Borreby. Fearing he would be targeted by the peasants during their period of discontent in the mid-16th century, Friis constructed Borreby Castle with particularly solid fortifications. Hans Christian Andersen used to stay at Borreby; his story about *Valdemar Daae and his Daughters* is based on the Daae family who were later occupants of the castle. Andersen also enjoyed visiting the nearby 17th-century Holsteinborg Castle which stands amidst extensive parklands; the guest room where he lodged is unchanged since his time.

From Holsteinborg drive to and turn right on to road 265 (not part of the Marguerite Route), before dipping on to the minor coast road before the approach to Næstved (27km/16 miles).

Næstved, Sealand

2 The important market town of Næstved evolved around the Benedictine monastery of Skovkloster in the 12th century. Today its attractions are the churches of **St Peter**, Denmark's largest Gothic church with 14th-century murals and chancel, and **St Morten**, a 13th-century edifice with a richly decorated altarpiece. The modern town has rather overwhelmed other

Borreby Castle was the setting for a Hans Christian Andersen tale

SPECIAL TO...

2 Gavnø Castle, on a small island linked by a bridge 6km (4 miles) south of Naestved, was a brigands' hideout in medieval times and later a royal nunnery before Otto Thott had the present grand manor built in the 18th century; he also accumulated a huge library and one of the largest privately owned art collections in Scandinavia, both of which are now on display.

SPECIAL TO...

2 On leaving Næstved you pass Fensmark in 10km (6 miles). Lying roughly 1km to the east of Fensmark, Holmegård is one of Denmark's most famous glassworks; visitors are welcome – glass-blowing is demonstrated and glassware can be bought at favourable prices.

relics of the past, but the **Næstved Museum** provides an interesting picture of the rich local history; it is housed in the 15th-century Helligåndshuset, formerly a home for the sick and destitute. The well-heeled had their children looked after at **Herlufsholm**, an old and prestigious private boarding school on the site of the original **Skovkloster**; the church is all that remains of the old abbey and is open to the public.

From Næstved travel east via Fensmark to Gisselfeld (25km/15 miles) and Bregentved Castle (a further 6km/4 miles).

Gisselfeld and Bregentved, Sealand

3 The Gisselfeld Castle is another estate which apparently served as inspiration for Hans Christian Andersen. It was built in its present Renaissance style in 1545 by Peder Oxe, the man who succeeded Johan Friis as chancellor of Denmark. The extensive gardens are open to the public, as are the grounds at the nearby late 19th-century Bregentved Castle.

From Bregentved continue to Fakse and Fakse Ladeplads, and keep along the coast, via Vemmetofte Manor and Rødvig, to Højerup (47km/29 miles).

Højerup, Sealand

4 The stretches of sand beach on this southern coast give way to a headland of chalk cliff known as **Stevns Klint**, which reaches a height of 41m (134 feet). The cliffs are constantly being eroded by the sea and now Højerup's small

Viking ships on display in Roskilde

medieval church stands precariously on the edge; part of it crashed into the sea in 1928.

From Højerup follow the road through Store Heddinge to Karise, and then north to Vallø Castle and Køge (31km/19 miles).

Køge, Sealand

5 Køge was a thriving herring port during the Middle Ages and keeps the charm of an old town along streets such as Kirkestræde, Nørregade and Vestergade, where there are many fine half-timbered houses. The oldest house is 20 Kirkestræde (1527) and the smallest is around the corner from the **church of St Nicholas**, famous for its splendid 17th-century altarpiece.

From Køge head west past Ejby, Borup, Jystrup and Skjoldenæsholm, and then bear northwards for Kirke Hvalsø and Lejre to reach Roskilde (44km/26 miles).

Roskilde, Sealand

6 The royal seat of Denmark shifted to Roskilde after Harald Bluetooth set up his quarters here at the end of the 10th century. Dominating the city is the huge twin-towered **cathedral**, built in the 1170s by Bishop Absalon on the site of Bluetooth's old wooden church. The towers were added some time after the original building programme and the sharp spires provided the finishing touch in 1636. All Danish monarchs

SPECIAL TO...

5 With its two great towers and surrounding moat, **Vallø Castle** – 8km (5 miles) south of Køge – is among the most imposing castles of Sealand. It was one of the estates of the Rosenkrantz family in the 16th century and later became home of Anna Sophie Reventlow – Frederik IV's morganatic wife. Most of the castle had to be restored after a terrible fire in 1893. For over 250 years Vallø has been a home for unmarried ladies of the more refined class.

SPECIAL TO...

5 The old trams from Copenhagen, Århus and Odense are now on display at the **Tram Museum** at Skjoldenæsholm.

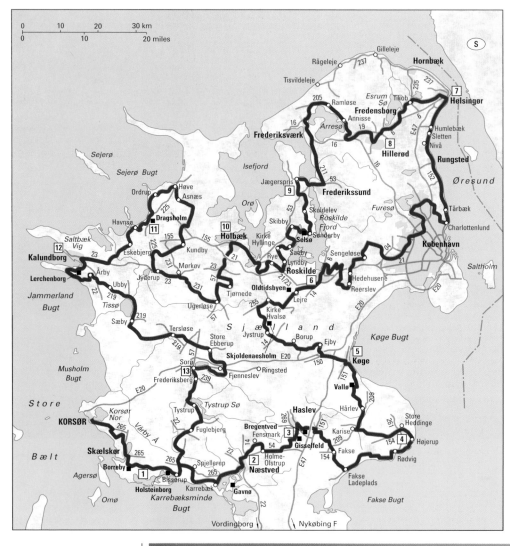

SPECIAL TO...

6 At **Lejre**, 10km (6 miles) southwest of Roskilde, there is a preserved ship tumulus to mark the site of a 10th-century Viking settlement; nearby Oldtidsbyen is a reconstruction of an an Iron Age village where activities from that period are enacted. Also near Lejre is the 18th-century **Ledreborg manor**, which is reached by way of a 7km (4 mile) -long avenue of lime trees. There is a rococo garden and rich woodland – 'visitors welcome when the forests are green', says the sign. Visitors are also welcome at the house – which has a good art collection – and the richly decorated chapel.

since 1536 have been buried here.
One of the most dramatic discoveries from the Viking era found anywhere in Scandinavia is the Viking ships of Roskilde. In the early 11th century five ships were sunk as they tried to defend the Roskilde Fjord at Skuldelev, 20km (12 miles) from Roskilde. They were discovered in 1962 and put on show at the **Viking Ship Museum**.

From Roskilde head eastwards towards Copenhagen. The capital can be avoided by passing through the suburbs and joining the coast road 152 at Charlottenlund, on the north side of the city (77km/48 miles). Continue north from Charlottenlund along the 152 (the famous Strandvejen) to Helsingør (38km/23 miles).

Kronborg, the castle at Helsingør

Helsingør, Sealand

7 As Denmark's closest point to Sweden, Helsingør has long provided a ferry service across the narrow strait to Helsingborg; today a boat leaves every 20 minutes, with a 20-minute crossing time. Down by the waterfront is **Kronborg**, the large, austere Renaissance castle which served Shakespeare as a setting for *Hamlet*. Built in 1585 by Frederik II, it had to be extensively restored after a fire in 1629 destroyed all except the chapel. Rebuilt by Christian IV, the great halls, chambers and chapel are open to visitors. In contrast to the tragic Hamlet is Ogier the Viking, whom Danes call upon to fill them with

Sunset over Roskilde fjord

SCENIC ROUTE

7 Strandvejen (the Coast Road) – road 152 between Copenhagen and Helsingør – is a stretch of fashionable villas and small fishing villages. Notable are: **Charlottenlund**, with aquariums holding fish from all over the world; **Tårbæk**, a fishing hamlet backed by the former hunting forests; **Rungsted**, where the home of Karen Blixen – author of *Out of Africa* – has now been converted into a museum; **Nivå**, a village with the Nivågaard Art Collection of Renaissance paintings; **Sletten**, a pretty fishing village; **Humlebaek**, famous for its excellent Louisiana museum of modern art.

The pretty northern coast beyond Helsingør consists of sandy beaches and forested headlands. There is a succession of fishing villages-cum-tourist resorts, notably Hornbæk, Gilleleje and Tisvildeleje.

fighting mettle in times of need; his statue is in the casements. The other principal sight is the splendidly preserved **St Maria church and Carmelite Monastery**, dating from 1517. Much of the old town has been tastefully restored and provides an historic and pleasant backdrop for this busy thoroughfare between nations.

From Helsingør travel westwards, via Tikob, to Fredensborg and thence to Hillerød (28km/17 miles).

Hillerød, Sealand

8 Frederik II acquired the Hillerødsholm estate as a hunting ground in 1560. Not content with the modest manor, he set about building **Frederiksborg Castle**, which his son, Christian IV, completed with great flourish in the early 1600s. Huge, surrounded by a moat and adorned with carved façades and figures, Frederiksborg is probably the most spectacular Renaissance castle in Denmark – it is certainly the most ostentatious hunting lodge. The chapel and its extravagant decoration survived the very damaging fire of 1859 and still has its original Compenius organ of 1610. The town evolved because of the castle and

Frederiksborg, the ultimate in Renaissance architecture

Frederiksborg is now on the edge of Hillerod; the gardens and woods of the estate spread behind the castle.

From Hillerød head west on road 19 to join road 16. Bear right for Annisse and skirt Lake Arresø to Frederiksværk. Continue south on road 211 to Frederikssund and Jægerspris (61km/37 miles).

Jægerspris, Sealand

9 Another royal hunting home, the castle of Jægerspris has been a popular estate among the Danish kings since medieval times, none more so than Frederik VII who enjoyed it as a family summer residence. On his death the Countess of Danner, his wife, handed the castle to a charity for abandoned young women. The apartments used by Frederik VII remain unchanged and are open to visitors in summer.

From Jægerspris turn southwards past Skuldelev, Sønderby, Selsø and Skibby, and continue through Sæby and Lyndby. Bear west to Holbæk, via Rye and Eriksholm (63km/39 miles).

Holbæk, Sealand

10 Situated on the southern end of the large Isefjord, Holbæk developed as a trading port around its medieval castle. The town reached its peak of prosperity between the 17th and 19th centuries when it became an important grain exporter. Some of the old **merchants'** houses still stand, and the one now occupied by the **local museum** dates from 1670. Holbæk remains the principal market town of the region; compared to the east, the countryside to the west is comprised of more sparsely populated farmlands. Four kilometres (2 miles) south of the town, the twin-towered **Tveje Merlose church** dates from the early 12th century.

From Holbæk take road 57 southwards, bearing right along the 231 at Ugerløse for Mørkøv. From Mørkøv travel west on road 23 to Jyderup, then north via Kundby for Asnæs and Høve, and then southwest for Ordrup and Dragsholm Castle (101km/63 miles).

Dragsholm, Sealand

11 The original medieval castle of Dragsholm served as a strong refuge during the uprisings of the 1530s and then as a sound prison 40 years later for the Earl of Bothwell, the husband of Mary, Queen of Scots. The Scottish nobleman ended his days here and the cell where he was allegedly manacled to the wall can be visited. The castle proved an inadequate defence, however, against the Swedes who blew it apart during a battle in 1659. Most of the present castle dates from the late 17th century.

From Dragsholm continue along the coast and join road 23 for Kalundborg (30km/18 miles).

Kalundborg, Sealand

12 Sheltered in its fjord at the western extreme of Sealand, the port of Kalundborg is a ferry point for Jutland (to Århus and Juelsminde) and the island of Samsø. It was a substantial medieval fortification and capital of Denmark for a short time. Most remarkable of the present sights is the **church** built in 1170 by Esben Snare, the man also responsible for the original defences and the brother of Bishop Absalon who was behind the construction of Roskilde Cathedral. **Lerchenborg Castle**, the 18th-century baroque manor of General Christian Lerche, is 5km (3 miles) along the coast to the south; it – like so manors – boasts a visit by Hans Christian Andersen, and the room where the author stayed is on display.

From Kalundborg take the road to Lerchenborg and then eastwards across country via Sæby and Tersløse to Fjenneslev and then west to Sorø, 82km (51 miles).

Sorø, Sealand

13 The 12th-century abbey at Sorø, originally home to Benedictine monks, was converted into an academy for upper-class boys in the 17th century. The main building underwent reconstruction in the 1820s, but the old abbey chapel dates from medieval times; the influential Bishop Absalon of Roskilde, who died in 1201, is buried here behind the altar. The academy – still a boarding school – has a lovely setting by the Sorø lake.

From Sorø head south and bear left to follow the shore of Tystrup Sø (Lake Tystrup) and then continue to Bisserup on the sea, finally taking the coastal stretch back to Korsør, 67km (40 miles).

Korsør – Borreby 19 (12)
Borreby – Naestved 38 (23)
Naestved – Gisselfeld 25 (15)
Gisselfeld – Højerrup 53 (33)
Højerrup – Koge 31 (19)
Koge – Roskilde 44 (27)
Roskilde – Helsingør 115 (71)
Helsingør – Hillerød 28 (17)
Hillerød – Jaegerspris 61 (38)
Jaegerspris – Holback 63 (39)
Holback – Dragsholm 101 (63)
Dragsholm – Kalundborg 30 (18)
Kalundborg – Sorø 82 (51)
Sorø – Korsør 67 (42)

Beautifully set by the sea off fashionable Stradvejen, Louisiana is one of Europe's great modern art museums

SPECIAL TO...

13 The granite **church at Fjenneslev**, 11km (7 miles) east of Sorø, dates from the early 12th century. A further 7km (4 miles) east is **Ringsted**, where medieval royalty – including Queen Dagmar (died 1212) of Dagmar Cross fame – were buried at **St Bendt's church**. There are interesting murals at both these churches.

SWEDEN

Sweden's southernmost county of Skåne was long occupied by the Danes, and the Danish heritage is conspicuous in the many old manors and churches. These are rich farmlands, Sweden's land of plenty. Immediately to the north are the forests of Småland where the earth is less generous; more people from this region than any other in the country fled to America during the lean years around the turn of the 20th century. Belying the poverty of the past is the Småland tradition of manufacturing some of the world's most beautiful glassware. The longest bridge in Europe links Småland to Öland, a narrow island of unique alva landscape, Viking settlements and spectacular shipwrecks. Further out in the Baltic is Gotland, Sweden's largest island, where curiously shaped rock stacks dot the coast.

On the other side of the country, the magnificent west coast has archipelagos of pink-rocked skerries and fashionable resorts, beaches and fishing villages. Inland from here the great Vänern and Vättern, Sweden's two largest lakes, dominate the interior. One of the main rivers feeding Lake Vänern is the Klarälven which rises in Norway. Timbers chopped in the forests near the border have long been floated downstream to feed the wood factories built at the point where the river meets the lake.

Sweden's heartland is further east, around Lake Mälaren, the country's third biggest lake. The lake provides easy access to the Baltic and was an important trading region as early as the Viking times. The presence of Stockholm will ensure this area remains the hub of Sweden. Push northwards to Dalarna (the Valleys) where the rolling countryside of forest and pasture leads down to quiet lakes with shores scattered with red-painted wood cottages. Continue to Östersund and the fell region around the resort of Åre and cut across to the east coast, to Sundsvall and the lovely High Coast. Push on, up into the heart of Lappland to isolated centres like Storuman and Arjeplog. This remote, empty country is sparsely populated, but nature has been as kind here as it was with the fertile fields of the far south; the rivers flowing to the Baltic have been harnessed for power, rich iron-ore deposits feed industry and the endless forests continue to be the country's main source of income. There are vast areas where nobody lives except for the Lapps with their herds of reindeer.

Helsingborg

Just a hop from Denmark, Helsingborg is the gateway to Sweden. From here tours lead southwards into the rich region of Skåne and northwards along the lovely west coast to Norway. Rising above the town is Kärnan, the stolid, brown-brick tower from the medieval fortifications, which is proudly displayed as Helsingborg's emblem; there are views from the tower across Öresund to Denmark. Art is displayed in the nearby Slottshagen park, in the gardens of the 19th-century Sofiero Castle and in the town's Museum of Art.

Växjö

Växjö was a medieval city at an important lakeside crossroad (*vag* means road, *sjö* means lake). Today it is a centre for high-tech industries and there is a young and prosperous atmosphere in the leafy streets of its modern

Gräsgård, a tiny fishing harbour on the east coast of the island of Öland

downtown area. Before embarking on Tour 8 visit the glass collection at the Småland Museum and the Emigrants' House which tells the story of the Swedish migration to America. Just to the north is the ruined Kronoberg Castle on the shores of lovely Helgasjön (Lake Helga), a popular spot for picnics and boating.

Visby

Port and capital of the Baltic island of Gotland, Visby was a significant medieval trading centre with links to the Hanseatic League. It retains the classic features of a medieval city: the sturdy defence wall, fortified by towers, which surrounds the city and its cathedral; several ruined monasteries; and cobbled lanes lined with half-timbered houses. Along with the old charm is a very lively streetlife in summer. The Museum of Antiquities and the pleasant Botanical Gardens are also worth a visit.

Stockholm

Built on the mainland and islands at the point where Lake Mälaren meets the Baltic, Stockholm is very much a city of the water. It is the most beautiful and grand of the Scandinavian capitals. Wander its waterfronts and the narrow lanes of Gamla Stan (Old Town). Visit the many museums on the neighbouring islands of Djurgården (including the 17th-century warship *Vasa* and the old buildings at Skansen) and Skeppsholmen with its Modern Art Museum. The old Town Hall overlooks Lake Mälaren at the point where there are boats to the royal palace of Drottningholm. One of the greatest pleasures in Stockholm is to catch a white ferry from outside the Grand Hotel and travel far out into the magnificent archipelago.

Karlstad

The pleasant city of Karlstad, with its 18th-century cathedral, is at the point where the Klarälven flows into Lake Vänern. The great tradition of floating timber down rivers still continues on the Klarälven, albeit on a modest scale compared to the great floating days of the past, and the main wood mills and pulp plants are at nearby Skoghall. Local history and culture is recounted at the Värmland Museum.

Leksand

Leksand is famed nationally for its ice hockey team and its *knäckerbröd* (hard bread). At midsummer the town's people raise the highest maypole in the country and every July they perform the *Himlaspel*, a much-loved mystery play. If you want traditional Sweden, with folk music and local costumes, then Leksand is the place to come. Also of interest is the fine lakeside church, originally dating from the 13th century, and Hildasholm, the interesting residence of Axel Munthe, royal surgeon and author.

Östersund

With a population of around 58,000, Östersund is the only town of any size in the county of Jämtland. It has an attractive setting on the eastern bank of Storsjön, the country's fifth largest lake, and it is linked by bridge to the pleasant island of Frösö. The island's old church is a popular place to get married.

Sundsvall

After a very destructive fire swept the town in 1888 the ancient trading hub of Sundsvall was rebuilt in stone – hence its nickname, Stenstaden, 'The Stone Town'. Wood is Sundsvall's fame and prosperity and it has a significant papermaking and woodworking industry. There is an open-air museum with a collection of old houses and a Municipal Museum focusing mainly on local culture and history.

Storuman

A market town in southern Lappland, Storuman is at the junction of the main inland road and rail arteries, which run north–south through Sweden, and the east–west 'Blue Way'. Opposite the station is the Old Railway Hotel (now the library) which has been refurbished in its original 19th-century style. Sweden's largest wooden church at Stensele, 5km (3 miles) outside Storuman, dates from 1886 and has an original Christina bible. Causeways and bridges link a cluster of islands in Lake Storuman; an interesting heritage museum can be found on the island of Luspholmarna.

The Sea God, *by Carl Milles, Stockholm*

WEST COAST

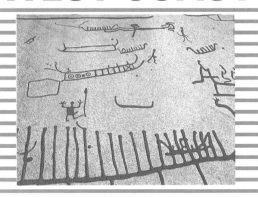

Helsingborg • Kulla Peninsula • Bjare Peninsula • Båstad • Halmstad • Tylösand Falkenberg • Varberg • Tjolöholm • Kungsbacka and Särö • Göteborg • Tjörn • Orust • Lysekil Strömstad and the Koster Islands • Oslo

Immediately north of Helsingborg are Skåne's fashionable twin peninsulas of Kulla and Bjare, jutting into the Kattegat. Beyond the peninsulas Halland county's straight sands stretch towards Göteborg (Gothenburg). From here Bohuslän's jagged coast of headlands and skerries, with shores of smooth pink-grey granite, leads to Norway. This is Sweden's long and lovely Sunshine Coast. The E6 runs its length, from Helsingborg to the Norwegian border and beyond to Oslo. But to appreciate its charm and beauty you must branch off the main highway, taking minor roads down to the sea and the fishing villages and resorts. This tour is linear, concentrating on the strip of coast west of the E6.

SPECIAL TO…

1 Flickorna Lundgren – the Lundgren Girls – were seven sisters who started a coffee shop at Skäret in 1938. Kings and lords from home and abroad came to try their cakes and declared them the tastiest in the land. The two surviving sisters continue to serve their special cakes in the lovely garden of their old thatched cottage.

Follow the E6 out of Helsingborg, bearing left for Viken and Höganäs, 20km (12 miles). Continue to follow the coast road around the Kulla peninsula to Ängelholm, a total of 65km (40 miles).

Kulla Peninsula, Skåne

1 From **Viken**, with its half-timbered cottages, the coast road continues to Höganäs. Originally a coal town, **Höganäs** is now famous for its clay, the raw material for the famous local pottery which August Strindberg

Rock carvings dating from 500–1500 BC

wrote about in his book *Hemsöborna*. Just inland is **Väsby** with its unusual neo-classical vicarage.

Beyond Höganäs, **Krapperup manor** dates from the 13th century, though its present form, with splendid large stars inlaid in the walls, is from the 1700s. It was reputedly haunted up until 1983, when the last lady of the house died (the gardens are open to visitors). Continue to **Mölle**, a pretty fishing village and one of the early resorts of the region, where the first mixed swimming shocked the more conservative minded. The model railway here is said to be the largest in Europe. Above Mölle, rising to a height of 200m (656 feet), is the lovely **Kullaberg nature reserve** which forms the tip of the peninsula. The seas here can be terrifyingly wild and a guiding light at the tip has helped direct mariners past the off-shore reefs for over 1,000 years. The present lighthouse has the most powerful lamp in Sweden.

Arild, on the northern shore, is another fine old bathing resort. The nearby 12th-century **Brunnby** church has a painted 16th-century interior. Continue via Skäret, Jonstorp and Farhult to **Ängelholm**, one of the most popular tourist centres on the west coast thanks to its 10km (6 mile)-long sand beach.

ℹ️ Triangelplatsen, Höganäs; Gamla Rådhuset, Ängelholm

From Ängelholm road 105 leads northwards for 25km (16 miles) to Båstad, at the northern base of the Bjare peninsula.

Bjare Peninsula, Skåne

2 To the west of the Ängelholm–Båstad road is a maze of lanes winding their way through pretty rolling countryside (where Sweden's first potatoes and strawberries of the season are collected) and leading down to beaches and rugged headlands. **Vejbystrand** and **Ängelsbäckstrand** are long stretch-

Viken beach is typical of the Swedish coast between Halmstad and Göteborg

es of sandy beach; **Torekov** is an old fishing village, from where there are boats to the island of **Hallands Väderö**, with its rich flora and birdlife. **Hovs Hallar**, the rocky northern headland of the peninsula, is a nature reserve with seals; to its east is the tiny fishing harbour of **Kattvik** from where the coast road continues to Båstad.

i Hamnplanen 2, Torekov

Båstad, Skåne

3 The fire which destroyed Båstad in 1870 cleared the way for new development to meet the growing influx of tourists who came here in increasing numbers after the opening of the railway in 1885. Ludvig Nobel (nephew of Alfred Nobel) helped finance the reconstruction and Båstad rapidly became a thoroughly fashionable modern resort. Tennis was *de rigeur* and during the 1920s the first Swedish Tennis Championships were held here. In the 1930s King Gustaf V participated in the competition, playing under the name of 'Mr G'. Since 1948 Båstad has hosted the Swedish Open, and a more recent innovation is the Kalle Anka Cup (Donald Duck Cup), a prestigious junior championship in which the likes of Björn Borg, Stefan Edberg and Mats Wilander gained valuable experience for the big time. Båstad remains one of Sweden's more exclusive resorts.

i Stortorget 1

From Båstad pick up the E6, following it alongside the beaches for 36km (22 miles) to Halmstad.

Halmstad, Halland

4 The fires which frequently destroyed the wooden towns seem to have been a mixed blessing. After the fire which razed much of Halmstad, only the new castle and the 15th-century **church** survived reasonably intact. Christian IV of Denmark, then ruler over this part of Sweden, had the chance to rebuild the city in the modern Renaissance style, with smart houses lining a grid of straight streets. The ruined **Norre Port** is a reminder of that time when Halmstad was a frontier defence town between Sweden and Denmark.

More recent landmarks are *Najaden* (built 1897), one of the world's two remaining composite-built fullriggers (the other is the *Cutty Sark*, moored on the River Thames in London), which is on the river by the governor's residence, and, on the far bank, Picasso's huge *Man and Woman* statue. The town had its own famous artists, the 'Halmstad Group', better known as the Swedish Surrealists, whose work can be seen at the town **museum**. On the road going out to Tylösand you pass **Miniland**, a park where many of Sweden's historical sights have been built in miniature.

i Hamngatan 35

Bear west out of Halmstad for 9km (6 miles), following signs for Tylösand.

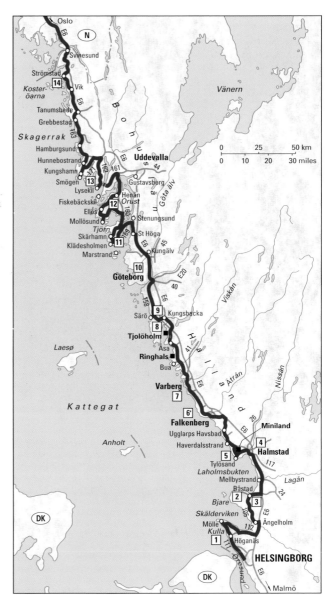

Tylösand, Halland

5 They call Tylösand Halland's Riviera because of its long stretch of sand. But, although it is one of the best beaches on the west coast, it is not unique. There are smaller bays dotted all the way to Falkenberg; for example at **Viken**, **Haverdalsstrand** and **Ugglarps Havsbad**. This picturesque coast is also rich in birdlife.

Follow the coastal road north for 60km (37 miles) to Falkenberg.

Falkenberg, Halland

6 One of the several pleasant market towns along the Halland coast, Falkenberg is famous for its 18th-century stone **toll-bridge** and the excellent salmon fishing on the River Ätrån: 'You cannot experience fishing like this in any other river, be it in Norway or in Canada,' enthused Englishman W M Wilkinson in 1860 in his book about his stay in Falkenberg. The region once had a large falcon population, hence the name Falkenberg.

i Stortorget

*Take the **coastal road** north for 28km (17 miles) from Falkenberg to Varberg.*

Varberg, Halland

7 Down on the waterfront you get a sense of Varberg's past as a defensive site during the Swedish-Danish conflicts and also as a fashionable spa resort at the turn of this century. The large fort now contains an impressive **museum**.

In 1936 a farmer uncovered a body while digging peat in the Bocksten bog. Suspecting foul play, he reported his find to the local police, and indeed the deceased had been killed by a blow to the head. However, the murder had, according to the pathologist, been committed 600 years previously. The chemical properties of the peat had preserved both body and clothes. Holes through the man suggested the body had been staked to the ground to prevent his soul escaping to haunt his killers. The **Bocksten Bog Man**, was estimated to have been in his mid-thirties, about 170cm (5 foot 8 inches) tall and a 'gentleman', judging from the cut of his cloth. He is the *pièce de résistance* at the museum and the only clothed medieval man in the world. The fort also served as a prison and cells have now been converted into rooms for the youth hostel.

On a pier jutting into the water alongside the fort is the splendid old wooden **bath house**; after bathing, refreshments would be taken in Societetshuset, in the nearby gardens. Today the most popular places for a dip are off the island bird sanctuary of **Getterön**, to the north of the town, and the surfers' **Apelviken beach**.

ⓘ Brunnsparken

*Leave Varberg northwards along the **E6**, soon bearing left to follow the more pleasant parallel road to Tjolöholm, about 40km (25 miles).*

SPECIAL TO...

7 Across the bay from Bua, north of Varberg, is Ringhals, one of Europe's largest nuclear power stations. Vattenfall, the owners, are keen to show the positive side of their energy making and they provide guided tours around the plant. There is a complimentary bus service from Varberg.

Hällviksstrand on the island of Orust is one of the many small fishing villages on the coast north of Göteborg

Tjolöholm, Halland

8 James Dickson, a Göteborg merchant and king's stable master of Scottish descent, was keen to have an English-style manor – preferably Elizabethan – as his residence. In 1892 he bought the Tjolöholm estate on a beautiful peninsula, at the point where the beaches of Halland begin to give way to the rocky coast of Bohuslän. Lars Israel Wahlman, a 27-year-old architect, was awarded the commission to build the manor which he completed in 1904. The result was not totally satisfactory. None the less, the heavy stone exterior and the traditional-cum-art nouveau interior, with large fireplaces and dark woodwork, does feel like a cross between a middle-class Surrey house and a modest English stately home. Special features included a copy of Henry VIII's four-poster bed – reserved for royalty in case they chose to visit – a piped hot-air heating system and a horse-pulled vacuum cleaner. Sadly Dickson never enjoyed the finished estate; he died from blood poisoning after putting an old bottle top on a cut finger to stop it bleeding. He was buried in a marble **mausoleum** in the grounds. The manor, which is open to visitors, overlooks a quiet bay and is surrounded by manicured gardens and thick forests of oak and beech. The nearby **village** was created to house Tjolöholm's workers and their families, and included a school and a chapel; there is also a **carriage museum**.

*From Tjolöholm head northeast towards the **E6** and continue to Kungsbacka, 15km (9 miles).*

Kungsbacka and Särö, Halland

9 A fire in 1836 destroyed medieval Kungsbacka. Only two houses survived. The **market square**, surrounded by the 'new' 19th-century buildings, is a pleasant centre to the town. From Kungsbacka take road 158 to **Särö** (12km/7 miles), where Kings Oscar II and Gustav V used to spend their summers earlier this century. The small resort remains quite exclusive and home to the well heeled who commute to Göteborg.

ⓘ Stortorget 41

From Särö continue north on road 158 to Göteborg, 23km (14 miles).

Göteborg (Gothenburg), Bohuslän

10 Built by Dutch designers in the 17th century, Göteborg is a large port and industrial city, second only to Stockholm in size. With its west-coast location the locals believe they are more outward looking than Stockholmers, who, they joke, live at the backside of the country. The city does have a cosmopolitan atmosphere, especially along the **Avenyn**, the wide Champs Elysées-like boulevard which leads up to the huge Carl Milles statue of Poseidon in front of the excellent **Art Museum**, home of the largest collection of Scandinavian art. While Stockholm is very much a city of water, Göteborg has no attractive waterfront; rather it is a city of parks (there are over 50 of them). For a feel of the sea take a ferry out into the archipelago or up to the popular old resort of **Marstrand**. Better still, push even further north along the Bohuslän coast.

From Göteborg continue northwards on the E6, via Kungälv with its old town and Bohus fort, bearing left at St Höga. Continue on road 160 to Stenungsund, 42km (26 miles), then cross the bridge to the island of Tjörn. The old bridge, which collapsed after a hit from a ship in 1980, has been replaced.

Tjörn, Bohuslän

11 The lovely skerries of Bohuslän are dotted with old fishing villages, which remain picturesque with red-painted wood cottages clustered on the waterfronts. On Tjörn pick up road 169, taking it to the far end of the island (18km/11 miles) where a bridge spans the strait to the tiny island of **Klädesholmen**, now one of Sweden's main centres for herring canning. They smoke fish on the nearby island of **Åstol** which was home to a sizeable fishing fleet in the 18th century; the island is linked by ferry (no cars).

Further up the Tjörn coast is **Skärhamn**, long a significant port for the merchant fleet; the old captain's house, **Cherlinska Huset**, is now a shipping museum.

Return eastwards and pick up road 160 north on to the neighbouring island of Orust.

Below, right: the botanical gardens, Göteborg

Orust, Bohuslän

12 Orust, Sweden's third largest island after Gotland and Öland, has pleasant rolling countryside. Once again push west, to the end of the island and to pretty fishing villages like **Mollösund**, **Hällviksstrand** and, on the islands beyond, **Käringön** and **Gullholmen**. Return inland via **Ellös**, where the church organ (1575) is one of the oldest in Sweden, and continue to **Henån**, Orust's main town.

ⓘ Hamntorget, Henån

From Henån take road 160 north off Orust, bear left on 161 and take the ferry across Gullmarsfjord to Lysekil, 30km (19 miles). The tour can be extended to Skaftö before taking the ferry.

Lysekil, Bohuslän

13 Lysekil is one of the larger fishing ports and resorts in Bohuslän. It is a short ferry ride across the fjord to the village of **Fiskebäckskil** on Skaftö.

ⓘ Hamngatan 6, Lysekil; Lyckans Slip, Skaftö

Take road 162 from Lysekil inland up the peninsula, bear left on the 171 and follow it down to the fishing village of Smögen and the larger Kungshamn, 49km (30 miles). Turn northwards passing through Hunnebostrand and continue along the coast road via Hamburgsund, Fjällbacka and Grebbestad before rejoining the E6 at Tanumshede, about 55km (34 miles). Continue north on E6, bearing left on road 176 to Strömstad, 33km (21 miles).

Strömstad and the Koster Islands

14 Strömstad is a fishing port and spa resort famous for its prawns and for having more hours of sunshine than anywhere in Scandinavia. There are ferries from here to Norway and to the small islands of **Nordkoster** and **Sydkoster**, both popular swimming spots. The old **lighthouse** on **Nordkoster** was so high that its light misdirected sailors who mistook it for a star; it was replaced by the present shorter lighthouse in 1891.

ⓘ Torget, Norra Hamnen

Road 176 continues east from Strömstad to the E6, which leads northwards to the Norwegian border at Svinesund, 23km (14 miles). Continue on the E6 to Oslo, 115km (71 mile).

SPECIAL TO...

13 Spa resorts along the west coast have attracted the fashionable since the 18th century. Pleasant, leafy Gustavsberg, Sweden's oldest resort, is in a quiet cove just beyond the southern outskirts of Uddevalla. The elegant wooden villas still stand on the slopes leading down to the waterfront, where the original spa building now houses the youth hostel; ask here for a sample of the water which made Gustavsberg so popular.

13 Tanum's Gestgifveri dates from 1663 and claims to be Sweden's oldest inn. The house speciality is fish casserole: the five different fish of the day and prawns and mussels flavoured with saffron and a blend of herbs.

FOR HISTORY BUFFS

13 Evidence of Bronze Age cultures is found scattered all along this coast. Most notable is the Tanumshede vicinity where, at Tanum and Vitlycke, for example, there are beautiful rock carvings of long ships, hunters and animals dating from 3,000 years ago. The Vitlycke Hällristningsmuseum (rock-carving museum) organises niga ht-time excursions; the figures are all the more dramatic under flashlight.

BACK TO NATURE

13 Nordens Ark, on road 171 about 15km (9 miles) from Kungshamn/Smögen, is an animal sanctuary helping to protect and preserve endangered species indigenous to colder climes. Animals include the Przewalski horse, arctic fox, markhor (a wild goat), lynx and snow leopard.

3 days – 380km (236 miles)

SKÅNE

**Helsingborg • Landskrona and the Island of Ven
Trollenäs and Trolleholm • Lund • Malmö • Ystad
Ystad-Simrishamn Coastal Route • Simrishamn
Simrishamn to Brösarp • Kristinehov • Höör and
Bosjökloster • Helsingborg**

The Swedes finally managed to wrest Skåne – the rich farm-lands of the south – from the Danes in 1658. The Danish heritage is still very evident in the design of the many church-es and manors and also in the throaty accent of the Skånians. Even the flat countryside of west Skåne resembles Denmark. But do not linger too long in the west, push eastwards to Österlen – 'The Land East of the Lane' (the Ystad-Kristianstad road) – Skåne's charming southeast corner, where the land-scape is rolling, the beaches are long and sandy and minor roads dip down to pretty fishing villages.

SPECIAL TO...

2 There are about 250 manor houses in Skåne. Most are still privately owned or com-pletely closed to the public, while others have restricted opening hours or only allow visits by appointment. Yet many permit access to their lovely gardens and parks throughout the year. The local tourist boards have up-to-date lists with relevant details about the main manors. There are a number of manors in the countryside west of the Eslöv–Lund road, including 13th-century. **Ellinge**, 15th-century **Örtofta**, 17th-century **Viderup** (rebuilt in the 1750s) and the late 16th-century **Svenstorp**. The gardens, but not the buildings, of these four manors are open to the public.

From Helsingborg take the E6 south for 22km (14 miles) to Landskrona.

Landskrona and the Island of Ven, Skåne

1 The most famous of Landskrona's various old buildings is its **Citadel**, which was built in the 16th century by King Christian III of Denmark. The ring of three moats and ramparts was added after Sweden had taken Skåne; more recently the Citadel has been used as a refugee camp and a women's prison.

Leave the car in Landskrona and catch the ferry to the flat-topped, steep-sided Island of **Ven** (a 30-minute journey; there are also ser-vices from Helsingborg and Råå further up the coast). Ven, with a present population of 400 and an area of 7.5sq km (3sq miles), was home of the Danish astronomer Tycho Brahe between 1578 and 1598. His castle, **Uranienborg**, still stands in the centre of the island; near by is a museum in his memory and **Stjärneborg** (Star Castle), his observatory where he became the first to sight a supernova star. Ferries land at **Backviken**, from

Off the beaten track in southern Skåne: an old barn near the fishing village of Kådrnrths

where you can hire cycles. **Kyrkbacken** and **Norreborg** are small harbours on the northern side of the island; it is possible to swim here.

ℹ️ Rådhusgatan 3 (Landskrona); Landsvägen 2 (Ven)

*From Landskrona bear east along road **17** towards Eslöv, 34kms (21 miles). Five kilometres (3 miles) before Eslöv there is a turning left to Trollenäs. Trolleholm is 8km (5 miles) further north.*

Trollenäs and Trolleholm (Eslöv vicinity), Skåne

2 The medieval home of the Thott family was acquired by the Trolle family in 1682; they made the castle grander and bestowed upon it their name. Restoration work in the 19th century gave Trollenäs its present Renaissance (exterior) and baroque (interior) styles; gardens and interior can be visited. Trolleholm fort also had a name change and a facelift: the early 16th-century structure was called Eriksholm and in the 19th century it underwent the major restoration work which gave it its current appearance; the gardens can be visited.

*From Eslöv head south on road **113** and then join the **E22** to Lund, 20km (12 miles).*

Lund, Skåne

3 Lund is as ancient a 'living' city as you are going to find north of Denmark. It was founded in AD990 by the Danish king Sven Tveskägg – Two (Fork) Beard – as the capital of the eastern provinces of his domain. A century later King Canute the Holy started building the **Domkyrka** (cathedral); its twin towers, known locally as the 'Lunna Pågar', the Boys of Lund (*pågar* is the Skanian for *pojke*, meaning boy in Swedish), are landmarks in the centre of the city. The cathedral is the oldest archiepiscopal see in Scandinavia – there was a time when its authority embraced 27 churches and eight monasteries – and it stands as the most impressive example of Romanesque architecture in the country. The crypt dates from the mid-12th century and you can still see the images of the giant Finn and his wife and child who, according to the myths, had created the cathe-dral. The 16th-century Lundagård, built as the residence of the Danish king, is north of the cathedral. After Skåne was won by the Swedes, Carl XI of Sweden donated it to the uni-versity. **Lundagård** became the first university building. Founded in 1666, Lund University is the third oldest Swedish university – the oldest being Uppsala, followed by Tartu (1632) in Estonia which was then part of Sweden. The scholastic atmosphere remains strong in Lund and the university – the largest in Scandinavia – dominates the city (the university library is said to house over two-and-a-half million

volumes). Behind the cathedral is a section of the **Kulturhistoriska Museet** (Cultural History Museum) – nicknamed Kulturen – an open-air heritage museum with buildings and cultural material from southern Sweden.

i Kyrkogatan 11

From Lund take the E22 southwest to Malmö, 17km (11 miles).

Malmö, Skåne

4 Today almost a conurbation with Lund, Malmö is Sweden's third largest city. It has long been a significant port and is as commercial and modernly industrial in nature as Lund is scholastic and ancient in its character. The **Town Hall** in Stortorget, the main square of the old town, dates from the mid-16th century and is the heart of Malmö. Some of the burghers' residences are in the neighbouring side streets. Also from this period is **Malmöhus**, the castle built on the ruins of the older citadel, which is now a museum displaying the history of the city. Rather more quirky are the splendid old wooden **bath houses** at the end of the long pier at Ribbersborg, Malmö's narrow strip of Copacabana, which is only a short distance from the downtown area. There is a speedy ferry service from Malmö to Copenhagen.

i Centralstationen

A drive along winding lanes which criss-cross the Skåne countryside is the most enjoyable way to travel east from Malmö to Ystad. However, the most direct route between the two places is along the E65, 59km (37 miles).

Ystad, Skåne

5 The pretty south-coast port of Ystad once grew rich from its herring catches and later – when Napoleon enforced his European blockade – it gained notoriety, and wealth, as a smugglers' entrepôt. Today the past is Ystad's prosperity; the quaint downtown area, with its many well-

The ferry from Helsingør arrives at Helsingborg; beyond is Örsund and Denmark

preserved half-timbered houses (there are over 300), is a main tourist attraction of Skåne. A copy of the 1753 map provided by the tourist office is a sufficiently accurate plan of present Ystad, and the office's suggested walking tour passes the most historic places.

Worth exploring is the main Stora Västergatan-Stora Östergatan thorough-fare with its many houses of interest. The town's ecclesiastical buildings include the 13th-century churches of St **Mary** and St **Peter**. Close to the latter is the Franciscan **cloister to the Grey Friars**, one of the oldest monasteries in Sweden, which had a post-Reformation spiritual role as a brandy distillery.

i St Knuts Torg

Take road 9 east from Ystad and then follow the coastal road to Simrishamn, about 45km (27 miles).

Ystad-Simrishamn Coastal Route, Skåne

6 About 10km (6 miles) east of Ystad a road leads off road 9 via Kabusa to the tiny fishing port of **Kåseberga**. High on the cliff above, and splendidly located in a meadow grazed by cows, are the **Ales Stenar**, one of Scandinavia's great Bronze Age stone ship sites. It comprises 59 standing stones and measures 67m (220 feet) in length. Continuing eastwards you pass **Backåkra** where Dag Hammarskjöld, the late UN Secretary-General, had a house (now a museum). Beyond is the turning down to **Sandhammaren**, one of the most popular of several beaches along these southern Skåne shores. **Skillinge** is a pretty fishing village with a small maritime museum, and it is a suitable point to bear inland to **Glimmingehus Castle** (10km/6 miles), via **Gislöv** with its blacksmith and museum. Beyond Skillinge is the delightful harbour at **Brantevik**, once

SPECIAL TO...

3 Southeast of Lund, road 16 leads for 12km (7 miles) to **Dalby**, where the stone church of the Holy Cross was built in 1060 by Sven Estridsen. It pre-dates Lund's cathedral and is probably the oldest church in Scandinavia.

SPECIAL TO...

4 The flat **Falsterbo peninsula** pokes out of Skåne towards Denmark. It is an important stopping point for migratory birds and, with its sandy beaches and golf courses, it also serves as an escape for people from Malmö. In medieval times Skanör and Falsterbo were thriving herring ports; today tourism is their main trade.

SCENIC ROUTE

5 The most direct route from Ystad to Simrishamn is the 37km (23 mile) -long road 9. In the countryside to the north of the road are the manors of **Tosterup**, **Orup** and **Bollerup**. On the south side of the road at **Valleberga** is the only round church in Sweden, dating from the 12th century, and 10km (6 miles) southwest of Simrishamn is the famous Glimmingehus Castle.

FOR HISTORY BUFFS

6 Jens Holgersen Ulfstand, the Danish knight and admiral, had been impressed by the Gotlandic architecture while he was serving as governor of the island. In 1499 he set about building **Glimmingehus** in that solid style and, today, this moat-surrounded stronghold is Sweden's best-preserved medieval fort, due partly to the fact that it was never attacked. The interior is open to the public.

SCENIC ROUTE

8 The coast road to the pretty port of Åhus runs north of Brösarp parallel to a long stretch of sandy beach (the 16th-century **Vittskolve** manor is in the countryside to the left). **Åhus** is known as the 'City of Three Sins' because of its specialities of schnapps, *snoose* (the tobacco Swedes wedge between lip and gum) and eels. A full glass of schnapps should be drunk for every 10cm (4 inches) of eel eaten; however, it is the eel which is blamed for the headache the next day.

FOR HISTORY BUFFS

'Skåne is the most beautiful part of Denmark. It is well populated, fertile and rich in merchandise. It has numerous churches. Skåne is a separate part of Denmark, it is like an island surrounded by sea except for its border with Sweden in the east. But even here there are deep forests and difficult hills which one has to overcome before reaching the land of the Swedes.'
Thus wrote Adam of Bremen in the late 11th century. Skåne's past was with Denmark; its present is with Sweden. Many a Skånian will say he feels neither 'Danish' nor 'Swedish', merely 'Skånian' in his proud land of Skåne.

Sweden's largest port for sailing ships with well over 100 of them docking here at the turn of this century. Here, too, is a collection of shipping memorabilia. The coast road continues the 5km (3 miles) from here to Simrishamn (there are prehistoric rock carvings at the quarry near the roadside).

Simrishamn, Skåne

7 An old Baltic port, Simrishamn has an attractive waterfront and a residential quarter with cobbled streets where the roses climb the colourfully painted fishermen's cottages. In the shadows of the church of St Nicholas is a Carl Milles statue of dancing girls. A local curiosity is Frasse's Music Museum with over 400 music machines and, apparently, the world's largest collection of Edison phonographs.

ℹ️ Tullhusgatan 2

*From Simrishamn continue on road **9** northwards along the coast to Brösarp, 28km (17 miles).*

Simrishamn to Brösarp, Skåne

8 Three small fishing villages dot the beach and rocky coast immediately north of Simrishamn: **Baskemölla**, with its picturesque harbour, **Vik** and **Kivik-Vitemölla**. Kivik is famous for its cider and summer market, one of the largest in Sweden and held over two days in July. Just to its south is **Kungagraven**, an enormous royal stone mound tomb from the Bronze Age. It was originally three times the size, 75m (246 feet) in diameter, before stones were filched for construction elsewhere. A further 3km (2 miles) south is **Stenshuvud National Park**, 390 hectares (962 acres) of land spread along the shores with

Baskemölla, on Skåne's east coast, where small wooden fishing boats are still in use

walking trails through forest and extensive views from **Fornborg** (97m/319 feet). The road northwards bears inland after Kivik; to the right at the junction with road 19 is Brösarp station. In summer there is a chance to take a pleasant break from the road and catch the old steam train which operates between Brösarp, **Vitaby** and **St Olof** (approximately a half-hour journey).

Skåne has many medieval parish churches and the ones at Vitaby and St Olof are among the most interesting. The 13th-century crucifix in the former is reputed to contain a piece of the Cross, while the latter was long a place of pilgrimage thanks to curative powers which lay in the silver axe held by the wooden statue of St Olof.

ℹ️ Biokonditoriet, Brösarp

*Take road **19** south of Brösarp, bearing right at Eljaröd for Kristinehov near Andrarum, about 12km (7 miles).*

Kristinehov

9 There was an alum mill at Kristinehov as early as the 17th century (alum was extracted from the local shale and used in the dyeing of textiles). The manor was shaped in its present baroque style in the mid-18th century by its owner, Christina Piper. The Piper family still run the estate, though it is the vineyards and its sparkling wine, rather than alum, for which Kristinehov is known today.

*The cross-country road southeast from Kristinehov runs via Lövestad to Sjöbo (18km/11 miles). Road **13** leads north from Sjöbo via Hörby to Höör (39km/24 miles). For an additional excursion, follow road **104** from the outskirts of Sjöbo and bear left to Övedskloster, an 18th-century castle built on the site of a 12th-century monastery.*

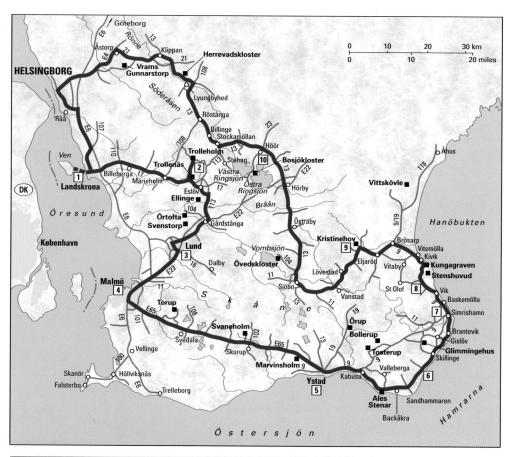

SCENIC ROUTE

10 The stretch of road 13 between Stockamöllan and Ljungbyhed is regarded as one of the most scenic in Skåne. However, the prettiest part of the region is the hills and forests of Söderåsen, to the left of this road. At the northern end of Söderåsen is the 17th-century **Vrams Gunnarstorp** manor, with gardens once praised by Carl Linnaeus; they are open to the public.

Höör and Bosjökloster, Skåne

10 Skåne's *djurpark* (zoo), with over 400 animals of the Nordic regions, is at Höör. The 12th-century Benedictine convent of Bosjökloster has a lovely setting amidst gardens and woods on the banks of Ringsjön, about 8km (5 miles) south of Höör (off the Malmö road). The wealthy sent their daughters here to be educated and they bequeathed large estates to the monastery. However, it was thought that the riches blemished the spiritual purity of the place and eventually a prior was employed to manage the acquisitions so that the women could be left in peace with their prayers. After the Reformation, Bosjökloster gradually fell into disrepair; it is now fully restored and open to the public. (For an alternative attractive route to Stockamöllan, continue south on the Malmö road, bearing right after the lake for Stehag and Stockamöllan.)

Vitaby church, with its white-washed walls and a red tiled roof, is characteristic of medieval Danish architecture

*From Höör, road **13** continues west to Stockamöllan and Ljungbyhed. The 12th-century Cistercian monastery of Herrevadskloster, to the right of the road, was rebuilt in the 18th and 19th centuries. Continue on road **13** to Klippan. Take road **21** to Åstorp and then the **E4** to Helsingborg, 72km (45 miles).*

Heslingborg – Landskrona 22 (14)
Landskrona – Trollenäs 29 (18)
Trollenäs – Lund 41 (25)
Lund – Malmö 17 (11)
Malmö – Ystad 59 (37)
Ystad – Simrishamn 45 (27)
Simrishamn – Brösarp 28 (17)
Brösarp – Kristinehov 12 (7)
Kristinehov – Höör 57 (35)
Höör – Heslingborg 72 (45)

FOR HISTORY BUFFS

The Skånians, with their rich farmlands, did not suffer the hardships of the past as much as their northern neighbours in the forests of Småland. In comparison to the Smålander, who lived a hard, pinched existence, the Skånian enjoyed a more leisurely, indulgent lifestyle. Their cuisine, for example, is traditionally the most lavish in Sweden. Goose, turkey and lamb dishes are local delicacies and *Spettekaka*, a tall meringue-like pyramid, is a Skånian speciality.
Smörgåsbord – the 'national dish' – also originates from Skåne.

2 days – 391km (242 miles)

SMÅLAND

Växjö • Kalmar • Öland • South Öland (west coast) • South Öland (east coast) • Borgholm Kosta • Växjö

After service in the field, Generals Koskull and Stael von Holstein were stationed in the backwoods of Småland in 1742 and, with time on their hands, they decided to found a glassworks at Davedshult. Taking the first three letters of their respective surnames, they renamed the village Kosta. Sweden's beautiful glassware had been born. Today there are a dozen famous glassworks within a 30km (18 mile) radius of Kosta – most were established in the last years of the 19th century – and between them they produce nearly all of the country's fine glassware. You are welcome to visit the works; almost flawless seconds are on offer at favourable prices. This tour through the heart of Glass Country incorporates a side trip to the island of Öland which is linked to the mainland by Ölandsbron, Europe's longest bridge.

From Växjö take road **25** east – the southern route through Glass Country – towards Nybro (80km/50 miles). Glassworks are on or just off this road and are

Glassware from the 'Tigris' collection designed by Erika Lagerbielke of Sandvik

FOR HISTORY BUFFS

1 Between 1861 and 1947 a total of 1.3 million Swedes migrated across the Atlantic. Among them were many Smålanders, including 1,200 people from the commune of Långasjö near Kalmar who quit their stony fields for America. Of these, 210 returned to Sweden. Their tales are touchingly told in one small room of a *Guldgrävarstugan* (log cabin), opposite the Långasjö church. Near by is Klasatorpet, a simple homestead typical of the kind the migrants left behind; it was used as a set in the famous film *Utvandrarna*.

The paint room at Åfors glassworks

well signposted.
From the town of Skruv follow directions on road **25** to Eriksmåla and the nearby Åfors glass factory (13km/8 miles). The Johansfors factory is then 10km (6 miles) south of Eriksmåla via road **28**, and Boda is left off road **25**, 5km (3 miles) further on. It is 15km (9 miles) from the Boda factory to the town of Nybro. Road **25** continues 27km (17 miles) to Kalmar.

Kalmar, Småland

1 Kalmar's medieval castle was Sweden's southern defence when Skåne was ruled by Denmark. In the 16th century the Vasa kings rebuilt the island fort in its present Renaissance style and today it stands in splendour, linked to its old town – itself twice winner of the prestigious Europa Nostra, the prize awarded to Europe's best preserved wooden towns.

The great warship *Kronan*, designed by the British master shipwright Francis Sheldon, was engaged in battle with the Danish-Dutch navy 6km (4 miles) off Öland's east coast on 1 June 1676. As the vessel turned to face the enemy it keeled over and exploded. All except 42 of the 840 crew perished. The wreck of the *Kronan* was discovered in 1980 and parts of it and much of its contents, including bronze cannons and a haul of 255 gold ducats, are now exhibited in the **Kalmar County Museum**.

i Larmgatan 6

From Kalmar take road **137**, following directions for the island of Öland (or Borgholm), and cross Ölandsbron, continuing until you reach Färjestaden at road **136**, the island's main north–south route (12km/7 miles).

Glass Factories

The **Sandvik** factory at Hovmantorp, 28km (17 miles) from Växjö, has been part of the Orrefors glassmaking company since 1918. It is famed for its stemware and coloured glass. A favourite piece with the buying public is 'Illusion', a stemmed glass which has sold over 15 million pieces since it was created in 1957. Sandvik designer Gunnar Cyren was commissioned to make the stemware for the Nobel Foundation's ninetieth anniversary in 1991; the result was the 'Nobel Jubilee' set.

Bergdala, left off road 25 and 7km (4 miles) from Hovmantorp, is renowned for its household and ornamental glassware, in particular its popular blue-rimmed breakfast bowls; visitors can watch them being made.

Strömbergshyttan, a small studio on road 25 soon after Hovmantorp, specialises in painted glassware; there is also a dolls' museum here.

Skruf at Skruv, about 11km (7 miles) to the right of road 25, is most famous for its small bulging barometer which dribbles water when a storm is about to break. It is a popular gift and can be seen on walls of homes throughout the region.

Åfors, a relatively small glassworks, has designers such as Bertil Vallien (maker of glass sculptures) and his wife, Ulrika Hyman-Vallien, whose 'Open Mind' series, with its penetrating eye, is hugely successful.

Johansfors is best known for its ornamental glass and glass tableware, and in particular 'Chateau', which is one of Sweden's most popular wine glasses.

Boda was founded by two artisans from Kosta in 1865. Erik Höglund, one of the foremost names in Swedish glass art in recent decades, was a designer at Boda.

Nybro, a relatively new glassworks, having been established in 1935, specialises in moulded ornamental and table glassware.

Öland

2 Measuring 140km (87 miles) from north to south with a maximum breadth of 16km (10 miles), long, narrow Öland is Sweden's second largest island. The sun shines upon Öland for more hours than anywhere else in Sweden and in summer the island's normal population of 25,000 swells to 2 million. Most tourists head for the beaches in the north,

Kalmar Castle, once a frontline defence on Sweden's southern frontier, is now a museum displaying the region's historic past

the favourite being **Böda**, a 10km (6 mile) stretch of sand. This tour, however, concentrates on the more unusual southern part of Öland.

ⓘ Färjestaden

Follow the 136 south towards Ottenby (51km/32 miles).

South Öland, the west coast

3 There are many ancient burial grounds dating from the Iron Age in this part of the island; **Gettlinge** with its megaliths and ship grave is one such example. Beyond **Degerhamn**, with its ruined, early

SPECIAL TO...

3 Öland has long been a favourite hunting ground for kings (the present monarch has his hunting park in the north of the island). On a famous trip here in the mid-19th century the popular Karl XV had local girls brought to his quarters for his entertainment after his long days on the chase. Today there are islanders who trace their ancestry to that much-loved king.

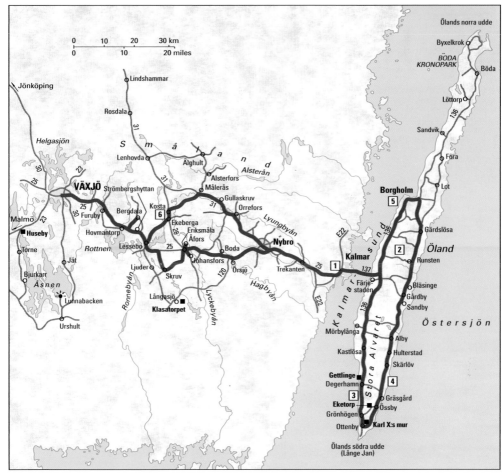

18th-century alum factory, and the fishing village of **Grönhögen** is the **Karl X Wall** which stretches from coast to coast; it was built in 1650 to confine deer to the southern tip of Öland and thus make the king's hunt all the easier. Paradoxically, a portion of this region is now part of the **Ottenby Nature Reserve** and includes Öland's southernmost point – marked by **Lange Jan**, the 42m (138 feet) -high lighthouse built in 1785 – which is a favourite spot for birdwatchers.

*Take the **east coast road** for the return journey northwards to Gärdslösa, about 47km (29 miles).*

South Öland, the east coast

4 At Össby bear left for **Eketorp**, a splendidly reconstructed prehistoric fort. Originally built around AD300, the impressive circular drystone wall enclosed homesteads during three different periods for over 1,000 years. The typical stone, thatched-roofed dwellings have been reconstructed, and a museum recounts the history and displays a selection of the 25,000 archaeological finds.

Back on the east coast road flat fields lead down to stony shores; **Gräsgård** is one of several tiny fishing ports. The *Kronan* sank off this coast in 1676 and parish records at **Hulterstad** tell us that the bodies of 183 of the crew were washed ashore; it seems they were buried without ceremony or gravestone in the village churchyard. With no naval defence, Öland subsequently suffered its darkest year at the hands of Danish plunderers.

Further up the coast at **Sandby** there is a runic stone in the churchyard and at **Bläsinge** it is possible to take a rod and go to sea with local fishermen. **Gärdslösa church** has medieval frescos and rich 17th- and 18th-century adornments. A maze of lanes criss-cross the island – especially in this central part – and Gärdslösa is as good a place as any from where to cut inland to Borgholm on the west coast.

From Gärdslösa it is about 15km (9 miles) along minor roads to Borgholm.

Farmyard animals run around the prehistoric village at Eketorp on Öland

Borgholm, Öland

5 Borgholm is the island's small, attractive capital and main harbour. On a hill on the south side of town is **Borgholm Castle**, the largest fort in Scandinavia at the turn of the 14th century. The huge ruin we see today dates from the mid-17th century. The castle is used as a site for concerts in summer. The royal family has a villa in Solliden.

ℹ️ Hamnen (the harbour)

*From Borgholm head southwards on road **136**, turning right after 24km (15 miles) for Ölandsbron and Kalmar, a further 12km (7 miles). From Kalmar return to Nybro, 27km (17 miles), and rejoin the Glass Route by taking road **31** northwest from Nybro to the Orrefors factory, about 19km (12 miles).
Continue along road **31** to the Gullaskruf factory, 5km (3 miles), and then to the Målerås factory, a further 9km (6 miles).*

From Målerås the road to the southwest leads to the town of Kosta, about 15km (9 miles).

Kosta

6 Kosta, the first of the glassmakers, still crafts traditional-styled crystal but keeps abreast of the times with designers producing exciting shapes in coloured glass. The wooden cottages where the original workers were lodged still stand and some of today's glassmakers can claim over 200 years of unbroken family service for Kosta – from a time when their ancestors made chandeliers and crystal services for the aristocracy. **SEA**, at the other end of town, produces attractive glass for everyday use at everyday prices.

ℹ️ Kosta Glasbruk

*From Kosta drive southwest to Lessebo, 12km (7 miles), and continue west along road **25** back to Växjö (36km/22 miles).*

The head of Gotland stone stack

ⓘ Hamngatan 4, Visby

Take road 149 north out of Visby and follow it through Kappelshamn; continue via Bläse to Rute on road 148; turn left for Fårösund. About 90km (56 miles) in total.

Visby to Fårösund

1 Road 149 runs parallel to the coast, passing the resort of Snäck and the herb gardens at Krusmyntagården before reaching **Lummelundagrottan** and its network of subterranean tunnels and stalactitic caves (14km/9 miles from Visby). A further 13km (8 miles) north is the fishing village of **Lickershamn**, left off the 149, where you find the 11.5m (38feet) - tall **Jungfru** (Virgin), Gotland's highest *rauk*. Another 11km (7 miles) and there is a turning into the peninsula of Hall – a nature reserve on its western side – which leads to the remote headland of **Hallshuk** with its old fishing hamlet, cliffs and *rauk*. This minor road rejoins the 149 at the port of Kappelshamn, but just beyond, at the bottom of the bay, bear left again and follow the coast for about 14km (9 miles) to **Bläse** where the museum at the old limeworks recounts the history of Gotland's once significant limestone industry. Limestone is Gotland's bedrock and the building blocks used for most of the island's medieval defences and churches. From the 1500s burnt lime, as well as slabs of the stone, was shipped to countries across the Baltic. Business was good, the quarry owners grew rich and they developed industrial villages around their lime kilns. However, limestone exports declined in the 19th century and although there was a revival of demand by the new heavy industries early this century, that interest has now dwindled. The workers were forced to move in search of employment and some of their abandoned homes have been bought as summer cottages: tourism is currently Gotland's main source of income. Today limestone is quarried only at Storugns, to the south of Blase, and at Slite on the east coast.

Much of this northern part of Gotland is a military zone and out of bounds to foreigners. At Bläse it is therefore necessary to turn southwards to Fleringe and then Rute, where you bear left along the 148 to Bunge. Here the 14th-century church has interesting murals and there is an open-air museum which gives an insight into Gotland's traditional farm life. Continue on to Fårösund.

From Fårösund take the ferry (no charge) across the short straight to Fårö island.

Fårö

2 Fårö means Island of Sheep and – take care – there are areas where sheep roam quite freely across road and pasture alike. At the village of Fårö – 6km (4 miles) from the ferry

GOTLAND

**Visby to Fårösund • Fårö • Lärbro • Tjelvars grav
Åminne to Fidenäs • Southern Peninsula
Fidenäs to Klintehamn • Klintehamn to Visby**

Gotland, the largest island in the Baltic, is unlike anywhere else in Sweden. It is an island of sun and wind, a coastline of sand and shingle beaches, high cliffs and *raukar* (stone stacks) shaped by weather and sea over thousands of years. The birdlife and flora is rich and unusual and the island's past is revealed in its Bronze Age ship graves, Iron Age forts, Viking legends and medieval churches. Swedes are charmed by the romance and mysticism of this world only 80km (50 miles) from their mainland. They love the uniqueness of Gotland.

point – bear left, and then left again along the track by the lake to **Gamlehamn**, site of a prehistoric and medieval harbour and also the ruins of a chapel to St Olof. In shallow waters across the shingle beach is **the 'Camel'**, one of Gotland's most bizarrly shaped *raukar*. Return to the road and bear left along the northern coast to Lauterhorn, Digerhuvud, the old fishing settlement at Helgumannen and Langhammars. It is a rocky, windswept, empty shore – beautiful in its starkness and all the more special because of its clusters of curious *raukar*. It is 7km (4 miles) from Langhammars – Gotland's northern tip – to Mölnor back on Fårö's main road. Turn to the left and go to Sudersand, the island's most popular sandy beach. Continue on the road: tracks through the forests on the right lead to Fårö's lighthouse and to Norsta Aura, one of Sweden's first nudist beaches; after the beach at Ekeviken the road heads back to Fårö and the ferry point for Fårösund.

From Fårösund double back via Bunge and Rute and continue to Lärbro (25km/16 miles).

Lärbro

3 Lärbro's 13th-century church, with its double-aisled nave and square-ended chancel, is quite characteristic of medieval Gotland design. The octagonal tower dates from the 14th century, while the keep – now the belfry – is from the 12th century. The rich 13th-century murals were removed long ago but the chair in the chancel is from this period.

During World War II King Gustav V persuaded the Germans to allow internees from a concentration

BACK TO NATURE

Gotland is reasonably flat and well suited to cycling. A marked cycle route covering over 500km (300 miles) incorporates some of the most beautiful parts of the island, both on and off the beaten track. Cycles can be hired on Gotland and they can be taken on the local buses when you wish to take a break from pedalling.

SPECIAL TO...

1 Gotland's golden Hanseatic age is relived during one week in August, when Visby becomes, once again, a bustling medieval town. People dress up in period costumes, there is jousting, jesting and other forms of entertainment typical of that time. The arrival of the conquering Valdemar Atterdag is commemorated, as is the execution of the local girl who is said to have betrayed her island to the Danish king.

SPECIAL TO...

2 Stone and 50,000 sheep are Gotland's main natural resources. The islanders have long exported their wool products; Gotland wool items were favoured by the Renaissance Italians, as they continue to be by modern-day visitors to the island.

FOR HISTORY BUFFS

4 Gotland, having been saved from the sea by the mythical Tjelvar, gave birth to a rich culture. The numerous Bronze and Iron Age sites indicate the existence of thriving prehistoric communities. The island became a significant centre for Vikings – whose attentions were focused on Russia and beyond – and continued as a trading crossroads well into the Middle Ages. In 1288 the seafaring farmer-merchants, who had traditionally controlled much of the wealth, lost their influence to the burghers of Visby, who developed close ties with Germany and made their city into a rich centre in the Hanseatic League. During the prosperous medieval times impressive stone churches were built throughout the island, of which over 90 still remain in good condition. Treasures were amassed and frequently buried; hoards of silver and gold are frequently unearthed (unauthorised use of metal detectors is prohibited in an attempt to prevent heritage treasures being discovered and smuggled abroad). However, Gotland's fate was in the hands of the greater Baltic powers, and in 1361 the Danish king Valdemar Atterdag conquered Gotland and thereafter the island became a backwater. The conquest is the subject of a famous painting by C G Hellqvist which hangs in the Historical Museum in Visby.

The meadow and medieval church at Öja

camp in north Europe to come to Lärbro military hospital for treatment tuberculosis. Permission was granted and on recovery many of the patients – they were mainly Poles and Czechs – chose to stay on in Gotland or Sweden after the war. There are, however, 34 simple wooden crosses in Lärbro churchyard on the graves of those who did not survive their illness; next to them, in a separate enclosure, lie their Jewish comrades.

*South of Lärbro, road **147** bears to the left, passing through Slite – once an important Viking port (Bogeviken), now Gotland's second largest town and centre of the limestone industry – and Boge where you turn left on the **146** to Åminne (22km/14 miles). A turning to the right just before Åminne leads to Tjelvars grav.*

Tjelvars grav

4 'Gotland was first discovered by a man named Tjelvar. Gotland was at that time bewitched so that it sank into the sea by day and rose again at night. But this man was the first to bring fire to the land, since when it has never sunk.'

This account appears in the *Guta Saga* – the history of Gotland which was first put on paper in the 13th century. Tjelvars grav, standing stones set in the shape of a ship, was discovered in a clearing of the pine forest and is believed to be Tjelvar's burial place. So far 350 such ship graves dating from the Bronze Age (1500–300BC) have been located in Gotland; they were usually built by the shore, but over the centuries the sea has receded and they are now a short distance inland. Typically, the deceased was cremated and then his bones were washed, crushed and put in an earthernware urn which was buried underneath or placed beside the stone ship. Archaeologists unearthed the remains of burnt bones at this site. Maybe they were Tjelvar's.

Between 300BC and AD500 the Iron Age Gotlanders built over 70 hill forts on their island. Often they were little more than ramparts erected upon a naturally strategic point; there is the site of such a *fornborg* (ancient stronghold) a few minutes' walk from Tjelvars grav.

*From Åminne take the **146** and **144** to Fidenäs, about 100km (62 miles).*

Åminne to Fidenäs

5 Continue from Åminne towards Kräklingbo along the 146; after about 13km (8 miles) a turning to the left leads to **Trullhalsar**, site of 350 stone cairn graves from the Vendel Age (AD550–800). Two kilometres (1 mile) east of Kräklingbo bear east to the resort of Katthammarsvik (a road to the right, 2km (1 mile) out of Kräklingbo, leads to **Torsburgen**, site of Gotland's largest Iron Age fort). It is a scenic coastline east of Katthammarsvik, from Herrvik to the beach at Sandviken and on to **Ljugarn**, Gotland's oldest seaside resort and site of offshore *raukar*. Road 144 cuts inland from Ljugarn (a turning to the left to **När** and the flat Närsholmen peninsula, a stopping point for migratory birds, offers a more leisurely alternative) passing through **Garde** and **Lye**, both with interesting early medieval churches.

From Hemse continue south on the 142. A turning to the left, 2km (1 mile) beyond Grötlingbo, leads to **Kattlunds** where the Judge's Farm (open to the public) is an example of a well-to-do family home spanning various periods of Gotland's past. Return to the main road for Fidenäs (3km/2 miles).

From Fidenäs head south for a circuit of the southern peninsula, about 55km (34 miles).

Southern Peninsula

6 There are two roads from Fidenäs leading into Gotland's pretty southern peninsula. The one on the right is the main and more direct route to Hoburgen and its *gubben* (old man) - shaped rock at the island's furthest point, and passes the traditional Gotland farm at **Bottarve**. The route to the left passes **Öja** – noted for its medieval church with its famous crucifix and meadowed surrounds – and cuts into the eastern part of the peninsula, where the birdlife is rich, to the beaches around **Holmhällar** before rejoining the other route at Mickels, near the 13th-century

Tjelvars grav, a stone ship grave

church of **Vamlingbo**. Turning northwards from Hoburgen be sure to take the scenic route along the lower western side of the peninsula.

Take road 140 north from Fidenäs to Klintehamn, about 41km (25 miles).

Fidenäs to Klintehamn

7 Lanes to the left of the 140 lead down to the sea. There is a rich birdlife around the bay of **Nisseviken** and at **Petesvik**, an 18th- to 19th-century farm has been preserved and converted into a museum. The coast between Hammarudd and Djupvik (from where there is a ferry to L Karlsö) is particularly pretty. East of **Fröjel**, with its pack-saddle-styled church, is the site of the prehistoric village of **Vallhagar**; while 2km (1 mile) to the north is the **Gannarve ship grave**. A further 4km (2 miles) along the road is the resort town of Klintehamn.

Continue along the 140 from Klintehamn to Visby (33km/20 miles).

Klintehamn to Visby

8 Left off the 140, 4km (2 miles) from Klintehamn, are the remains of *Vivesholm's* medieval **castle**. A further 2km (1 mile) along the coast is the fishing village and museum of **Kovik**. **Tofta strand** (15km/9 miles from Klintehamn) is one of Gotland's most popular beaches and just to its north is the fishing village of **Gnisvard**. The **Gnisvard ship grave** is 2km (1 mile) inland, at 45m (148 feet) in length, the longest ship grave ever uncovered. One final detour off the 140 is to **Högklint** (High Cliff). Taking the coastal lane back to the main road at Vibble you pass the 19th-century royal summerhouse at **Fridhem**. From Vibble it is 4km (2 miles) to Visby.

Visby – Fårösund 90 (56)
Fårösund – Fårö 60 (37)
Fårö – Lärbro 25 (16)
Lärbro – Tjelvars Grav 22 (14)
Tjelvars Grav – Fidenäs 100 (62)
Fidenäs – Klintehamn 96 (60)
Klintehamn –Visby 33 (20)

BACK TO NATURE

5 Gotland's flora includes most of Sweden's 40 species of wild orchids and one of the best places to see them is **Östergarnsholm**, a little visited, now deserted, island off Herrvik on the east coast. There is no regular ferry service to the island, but it is possible to hitch a lift with a fisherman.

BACK TO NATURE

8 Gotland as a whole is very rich in birdlife and one of several spots of particular interest to ornithologists is **Stora** (Large) **Karlsö**, an island nature reserve of 2.5 sq km (1 sq mile) in an area located 6.5km (4 miles) off Gotland's west coast (45 minutes by ferry from Klintehamn), where razorbills and guillemots are predominant. Also of interest are the caves, the strange geology and unusual flora. The nearby **Lilla** (Small) **Karlsö** is reached by ferry from Djupvik (20 minutes).

SPECIAL TO...

1 The ruined Cistercian abbey of **Roma** is an important medieval site located in the middle of the island. Dating from 1164, it was destroyed during the Reformation. It is 17km (11 miles) southeast of Visby on road 143.

LAKE VÄTTERN CIRCUIT

Jönköping • Gränna • Visingsö • Vadstena Karlsborg • Mariestad • Lidköping and the Kålland Peninsula • Skara • Hjo • Jönköping

Look at a map of Sweden and two large lakes catch the eye. They lie alongside each other, Vänern – round and large, and Vättern – long and deep. They are the centre of Sweden, not geographically by any stretch of the imagination, but in the mind's eye of most Swedes who see the North as starting somewhere not far beyond them. Furthermore, Swedes regard these lakes as historic heartlands, and important medieval sites lie scattered around the region. Vänern and Vättern lie between Stockholm and Gothenborg (Göteborg) and they are touched by the thoroughfares which run between these cities of the east and west coasts. There is lovely country just off the main roads, for example at Omberg and at Kinnekulle on the shores of Vättern and Vänern respectively.

SCENIC ROUTE

2 A highly recommended detour off road 50 is through the **Omberg** forests. Bear left for **Alvastra**, the 12th-century Cistercian abbey which was ruined after Gustav Vasa plundered its stone for his castle at Vadstena, continue to **Strand**, the home of author Ellen Key, and thereafter to Stocklycke and on to **Hjässan**, the highest point of the tour at 264m (868 feet), from where there are panoramic views over forest, lake and the flat countryside stretching to the east. From Stocklycke it is a scenic 10km (6 mile) road north to Borghamn, where the most dramatic views over Vättern are from the cliff at **Västra Väggar**. The route rejoins road 50 at Rogslösa, soon after Borghamn.
You can extend the detour from Borghamn by turning right back down road 50 and then, after a short distance, bearing left, following the road via Väversunda through flat pretty farmland around **Lake Tåkern**, a nature reserve which is home to over 250 species of birds. Tracks to the left lead from the road to the lake's shore where there are viewing towers. One road to the right runs to **Rök** where, standing next to the church, is one of the most remarkable of Sweden's 2,000 runic stones. The 9th-century **Rök Stone** has 800 characters, making it the longest runic message in the world; it has yet to be comprehensively deciphered.

ℹ️ Djurläkartorget 2, Jönköping

Take the E4 northwards along the shores of Lake Vättern to Gränna (34km/21 miles).

Gränna, Småland

1 In 1652 the influential Count Per Brahe the Younger built a short street with houses (Brahegatan) by the shores of Lake Vättern to the south of his castle (Brahehus). The street evolved into the village of Gränna which, in the 19th century, became a modest resort and artists' colony. The Arctic explorer Salomon August Andrée was born here in 1854; he died attempting to balloon over the North Pole in 1897 (there is a museum in his memory with items salvaged from the fateful expedition). With its painted wooden houses along the cobbled Brahegatan, Gränna remains a charming old village and one which seems a suitable home for polkagrisar (polka-dotted piglets), the peppermint rock-candy delicacy first made by an impoverished widow named Amalia Eriksson in 1859.

ℹ️ Andrée Museum

A ferry service operates between Gränna and the island of Visingsö in Lake Vättern; 25-minute journey time.

Visingsö, Småland

2 The long, flat, narrow island of Visingsö – a stepping stone for giants across Lake Vättern according to the Nordic myths – also bears the mark of Count Per Brahe the Younger and his family. On arriving at the harbour you will see the ruins of his Visingsborg, one of the finest castles in Sweden in the 17th century, which was burnt down by rampaging Russian prisoners-of-war who were detained there in 1718. The nearby herb garden was

A detail of the Rök runic stone

originally planted by the count, and he was responsible, in 1636, for the completion of the **Brahe church** which lies just beyond; it was built on the foundations of a medieval church and lavishly decorated inside in Renaissance and baroque style. Less elaborate is the 12th-century **Kumlaby church**, 3km (2 miles) to the north, with frescos of the Holy Trinity, the Virgin and saints dating from the 15th century. There is a fine view over the island from the tower.
A further 2km (1 mile) along the road is the **Templegarden** – a mock Greek temple now used as an art gallery. At the southern tip of Visingsö are the 12th-century ruins of **Näs**, Sweden's first royal castle, destroyed in 1318 during a battle for the succession to the throne. Visingsö is 15km (9 miles) in length, with a maximum breadth of 3km (2 miles). Distances are short, so consider leaving the car at Gränna harbour and renting a bike on the island. Excursions can also be made by *Remmalagen*, horse-drawn carriages which circulate the island.

ℹ️ Hamnen (the harbour)

From Gränna continue north on road 50 to Ödeshög, 27km (16 miles), and then bear left along road 50 to Vadstena, a further 31km (19 miles).

Vadstena, Östergötland

3 Bridget Birgersdotter, born in 1303, was the daughter of a lawyer and became lady-in-waiting to King Magnus and Queen Blanka in Vadstena. Revelations of increasing strength and clarity appeared to her. She went as a pilgrim to the tomb of the Apostle Jacob in Spain with her husband and on his death entered Alvastra Abbey. She travelled to the Vatican and, after years of persistent appealing, managed to gain papal approval to build an abbey at Vadstena. Inspired by the voice of Christ, she then pressed on from Rome to Jerusalem and it was on her return to Rome that she died in 1373. Pope Boniface IX authorised her canonisation 18 years later. Her bones were brought to **Vadstena Abbey** in 1393, where they became the object of pilgrimage, and remain there to this day. The Brigittine cult remained strong until Gustav Vasa's Reformation 200 years later.
Vadstena retains something of an old character in its pleasant downtown: besides the abbey there are the old **convent** and **monastery** buildings as well as the oldest **courthouse** in Sweden. Most impressive is the moat-surrounded **castle** which Gustav Vasa built in the 16th century; he celebrated his wedding here in 1552.

ℹ️ Rådhustorget and the castle

Proceed north from Vadstena on road 50, crossing the Göta Canal at Motala, and continue along the eastern shore, turning at the top of the lake before Askersund to join road 49 which runs south down Vättern's western shore to Karlsborg (110km/68 miles).

Karlsborg, Västergötland

4 The Göta Kanal (Göta Canal) enters the west side of Vättern at Karlsborg. The town's fame is based on its huge **fortress** with walls 2m (6.5´feet) thick, ramparts stretching 5km (3 miles) in length and the 678m (2,224 feet) -long Slutvärnet, reputedly the longest inhabited building in Europe. The fort was built as part of a programme to improve military prowess in the wake of Sweden's loss of Finland to Russia in 1809. By the time construction was completed in 1909 the need for such a place had dwindled. Today the fort serves as a training base for national service draftees and houses a **military museum** in Slutvärnet.

[i] Norra Kanalgatan 2

*Just north of Karlsborg road **202** wends its way westwards through forest and farmland via Forsvik, with Sweden's oldest iron bridge (1815) and Göta Canal's first lock, and Töreboda (the shortest ferry distance in Sweden, 24m/78 feet, is here across the Göta Canal) to Mariestad, 54km (34 miles).*

Mariestad, Västergötland

5 On the eastern shore of Lake Vänern, the cathedral city of Mariestad is a good base for excursions by ferry to nearby islands such as **Torsö** and **Brommö**. The further Djurö islands are a nature reserve and there is restricted access at certain times of the year.

[i] Hamnplan

*Take the **E20** southwards to Götene, 30km (19 miles), then bear right for Lidköping, 23km (14 miles).*

Roadside decoration on the island of Visingsö

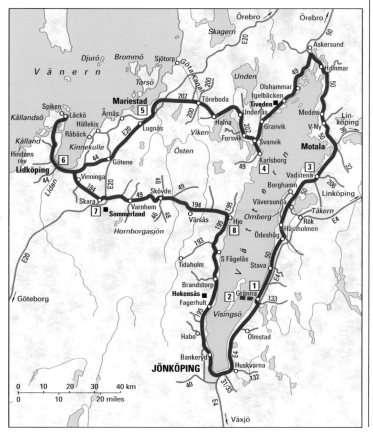

SCENIC ROUTE

5 Turn off the E20 at **Lugnås**, where millstones were quarried and crafted for both the home and export market between the 12th century and the turn of the 20th century. Continue along country lanes to Hällekis, then bear southwards through the picturesque forested and flower-covered **Kinnekulle hills**. During a visit here in 1746 Carl Linnaeus said '…this shire is lovelier than all others'.

A 45km (28 mile) rambling route is signposted through Kinnekulle: the highest point of 306m (1,004 feet) is at **Högkullen**, where a 100-year-old observation tower provides extensive views. South of Kinnekulle, the ancient three-spired **church of Husaby** stands by the spring where Olof Skötkonung, Sweden's first king, was baptised by the missionary St Sigfrid in 1008. Near by, at **Flyhov**, there are hundreds of Bronze Age rock carvings.

Lidköping and the Kålland Peninsula, Västergötland

6 Lidköping, the main market town of the region and famed for its large market square, is Sweden's centre for porcelain. **Rörstrand**, the leading manufacturer, has its factory and museum near the town centre.

Leave Lidköping from the west and turn northwards through Kålland. The peninsula is noted for its prehistoric sites, and in 1985 a remarkable collection of a dozen bronze shields dating from 600BC was discovered at **Fröslunda**. The road leads to the pretty island of **Kållandsö** with its fishing village and marina at Spiken and the splendid 17th-century **castle at Läckö**. Home for bishops of Skara during the Middle Ages, Läckö was given to Gustav Vasa by the last Catholic bishop in 1528. The castle was presented to the great General Jacob de la Gardie in 1615, and he, and his son Magnus rebuilt it in its present style. A reasonable number of the 248 rooms have been restored with the original period pieces. On Kålland's west side, **Hindens rev**, a 5km (3 mile long reef, pokes like a finger into the lake. On the south side the sheltered sandy beach of **Svalnäs** with its shallow waters is dubbed Vänern's Riviera.

i Gamla Rådhuset, Nya Stadens Torg, Lidköping

> *Road 184 leads southeast from Lidköping to Skara, 22km (13 miles).*

Skara, Västergötland

7 The small, pleasant university city of Skara has Sweden's oldest **cathedral**, the original structure dating from the 11th century. Its famous modern stained glass was designed by Bo Beskow. The Fröslunda bronze shields are exhibited at the **local museum** and there are also **veterinary, tank, train and car museums**. Skara's rather more dubious claim to fame is as venue for the world stone-seed spitting championships. Just out of town is **Sommarland**, one of the country's best amusement parks for children, and, to the southeast, Hornborgasjön (**Lake Hornborga**) which, having been drained several times in the past to provide pastureland, is now undergoing a wetlands restoration programme; it is home to a large variety of birds.

i Skolgatan 1

> *It is 26km (16 miles) east along road 49 from Skara, via the 13th-century Cistercian monastery church of Varnhem (buria; Place of some of Sweden's kings), to Skövde, soon after which you branch right on road 194 to Hjo, 35km (22 miles).*

Hjo, Västergötland

8 Hjo won the Europa Nostra medal in 1990 'for the remarkable restoration of the entire wooden town of Hjo, preserving the original quaintness and charm'. A pretty town on the western shore of Lake Vättern, Hjo became a popular resort at the end of the 19th century and it retains much of its character. Fish caught in the lake are smoked down by the harbour (anybody can fish in Vättern, where salmon, arctic char and trout are among the catches) and from here *Trafik*, the 100-year-old ice-breaker passenger steamer, makes trips to Visingsö, Vadstena and Karlsborg.

i Museibyggnaden

> *Take road 195 south from Hjo via Habo to Jönköping, 65km (40 miles).*

Jönköping – Gränna 34 (21)
Gränna – Vadstena 58 (36)
Vadstena – Karlsborg 110 (68)
Karlsborg – Mariestad 54 (34)
Mariestad – Lidköping 53(33)
Lidköping – Skara 82 (51)
Skara – Hjo 61 (38)
Hjo – Jonköping 65 (40)

The great Läckö Castle has been the country home to bishops, a king and a general

A brass band on the streets of Stockholm celebrates the coming of summer

ⓘ Sverigehuset, Kungsträdgården

*From Stockholm take the **E4** northwards and just before Märsta bear left on to road **255** (34km/21 miles). After 6km (4 miles) turn left again on to road **263** and continue for a further 6km (4 miles) to Sigtuna.*

Sigtuna, Uppland

1 Dating from 970, Sigtuna is reput-edly the oldest town in Sweden. It thrived as a trading port and attract-ed merchants from Asia and the Middle East. Coins were struck here by English minters, and churches and monasteries – each better than the next – were commissioned by the wealthy. There were setbacks,

A detail of a runic stone, Uppsala

however; notably when Uppsala stole the limelight as the region's major ecclesiastical centre and again when the Estonians burnt down the town in 1187. But Sigtuna survived and remained prosperous through-out the Middle Ages.

Today it is a quaint small town pleasantly located on the shores of Mälaren. Colourfully painted wood-en houses line the main Stora gatan, built on the ground plan of the origi-nal high street. The remains of the 12th-century **churches of St Olof, St Lars and St Per** are notable, though in best condition is **St Mary's**, part of a monastery dating from 1247. Other points of interest include the old **Town Hall** of 1744, the **local museum**, recounting the region's Viking-medieval period, and **Lundströmska Gården**, the old burgher's house.

ⓘ Stora gatan 33

*From Sigtuna head north via Haga to join road **255** for Uppsala (31km/19 miles).*

Uppsala, Uppland

2 The pre-Viking chiefs of Svea had their seat in Gamla Uppsala (Old Uppsala) and under three huge **bur-ial mounds** lie their kings, Adil, Egil and Aun. The nearby **church** is a remnant of the cathedral built in

MÄLAREN

Stockholm • Sigtuna • Uppsala • Enköping • Västerås
Eskilstuna • Strängnäs • Mariefred • Stockholm

With its waters stretching from far inland to the Baltic, Lake Mälaren provides easy access from the deep interior to the open seas. Both the Vikings and the medieval merchants founded their settlements on the lake's shores and islands, and the region soon became Sweden's heartland. Stockholm is situated at the very point where the lake meets the sea.

Surrounded by rich countryside dotted with castles, manors, cathedrals and ancient towns, the lake is an ideal place for a day trip from the capital. Where possible, branch off from the main roads that now encircle the lake, and take the lanes that skirt the shores. Alternatively, hop on to one of the delightful white steamers which chug between Stockholm and various points around the lake.

1125 on the site of a Svea heathen temple.

In 1273, however, the archbish-opric was moved 5km (3 miles) south to the port of Östra Aros (pre-sent Uppsala), while the kings trans-ferred their residence to Stockholm. Work began on a new **cathedral**, which was eventually consecrated in 1435. The result was, and still is, the largest Gothic cathedral in Scandinavia, measuring 119m (390 feet) in both length and height; the 18th-century twin spires dominate the Uppsala skyline. Sweden's patron saint, Saint Erik, and its kings, archbishops and heroes are all buried here.

The old quarter of Uppsala is on the west bank of the Fyrisån, and opposite the cathedral is the oniondomed, early 17th-century **Gustavianum**, originally an anatomi-cal theatre and now a museum with ancient Nordic and Egyptian collec-tions. Behind this, gardens dotted with runic stones and bronze stat-ues lead to the main building of **Uppsala University**, constructed in lavish fashion in the late 1800s. Founded in the late 15th century, the university is one of Europe's great seats of learning. Like Oxford and Cambridge in Britain, Uppsala and Lund (in the south) are the two most famous university cities of

SPECIAL TO...

1 The 13th-century Cistercian monastery of **Skokloster** was dismantled in 1574 and replaced by the present magnificent, white baroque **castle**, which was commis-sioned in the late 17th century by Karl Gustav Wrangel, Count of Salamis and Grand Marshal and Grand Admiral of Sweden. Exhibitions of armour and paintings are on display. About 14km (8 miles) northwest of Sigtuna, Skokloster can be incorporated into a day excur-sion to Sigtuna and Uppsala, the former of which can also be reached by ferry from Stockholm.

BACK TO NATURE

2 Better known as Linnaeus, the Swedish botanist Carl von Linné initiated the system of nomenclature using the Latin names of both the genus and the species to clas-sify plants. Linnaeus (1707–78) spent his last years at **Hammarby Farm**, 12km (7 miles) southeast of Uppsala; the house and gardens can be visited. Near by are the stones of Mora where Swedish kings would be sworn in.

4 One of the country's largest burial mounds and ship tumuli from the Iron Age and Viking periods is at **Anundshögen**, 6km (4 miles) northeast of Västerås.

4 Silver mined at Sala was of the finest quality and in the 16th century it significantly enriched the country's exchequer. The main mine was closed in 1908 but has now reopened to the public. A museum explains the mining process and the history of the site. Sala is about 40km (25 miles) north of Västerås.

Sweden. The university library, with over two million volumes and 30,000 manuscripts, is particularly impressive. On display is the famous 6th-century Codex Argenteus, a translation of the Gospels written in gold and silver on purple parchment.

It is a short walk southwards through the park and up the hill to **Uppsala Castle** which was started – but never completed – by Gustav Vasa in 1548. One of Uppsala's many famous old boys was botanist Carl von Linné (Linnaeus), who was curator of the gardens which now bear his name; the **Linnéträdgården** (Linnaean Garden) and its museum are on the east side of the river.

i Fyristorg 8 (also in the castle during the summer months)

From Uppsala take road 55 southwest to Enköping (45km/28 miles).

Enköping, Uppland

3 Another of Mälaren's old trading towns, Enköping was the main spice and herb market. Originally endowed with a castle, churches and monasteries, the town lost much of its heritage in the great fire of 1799. Some old buildings have been restored, while others retain just small sections of the past. More recently Enköping has attracted industries and it is as an industrial city that it is best known.

Minor roads lead through the pleasant countryside to the south of Enköping and to the bathing spots at **Harjarö**, at the tip of the peninsula.

i Torggatan 2 (also Kyrkogatan 29 during the summer months)

From Enköping take the E18 west for 34km (21 miles) to Västerås.

Västerås, Västmanland

4 Västerås is a medieval city with an imposing, but much restored, Gothic **cathedral** of 1271; among those enshrined within the building is King Erik XIV.

The city has boomed in recent years, thanks largely to ASEA Brown and Boveri (ABB) setting up their electrical plant here. Today the population is around 120,000, representing an increase of tenfold during this century.

The **Kyrkbacken district**, to the north of the cathedral, has preserved its old character well; the **museum of local history** is housed in the medieval castle, while the city's art collection, with works from the 17th century to the present, is displayed at the old **Town Hall**.

i Stora gatan 40

From Västerås continue west on the E18 and then bear south on road 53 for Eskilstuna (42km/26 miles).

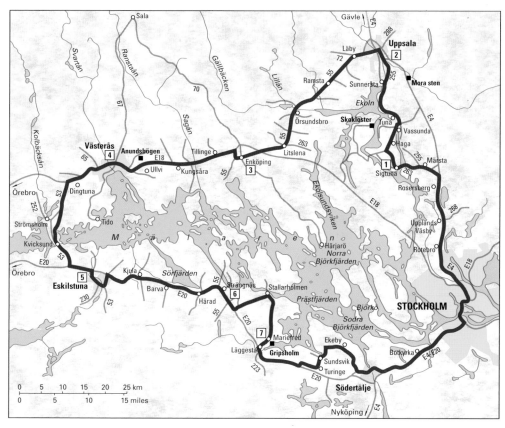

A view of Riddaholmen, Stockholm

Students throughout Sweden celebrate graduation from school in grand style

Eskilstuna, Södermanland

5 The town was named after the missionary bishop, St Eskil, who was stationed at Eskilstuna and martyred in nearby Strängnäs in 1080. Built along the banks of Eskilstunaån, the river which links Mälaren to Lake Hjälmaren, Eskilstuna emerged as an important iron-working town in the 16th century. Some of the large old foundries from the 1600s have been converted into museums and craft shops. Today, steelworking is the town's main industry and Sweden's finest cutlery bears Eskilstuna's name.

i Hamngatan 19

From Eskilstuna take the E20 eastwards for 30km (19 miles) to Strängnäs.

FOR CHILDREN

4 Located 15km (9 miles) southwest of Västerås, part of the 17th-century **Tidö Castle** has been converted into a **toy museum** with around 35,000 exhibits.

Left: the national flag flutters outside Stockholm's Kungliga Dramaten, Sweden's premier theatre

Right: imposing Skokloster, built amidst lovely countryside, is a worthwhile detour from the Stockholm to Uppsala road

Below: the Stockholm district of Södermalm glows a light ochre in the evening sun

SPECIAL TO ...

7 Of all Mälaren's ancient
trading centres it was **Birka**,
on the island of Björkö, in
eastern Mälaren, that flourished the earliest and the
most successfully.
Established between the 9th
and 10th centuries, today the
town-port is little more than
an archaeological site, but it
makes for an interesting visit
all the same.

Strängnäs, Södermanland

6 Set on the banks of Mälaren,
Strängnäs is a small, pretty town
with old wooden houses and a large
historic **cathedral** of 1291. Olavus
Petri introduced the Reformation into
Sweden at Strängnäs in the 1520s,
convincing the local archdeacon,
Laurentius Andreae, of the virtues of
this new trend of Christianity. And it
was from the cathedral's outdoor
pulpit that Andreae proclaimed
Gustav Vasa King of Sweden in
1523; the great king then set about
confiscating the riches of cathedrals
and churches throughout the land,
and Strängnäs was not exempt.
Charles IX, son of Gustav Vasa, is
buried here and his gilded armour
sits astride a model horse to the left
of the splendid 15th-century high
altar. Charles' funeral ensigns are
displayed with other treasures in the
Silver Chamber between the Lower
and Old Vestries.

Various chapels skirt the nave;
one of the most interesting houses
the sarcophagus of Admiral Carl
Carlsson Gyllenhjelm, the illegiti-
mate son of Charles IX who was
ennabled by his father. The cathedral
has one of the finest ecclesiastic
libraries in Sweden.

ℹ️ By the harbour

*From Strängnäs continue on the
E20, bearing left on the minor
road for Stallarholmen and thereafter south for Mariefred
(30km/19 miles).*

*The golden altar in Strängnäs
cathedral is one of the most
treasured pieces of church art in
Sweden*

Mariefred, Södermanland

7 This is yet another quaint town of
wooden houses and narrow lanes,
pleasantly set on the shores of
Mälaren. Mariefred's great attraction
is its large **castle**, Gripsholm, which
was originally a medieval fort but
gradually gained its present shape
over the succeeding centuries. New
owners constantly embellished the
castle, even going so far as knock-
ing down the 14th-century
monastery, Pax Marie, for further
supplies of building blocks. (Echoes
of the monastery's presence still
reverberate, however, in the name
of the town; Pax Marie, or Marie's
Peace, translates in Swedish to
Mariefred.) The castle also houses
the Swedish State Portrait
Collection, including some 3,500
paintings of royalty and nobility.

Local train enthusiasts have
restored early steam locomotives
and rolling stock and now use them
to run a service between Mariefred
and Läggesta (45 minutes).

ℹ️ Radhuset

*From Mariefred continue south
to the E20 and turn left. Turn off
the E20, then bear north before
Turinge for Ekeby, returning to
the main road at Södertälje
(40km/25 miles). From Södertälje
head northeastwards on the E4
for Stockholm (35km/22 miles).*

Stockholm – Sigtuna 46 (28)
Sigtuna – Uppsala 31 (19)
Uppsala – Enköping 45 (28)
Enköping – Västerås 34 (21)
Västerås – Eskilstuna 42 (26)
Eskilstuna – Strängnäs 30 (19)
Strängnäs – Mariefred 30 (19)
Mariefred – Stockholm 75 (47)

SCENIC ROUTE

7 A wonderful change from
driving is the 3 ½-hour journey along Lake Mälaren on
the old steamboat SS
Mariefred from Stockholm to
Mariefred (and the castle of
Gripsholm).

KLARÄLVEN

The dying tradition of log floating is still practised on stretches of the Klarälven

ℹ Västra Torggaten 28 (Bibliotekhuset), Karlstad

Take road 61 north out of Karlstad, thereafter bearing right along the 62 to Ransäter, 50km (31 miles), a short distance before Munkfors.

Ransäter, Värmland

1 The 'Father of Modern Sweden', the much-loved Tage Erlander, prime minister between 1946 and 1969, was born in Ransäter in 1901. He died in 1985 and is buried in the churchyard. His father was the teacher here and the old school where Erlander lived as a boy has been restored and is open to the public; nearby is the museum dedicated to the man under whom Sweden emerged as a prosperous egalitarian society. The differences of class were glaring at Geijersgården, the 18th-century manor house belonging to Ransäter's old iron foundry; the front, where the guests were welcomed, was a glistening white, while the back, the trades-men's entrance, had a lick of cheap red paint. The poet and composer Erik Gustaf Geijer and the author Fredrik August Dahlgren were both born in the house, which is now open to the public. A more realistic insight into the former iron industry can be had at the heritage village and at the preserved foundry, the world's oldest open hearth works, at Munkfors (8km/5 miles).

From Munkfors continue on road 62 to Ekshärad, 48km (30 miles).

Ekshärad, Värmland

2 The iron industry emerged in the Klarälven vicinity in the 1600s. Iron was the life of the communities and even in death, in Ekshärad, they placed iron crosses ('the trees of life with musical leaves') on the graves. The 17th-century church, with its baroque interior and works of art, reflects the level of prosperity at that time.

Continue along road 62 from Ekshärad to Stöllet (30km/19 miles).

Stöllet, Värmland

3 King Olof the Holy (St Olof as he became) attracted a great cult following in Scandinavia during the medieval period. The Klarälven was one of several well-worn pilgrim routes to his tomb in Trondheim and at Norra Ny church at Stöllet there are sculptures of St Olof and the Virgin, as well as other 13th-century sacred relics.

From Stöllet go north on road 62 to Sysslebäck (48km/29 miles).

Sysslebäck, Värmland

4 This is the last upriver town before crossing the Klarälven and return-ing southwards. Up here the timber is stacked on river banks, ready to be pushed into the water for their journey downstream.

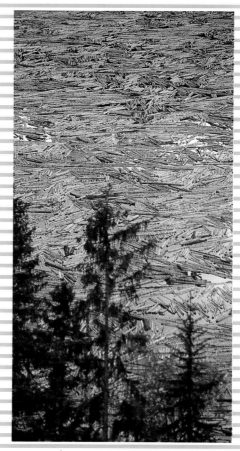

Karlstad • Ransäter • Ekshärad • Stöllet • Syssle-bäck • Torsby • Sunne • Rottneros Park • Karlstad

Approaching from the south, the medieval pilgrims would cross Lake Vänern and continue northwards, using the val-ley of the Klarälven as their path into the hills of Norway, from where they would proceed to Trondheim and the tomb of King Olof the Holy. More recently, timber from the forests strad-dling the Klarälven was floated downstream to Lake Vänern to supply the wood factories at Skoghall near Karlstad. Although today Sweden's timber industry transports its logs by road and rail, here trunks are still floated for at least part of their journey along the Klarälven.

The tour follows the Klarälven upstream into the ever more remote forests. The return south touches an area settled by Finns 400 years ago and follows the beautiful narrow Övre, Mellan and Nedre (Upper, Middle and Lower) Fryken lakes to Karlstad.

A lumberjack takes a coffee break

BACK TO NATURE

4 Rafting down the Klarälven is an increasingly popular activity. To partake, drive to Gunnerud, about 100km (62 miles) upstream of Karlstad, and leave your car. You will be taken to Branäsäng, just south of Sysslebäck, where you are encouraged to build your own raft from logs (assistance given). When you and your raft are considered riverworthy, you are cast off into the constant, gentle 2kmph (1mph) flow of the Klarälven, destination Gunnerud.

Map labels: Klarabro, Letafors, Syssleback, Bograngen, Letten, Dalby, Kindsjön, 567, Branäsbgt, Likenäs, Bjurberget, Backa, Ambjörby, Nyskogå, Stöllet, Kristinefors, Klarälven, Älvdalen, Vitsand, Hovfjället, 542, Åstrand, Lekvattnet, Fensbol, Ritamäki, Torsby, Ekshärad, Kvarntorp, Busjön, Gunnerud, Edebäck, Åshagen, Övre Fryken, Råda, 344, Tossberg, Rådasjön, Stöpafors, Mjönäs, Rottnen, Sunne, Rotternos Park, Munkfors, Rotternos, Mårbacka, Mellan Fryken, Ransäter, V Ämtervik, Ö Ämtervik, Över Ullerud, Elofsrud, Visten, Nilsby, Deje, Frykerud, Ned Fryken, Värmeln, Forshaga, Glafsfjorden, Apertin, Fagerås, Kil, Hynboholm, Klarälven, E18, Alster, Örebro, KARLSTAD, Skoghall, Vänern

0 10 20 30 km
0 10 20 miles

N

Continue north out of Syssleback
and then bear left over the
Klarälven to Letafors. Turn southwards here to Vitsand, after
which you pick up road **45** to
Torsby, about 90km (56 miles)
from Syssleback.

Torsby, Värmland

5 Torsby is the main market town on
the western side of the tour. In the
16th and 17th centuries the Swedish
government encouraged people to
settle in the forests of Värmland by
offering plots of land and exemption
from taxes. A group of Finns, known
as *svedjebönder*, were among those
to take up the offer. They cut and
burnt down trees, tilled the land and
carved for themselves a Little
Finland in the remote borderlands
west and northwest of Torsby. About
20km (12 miles) west of Torsby, at
Lekvattnet, the **Karmen Kynna heritage centre**, with its cluster of
Finnish settlers' houses, gives an
introduction to this incongruous pioneering community. A further 9km (6
miles) southwest of Lekvattnet is
Ritamaki where the farm, smoke
house, cow shed and sauna date
from the 1840s. The older farmstead
of **Kvarntorp** (Myllyla is the Finnish
name) is on the nearby lake of
Kroksjön.

*From Torsby continue south
along road 45 to Sunne, 40km
(24 miles).*

Sunne, Värmland

6 Straddling the channel which links
Övre and Mellan Fryken, the small
town of Sunne is a main tourist centre in this beautiful part of Värmland.
Mårbacka and Ransäter to the east
are easily reached from here.

*Yellow rape in blossom adds a
dazzling dash of colour to the
Swedish countryside*

SPECIAL TO...

1 Värmland has given birth to
a fair number of literary figures, none more important
than Gustaf Fröding,
Sweden's national poet, who
was born in 1860 at the
Alster manor house, just to
the east of Karlstad.

SCENIC ROUTE

5 About halfway between
Torsby and Sunne a side
road branches right from road
45 and ascends to the top of
344m (1,129 feet) Tössberg,
from where there is a magnificent panorama over Övre
Fryken to the east and over
the forests spreading towards
Norway to the west.

From Sunne continue on road 45 to Rottenos Park (4km/2 miles).

Rottenos Park

7Rottenros is the 'Ekeby' from Selma Lagerlöf's book the *Gösta Berling Saga* (The Story of Gösta Berling), a novel based on the traditions and legends of her native Värmland (see Special To...). The 39 hectare (98 acre) estate has fine formal gardens with sculptures by some of Scandinavia's most celebrated artists; there is also an animal park.

En route from Sunne you pass the **Kinship Monument**, a huge carved profile of the map of Värmland surmounted by an eagle. This work by Jussi Mäntynen was erected in 1953 and commemorates the large number of Swedes who migrated from here to America, as well as those Finns who moved to Värmland in search of a better life.

The enchanting flower gardens of Rottenos Park

From Rottenos continue along road 45, turn left on to road 61 via Kil (with the nearby 18th-century manor of Apertin), to Karlstad, 65km (40 miles).

Karlstad – Ransäter 50 (31)
Ransäter – Eksgärad 56 (35)
Eksgärad – Stöllet 30 (19)
Stöllet – Sysslebäck 48 (30)
Sysslebäck – Torsby 94 (56)
Torsby – Sunne 40 (25)
Sunne – Rottneros Park 4 (2)
Rottneros Park – Karlstad 65 (40)

The church at Sunne is outside the town, on the way to Mårbacka

SPECIAL TO...

6Cross the Frykens at Sunne and travel through gentle countryside to **Mårbacka**, home of Selma Lagerlöf, author of the *Gösta Berling Saga* (1891), *Jerusalem* (1902) and *The Wonderful Adventures of Nils* (1907). In 1910 she become the first woman to be awarded the Nobel Prize for Literature. She was born at Mårbacka in 1858 and had a great love for this region, often using local places, under fictitious names, as sets in her stories. She died at Mårbacka in 1940 and is buried alongside members of her family in the lovely churchyard at **Östra Ämtervik**, 6km (4 miles) south of the house, from where it is a pleasant drive back to Karlstad via Nilsby. Mårbacka, preserved with Lagerlöf's effects, can be visited.

2 days – 130km (79 miles)

SILJAN CIRCUIT

Leksand to Tällberg • Rättvik • Nusnäs • Mora Sollerön • Siljansnäs • Västanvik • Leksand Falun

'Glorious is Dalarna, yet sweetest is Siljan', wrote Hans Christian Andersen, the master of the fairytale, after his travels around Sweden in 1840. Surrounded by rolling dales of forest and pasture and with a shoreline dotted with red-painted wood cottages, Siljan is a most picturesque late. And in a country where the traditions are so lovingly displayed in local *hemsbygdsgården* (heritage villages), it is Siljan which most proudly shows off its folklore. Siljan is quintessential quaint Sweden.

FOR CHILDREN

1 Sommarland, the largest of several amusement parks around Siljan, is just north of Leksand on the Tällberg road. The admission charge entitles you to enjoy over 80 activities at no extra cost.

SPECIAL TO...

1 After the long dark winters, Swedes rejoice in the coming of spring and look forward to midsummer – the longest day of light – which is the high point of their calendar. Nowhere is midsummer better celebrated than in Dalarna, where people dress in traditional costumes and raise the maypole (Sweden's tallest one is in Leksand). There is a carnival atmosphere – Nordic style – with dancing around the maypole and drinking through the night.

i Norsgatan, Leksand

In Leksand take the turning for Tällberg, following the old road (the forested lakeside route) rather than the main road 70, 12km (7 miles).

Leksand to Tällberg, Dalarna

1 At Hjortnäs (8km/6 miles), the only village along this stretch of the route, a weekly dance is held down by the *brygga* (jetty); many people arrive by boat. A collection of tin soldiers and other figures are on display at the **Tennfigurmuseum**.

Beautifully situated above Siljan, Tällberg was a typical village of about 30 farms at the turn of the century. But with the coming of the railway in 1914 many 'outsiders' were attracted to this beautiful spot. They bought property and Tällberg was transformed into a 'tourist' village. Today there are seven hotels, handicraft shops and an old homestead museum. It has been developed in the best possible taste and all new buildings must be constructed in the traditional style.

From Tällberg continue along the lake before cutting inland to road 70; bear right for Rättvik (18km/11 miles).

A traditional Dalarna kurbits design painted on a window shutter near Leksand

Rättvik, Dalarna

2 'If you meet two men from Rättvik, three of them will be fiddlers', goes a curious old saying. Indeed, there is a strong fiddling tradition around Siljan and in the first week of July musicians come together during the Musik vid Siljan festival to perform over 100 concerts – mainly folk music – in Rättvik, Leksand and elsewhere in the region. The people of Dalarna are also traditionally good churchgoers. They came from afar by horse – the old stables by Rättvik's lakeside church still stand – or by boat. In summer parishioners still take the long church boat to Sunday service (a symbolic rather than a necessary action). Church boats are an important feature of Siljan's folk history and – ever keen to keep alive their traditions – the locals hold church boat races during the summer, with the grand final tournament held in the waters off Leksand.

Information about the meteorite which crashed to Earth and created the beautiful world of Siljan is displayed at the museum in the **Kulturhus**.

i Torget

From Rättvik it is 40km (25 miles) on road 70 to Mora. A short distance before Mora bear left for Nusnäs.

Nusnäs, Dalarna

3 During the 19th century woodmen would spend long periods in the forests away from their families, and in the evenings they often passed the time in their lonely huts carving figures from pieces of wood, which they would bring home to their children or barter for goods at the market. The horse, the reliable beast of burden and faithful companion, was the figure most commonly carved. In 1928 two young teenage brothers, Nils and Jannes Olsson, turned their hands to this old craft. They found buyers for their figures, business expanded and today their workshops in Nusnäs produce huge numbers of wooden horses for home and abroad. The figures are still crafted and painted by hand. Red – the colour of nearby Mora – is most characteristic, while yellow and grey, the traditional colours of Leksand and Rättvik respectively, are less common; the painted designs are copies of traditional patterns. The Dalarna Horse, found in homes throughout the country, has become the symbol of Sweden and the most popular souvenir from these shores. The Olssons' workshops welcome visitors.

It is a 5- to 10-minute drive from Nusnäs into downtown Mora.

Mora, Dalarna

4 With a population of 20,000, Mora, at the northern point of the lake, is Siljan's largest town. A statue of Gustav Vasa by Anders Zorn stands on a mound by the clock tower. It commemorates the occasion in 1520 when the Swedish hero arrived here to appeal to the *masar* (men of Dalarna) to rise up against the occupying Danes. They lent their support to great effect. As further celebration of this historic connection, a cross-country ski race – *Vasaloppet* – is held on the first Sunday every March along the route skied by Gustav Vasa between Mora and Sälen (90km/54 miles); it was first organised in 1922 and today it draws 28,000 participants each year. The inspiration and history of the race is related at the **Vasaloppsmuseum**.

Anders Zorn, one of Sweden's most famous artists, was from Mora and his **home**, **studio** and the nearby **Zorn Museum** provide an excellent insight into the man and his art. Zorn, who lived from 1860 to 1920, had a great love for the region

– Dalarna scenes and the local *kullor* girls were among his favourite subject matter – and he encouraged the folk traditions, arranging the first fiddlers' reunion in 1906, an event from which we can trace the region's present huge interest in folk music. The **Zorn Gammelgård**, a heritage village in the town, displays the old culture. Mora is also known for its wooden 'Grandfather' clocks.

☐ Ångbåtskajen

From Mora take the road across the causeway to Sollerön, 16km (10 miles) and then take the other road off the island to Gesunda, 6km (4 miles).

Villagers dressed in their local costume row their churchboat on Lake Siljan

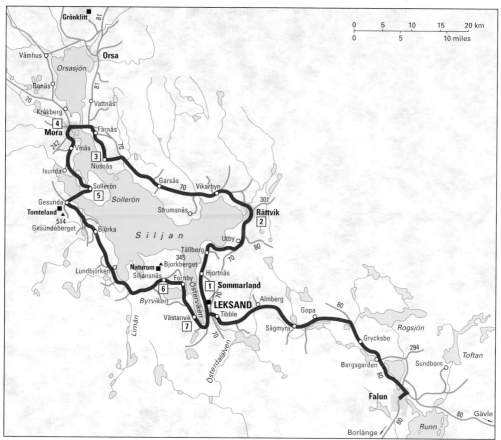

FOR HISTORY BUFFS

1 Gustav V was walking down the aisle in Leksand church after the service one day, when, suddenly, the four young Björling brothers at the back of the congregation began to sing. The king and his queen were highly amused and subsequently had this impromptu chorus recorded on canvas. Jusse, the second boy, was to become one of the all-time great opera singers during the 1930s, performing to kings throughout the world.

Sollerön, Dalarna

5 Sollerön – the 'Island of Sun' measuring 10km (6 miles) by 5km (3 miles) – is the only island of any real habitable size on Siljan. Vikings lived here and their burial ground – site of 123 graves – is in the north part of the island. Jurgen Jon, a local, twice walked to Stockholm to ask the king to grant autonomous parish rights to Sollerön. His request was granted in 1775 and the church was named Sofia Magdalena in honour of the queen.

Cross to **Gesunda**. From the summit of Gesunda (514m/1,690 feet) you can see seven parish churches on a clear day. Ski slopes have been cut through the mountain's woods; at the bottom is a children's park at **Tomteland**, home of Dalarna's Father Christmas.

From Gesunda it is 28km (17 miles) south along Siljan's western shore to Siljansnäs.

Siljansnäs, Dalarna

6 Siljansnäs is on the south side of Björkberget – a peninsula jutting into Siljan – and it overlooks the sheltered bay of Byrviken rather than the open expanse of water. On the hill's slope is **MasOlle's heritage homestead**, while on its summit is the **Naturum** and a 36 hectare (88 acre) **nature park**. About 360

A decorated panel from a building at the Skansen open-air museum, Stockholm

One of many Dalarna folk festivals

8 The Dalarnan peasants used to paint pictures on the furniture and walls of their wooden cottages. However, the inspiration for their subject matter was limited, being drawn from the small isolated world in which they lived. Rose and flower designs, known as *Kurbits*, were popular. Biblical characters heard about in church were also depicted; nobody had any idea that other races looked different from themselves so the characters were portrayed as local Dalarnans; Jerusalem was painted as Falun, the main town in the region. These Dal Paintings date from between 1780 and 1870.

million years ago a huge meteorite crashed here, creating the Ring of Siljan, a circular valley part of which is Lake Siljan; the 345m (1,132 feet) Björkberget is a high point on the rim of the ring with views over Siljan. The impact of the meteorite and the subsequent shaping of the landscape is described in the Naturum.

From Siljansnäs cross the causeway over the mouth of Byrviken and continue to Västanvik (9km/6 miles).

Västanvik, Dalarna

7 Västanvik, a characteristic, pretty Siljan village of red-painted wooden houses, faces Leksand across the long narrow bay of Österviken. This is home of the Jobs, the family famous for the handprinted textiles which portray the traditional art of Dalarna and other Swedish motifs in imaginative designs. The Jobs' shop and printing room are open to visitors.

The road continues around the bottom of Österviken to Leksand, 5km (3 miles).

**EXTENSION
TO FALUN**

From Leksand take the scenic road to Falun via the village of Tibble, just east of Leksand, and Sågmyra, 49km (30 miles).

Falun, Dalarna

8 The town of Falun was born from copper. It was first discovered here in 1000 and during the 1200s the mining rights were procured by Stora Kopparberg, believed to be the world's oldest industrial corporation. Falun went on to become the greatest producer of copper anywhere and in the 17th century it provided two-thirds of the world's copper. The mine has recently closed, but the huge open-cast pit and some of the underground galleries have reopened to the public; there is also an interesting museum on site. A side product from the mining operation was paint, with red colouring from the minerals. The paint, because it was cheap and had protective qualities, was instantly popular with the Dalarnans who continue to paint their houses the distinctive Falun Red.

Carl Larsson, Sweden's most celebrated painter, had a house at Sundborn 14km (9 miles) northeast of Falun; he died in 1919 aged 66 and is buried here. His home and studio are now a museum.

[i] Stora Torget

Leksand – Tällberg 12 (7)
Tällberg – Rättvik 18 (11)
Rättvik – Nüsnas 28 (17)
Nüsnas – Mora 8 (5)
Mora – Sollerön 16 (10)
Sollerön – Siljansnas 34 (21)
Siljansnas – Västanvik 9 (6)
Västanvik – Leksand 5 (3)

2 days – 353km (220 miles)

ÅRE CIRCUIT

Östersund • Åre • Tännforsen • Karl Johan's Road
Anjan Mountain Station and Skäckerfjällen
Nature Reserve • Kall • Östersund

The retreating Ice Age scarred, scoured and shaped the mountain landscape of western Jämtland. Today these high fells offer splendid open, empty expanses of wilderness for hikers. The tour starts at Östersund, provincial capital of Jämtland, and proceeds west along the E14 – the main road to Norway – and once a path for pilgrims to St Olof's tomb in Trondheim – and passes the resort of Åre before making a 200km (124 mile) circuit through the fell countryside surrounding the lovely Kallsjön (Lake Kallsjön).

SCENIC ROUTE

1 Southern Årefjellen is one of the region's most popular trekking areas (there are routes for all standards). A road south from Undersåker – 15km (9 miles) east of Åre – leads to villages such as Edsåsen, Dalen, Ottsjö, Vallbo and Vålådalen from where there are trails deep into the empty high fells.

FOR HISTORY BUFFS

1 In the summer of 1718 Sweden's King Karl XII launched his offensive on Norway. While he approached Frederiksten in the south his General Armfeldt marched with his army of 9,000 from the small fort at Duved towards Trondheim. Armfeldt's men pushed westwards with confidence, destroying and pillaging along the way. On reaching Trondheim, however, they were rebuffed by strong resistance and were forced to retreat. It was mid-winter by the time they recrossed the border and, ill-equipped for the harsh coldness, 3,450 of the Karolin soldiers lost their lives. Memorial stones at Duved and west at Ånn, Handöl and Bustvalen commemorate those who died here as a result of this miserable campaign.

i Rådhusgatan 44, Östersund

From Östersund take the E14 – the road to Norway – west via Järpen to Åre (98km/59 miles).

Åre, Jämtland

1 In the Middle Ages Åre's stone 12th-century **church** – with its decorated wooden interior – was a stopping point for pilgrims *en route* to Trondheim; the 14th-century statue of King Olof the Holy was crowned with its Karolin hat in the late 1600s. By the 19th century the village become a spa resort and it even attracted the British gentry who found the excellent fishing in the mountain streams an admirable pastime. Åre remains fashionable and today it is one of Sweden's foremost ski resorts: immediately to the north rise the slopes of the 1,420m (4,659 feet) high **Mount Åreskutan**. Come summer, hikers take to the paths to the top; alternatively a cable car – the only one in Sweden – operates a service to 1,274m (4,180 feet) from where it is a stroll to the summit.

From Åre continue westwards on the E14 and, having passed through the resort of Duved and crossed the River Indal, bear right and follow the signs for Tännforsen (21km/13 miles).

Tännforsen, Jämtland

2 The River Indal narrows to a width of 60m (197 feet) and crashes down 39m (128 feet) into Lake Östra Noren. In full flow the spectacular Tännforsen falls carries 715 cubic metres of water per second. Local guides put this volume into perspective: if all Jämtland's 135,000 population flushed their lavatories at the same time, they would use roughly the same quantity of water.

The river and the surrounding forests are a nature reserve; certain flora, and particularly lichens, normally found in coastal regions can survive here because of the constant dampness of the air. During cold winters, when it freezes into a sheet of glistening hanging ice, Tännforsen is at its most beautiful.

Continue northwest from Tännforsen to Sandvika, just over the Norwegian border (38km/24 miles).

Karl Johan's Road

3 The road gently ascends through forest and farmland to a land of lakes and fells, where the settlements are small and few. Once the main route into Norway, the road was improved in preparation for Karl XIV Johan's journey to the Trondelag region in 1835. You can see the small stone arched bridges alongside the present road.

From Sandvika the road runs north in Norway for 6km (4 miles) before cutting back into Sweden as road 336. It is 33km (21 miles) to Anjan fjäll Station.

Anjan Mountain Station and Skäckerfjällen Nature Reserve, Jämtland

4 Anjan – or Kolåsen further to the east – are bases for treks into Skäckerfjällen nature reserve. The mountains are gentle – Sandfjället at 1,230m (4,035 feet) is the highest point – the paths are few and the vegetation sparse above the coniferous forest treeline. The region is cut by the lovely Rutses Valley, where the flora is more luxuriant. Push on upriver to the high meadows at Gallonaute and possibly return downstream by canoe (canoes can be hired at Kolåsen). In the 19th century merchandise was transported along these waterways. Herrings were brought by boat from the Norwegian fjord port of Levanger along rivers and via lakes Anjan and Kallsjön to Storsjön; wood and minerals would travel in the opposite direction.

From Anjan continue on road 336, following the eastern shore of Kallsjön, and pass by Mount Suljätten (844m/2,769 feet) to Kall (82km/51 miles).

Kall, Jämtland

5 The village of Kall, directly across Kallsjön from Åreskutan, is the most significant settlement on the lake. Its large wooden **church** has a 13th-century statue of the Madonna.

One possible excursion from Kall is northwards to **Bergsjön** and **Killingskalsberget** – by road to Movallen, then by foot – and the **Bergsjö caves and tunnels** which descend 200m (656 feet); it is about 7km (4 miles) from Kall to the caves. The *Drottning Sophia*, a passenger steamer dating from 1904, provides pleasant trips around Lake Kallsjön.

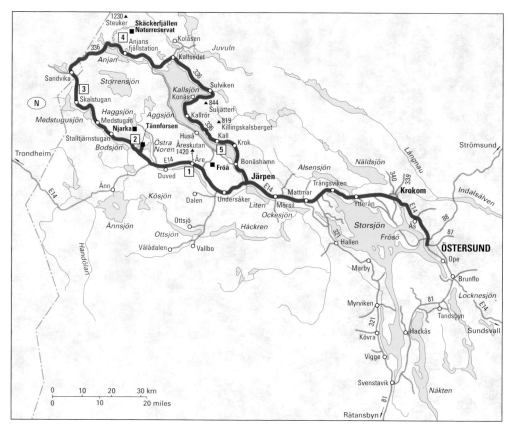

It is a further 21km (13 miles) from Kall to Järpen on the *E14*: to the right is Åre, 25km (16 miles); to the left is Östersund, 73km (45 miles).

Åreskutan – still snowcapped in June – rises above Kallsjön

Östersund – Åre 98 (61)
Åre – Tännforsen 21 (13)
Tännforsen – Karl Johan's Road (Sandvika) 38 (24)
Karl Johan's Road – Anjans Fjällstation 33 (21)
Anjans Fjällstation – Kall 69 (43)
Kall – Östersund 94 (58)

SPECIAL TO...

2 The territory of the southern Lapps extended into Jämtland. Up in the hills above Lake Häggsjön is **Njarka** – 30km (19 miles) northwest of Åre – a small traditional Lapp camp which is open to visitors. Farmers in this region breed the hardy North Swedish horses, as well as Iceland and Fjord horses.

SPECIAL TO...

4 Jämtlanders claim to have a monster similar to 'Nessie' in the depths of Lake Storsjön. This primeval beast, known as Storsjöodjur, looks like a huge dragon serpent and features as a symbol of Jämtland. There have been alleged sightings and numerous unsuccessful attempts to entrap the creature.

SPECIAL TO...

5 Legend has it that Rut and Jatt, two giants, hurled boulders at each other across Lake Kallsjön as they fought for supremacy of this area. Apparently, Rut won with a perfect hit to the head and the fallen Jatt can still be seen, his profiled head being the 844m (2,776 feet) -high Mount Suljätten.

3 days – 502km (301 miles)

HIGH COAST

Sundsvall • Timrå • Härnösand • The High Coast
Junsele • Näsåker • Sollefteå • Kramfors
Sundsvall

With its forests, rivers and lakes, the county of Ångermanland is not dissimilar to most of the rest of the province of Västernorrlands Län. What does make it different, however, is its *Höga Kusten* (High Coast) between the towns of Härnösand and Örnsköldsvik which, with its hilly wooded peninsulas and secluded coves, must be one of the of the most beautiful shorelines on the Baltic.

The tour starts at Sundsvall, central Sweden's main port and ferry point to Vaasa in Finland, and leads north to explore the High Coast, before cutting inland to the deep, sparsely populated forests. Timber is, after all, the past, present and no doubt the future of the region.

The return journey follows the lower reaches of Ångermanälven, one of several significant rivers which flow to the Baltic from the west.

SPECIAL TO...

1 In 1796 Magnus Huss – Vildhussen (Wild Huss) to his friends – tried to float his logs downstream by creating a channel to bypass the Storforsen falls at Lake Ragunda. There were heavy rains that year and the water burst through Huss' barriers and formed its own course to the sea. The result was the emptying of Lake Ragunda, the disappearance of the falls and the creation of the coastal delta.

SPECIAL TO...

3 Several boats ferry passengers along the High Coast. Aim for **Ulvön**. In summer there are daily services to the island from Ullånger, Docksta, Mjällomslandet, Köpmanholmen, Veasand and Norrfallsviken.

BACK TO NATURE

3 Skuleskogen National Park, with trails up hills and through forests, is the High Coast's largest nature reserve; the narrow 200m (657 feet) Slättdal ravine is 40m (131 feet) deep. On the other side of the E4 there are more demanding climbing routes up the 295m (970 feet) high Skuleberget. The nearby Skule Naturum has information.

From Sundsvall travel north on the E4 to Timrå, 12km (7 miles).

Timrå, Medelpad

1 Situated on the River Indal by the coastal delta, Timrå was first touched by the industrial revolution in 1685 with the opening of the **Lögdö iron foundry** to the north of the town (the old furnaces are now evocative ruins, but the manor house, the labourers' lodgings and the work's chapel – currently a highly fashionable place to be married – have been restored). But it was the trees brought downstream from the interior which became the basis of Timrå's prosperity, and the German romantic-styled **Merlö Manor**, the summer residence of timber baron Fredrik Bunsow – who had saw mills at nearby Skönvik – is a relic of the 19th-century timberboom days. Part of the old wood plant at **Wifstavarf** has been preserved; but today business has shifted away from timber and now concentrates on papermaking. The largest concentration of saw mills existed across the strait on the island of Alnö, where there are many sites from that past; at Alnö's *hemsbygdsgard* – near the beautifully decorated 12th-century church – we are given an insight into the mill workers' lifestyle.

ⓘ Bergeforsparken

From Timrå continue north along the E4 to Härnösand, 37km (23 miles).

Skiing is a major Swedish pastime

Härnösand, Ångermanland

2 Härnösand **cathedral** was burnt down by the Russians in 1721; the new white one – built in 1846 in neo-classical style – is the smallest cathedral in Sweden. The wood houses in the old quarter of Östanbacken date mainly from the 18th and 19th centuries; the collection of traditional buildings assembled on **Murberget** is, after Stockholm's Skansen, the largest open-air museum of this kind in the country.

ⓘ Spiran

From Härnösand continue north along the E4, crossing the Ångermanälven (River Ångerman) at Veda, 23km (14 miles). At Hornön, on the far bank, a sign to the right directs to Höga Kusten (the High Coast).

The High Coast, Ångermanland

3 The network of minor roads and tracks leads through the lovely gentle countryside, hills and forests of the High Coast. Travel out to the ends of peninsulas, to the small fishing villages and secluded coves. Follow the route between at least some of the following places and you will get a fair feel of the region: Berghamn, Mädan, Nordingrå – dubbed the Heart of the High Coast – Bönhamn, Barsta, Mjällom, Norrfällsviken.

ⓘ Bredbyn's Hostelry, Bredbyn

Return to the E4 at Ullånger (take the road via Salsåker) and continue north via Docksta (the Skuleskogen National Park is to the right) towards Örnsköldsvik, 54km (34 miles). Just before Örnsköldsvik a road bears inland to Bredbyn (with its 1437 Anundsjö church, which has a decorated interior) and continues through forest to Solberg and the junction at Hälla, about 110km (68 miles). From Hälla turn southwards and follow the Ångerman downstream (road 90) to Junsele, 36km (22 miles).

Junsele, Ångermanland

4 Among the pine forests at Junsele there are – besides the elks and the bears – white tigers and a camel called Fejzal; the **zoo** is particularly popular with children. There is good fishing to be had throughout this region; **Lake Betarsjön**, immediately west of Junsele, is well stocked with salmon, trout and the local whiting-like *betersil*. Minor roads lead east into the forests to old woodmen's homesteads such as **Kläppsjö**.

ⓘ Turist Services Kampanj 90

From Junsele continue along road 90 for 34km (21 miles) to Näsåker.

Näsåker, Ångermanland

5 One of Scandinavia's finest collections of **rock carvings** – depicting elks, fish and hunters – has been discovered on the islands and shores near Namforsen falls at Näsåker. They date from about

3000BC, and a settlement from this time has been reconstructed on the river bank. Scantily clad in skins, locals enact Stone Age activities for visitors. The falls refer to the waters emitted through the dam at the hydro-electricity power plant which crosses the river at this point.

It is a further 40km (25 miles) along road 90 to Sollefteå. The parallel minor road which closely follows the river is a more scenic and interesting route.

Sollefteå, Ångermanland

6 Attractively located on the Ångerman river, the old garrison town of Sollefteå was, like many other places in the region, heavily involved in iron working (the 18th-century Galsjö foundry is to the east) and timber. The **Log Driver's statue** by the bridge is a testimony to that past.

Today the town is one of the country's main producers of hydro-electricity. It is also known for its *nipa* – the curious hillocks near the river – its ski jumps and **National Dog Training Academy**, where dogs are taught to lead the blind or sniff out drugs; the kennel, one of the largest in Europe, can be visited.

i Torggatan 4

Take road 335 east out of Sollefteå and follow the left bank

– *the 334 after Boteå – and re-cross the river at Sandslån for Kramfors, 63km (38 miles).*

Kramfors, Ångermanland

7 The Ångerman used to be Sweden's main timber-floating river, with over 20 million logs passing down its stream each year. Kramfors, at the point where the Ångerman widens before entering the Baltic, developed as a wood-processing town. The nearby Sandslån was a main timber sorting depot until its closure in 1982; the 18th-century sawmills at Bollstabruk continue to function. Suffering during the Depression, workers embarked on a protest march in 1931. When they arrived at Lunde, to the south of Kramfors, the military opened fire killing five demonstrators. A statue by Sandöbron bridge commemorates those who died.

i Företagens hus

South of Kramfors the road rejoins the E4. From Kramfors it is 97km (60 miles) via Härnösand and Timrå back to Sundsvall.

Sundsvall – Timrå 12 (7)
Timrå – Härnösand 37 (23)
Härnösand – Nordingrå 65 (41)
Nordingrå – Junsele 200 (124)
Junsele – Näsåker 34 (21)
Näsåker – Sollefteå 40 (25)
Sollefteå – Kramfors 63 (39)
Kramfors – Sundsvall 97 (60)

SPECIAL TO...

1 Västernorrland province (Ångermanland and Medelpad counties) had the power but not the metal. The iron ore was brought here because of the region's huge supplies of wood which were so essential to fuel the foundries. The first works were established at Graninge, west of Sollefteå, in 1673 and it smelted iron ore shipped from Utö, the island in Stockholm's archipelago. By the mid-18th century there were 21 iron foundries in Västernorrland. The decline came with the shift from charcoal to steam as a means of powering the industry. But by now trees themselves were the most profitable resource. Timber was floated down the rivers to the coast for processing and transport. For the past 100 years Västernorrland's wood has accounted for about half of Sweden's total exports. It is the province's endless forests, more than anything else, which have provided Sweden with its modern prosperity.

SPECIAL TO...

3 Tinned *surströmming* – sour and fermented Baltic herring – is a speciality of the High Coast. Traditionally it is eaten on the first Thursday in August and out of doors because of the terrible stench (eat direct from the tin to avoid tainting plates with the aroma); breath can be freshened by eating tomatoes.

SPECIAL TO...

5 In the valleys west of Näsåker the locals flavour their schnapps with potent-smelling secretions from the glands of beavers. This unusual blend is a healthy tonic with aphrodisiac qualities, supposedly.

FOR CHILDREN

6 Children throughout Sweden are taught how to respect their environment by the Mulle Man, who visits schools and takes classes to the forests where he introduces children to nature. Sollefteå has a special Mulle centre; all children are welcome.

SCENIC ROUTE

6 You can extend the tour by heading southwestwards from Sollefteå to Bispgården, then bearing left to follow the lovely **valley of the Indal**, probably the most picturesque of the region's river valleys – crossing the river for Sundsvall before Timrå.

3 days – 614km (368 miles)

BLUE-SILVER
WAYS

**Storuman • Sorsele • Arjeplog • Border crossing
near Kåtaviken • Hemavan and Tärnaby
Storuman**

This is the southern quarter of Lappland, the vast, sparsely populated northern county of Sweden, home of reindeer-herding Lapps. The tour follows a short section of the Blå Vägen (Blue Way) – a 1,760km (1,094 mile) scenic route which traces a path from the Norwegian coast across Sweden, the Gulf of Bothnia and Finland to Petrozavodsk in Russian Karelia – and the parallel stretch of the Silver Way, an old trading trail. It is necessary to cross into Norway to find a road which links the upper parts of these two ways. Travelling westwards you leave behind the dense coniferous and primeval forests and gradually ascend through a strange landscape of twisted dwarf birch to the sparse treeless fells which characterise the high borderlands between Sweden and Norway.

*Top, left: the mountains of
Lappland
Above: farming reindeer
Below: Swedish Lappland*

BACK TO NATURE

'If not for the mosquitoes, t'would this be earth's paradise,' declared Carl Linnaeus on his visit to Lappland in the 18th century. Come summer and the mosquitoes are truly enormous and extraordinarily bothersome.

ℹ Storuman Railway Station

From Storuman take road 45 north to Sorsele, 75km (47 miles).

Sorsele, Lappland

1 The main reason for visiting this region is to experience the wilderness and to get an idea of the Lapp culture: follow the Vindelälven (River Vindeln) – one of the few rivers to be left untapped for water power – northwest of Sorsele. The pioneering Swedes settled along the valley in the 17th century, pushing the native Lapps ever upstream, and some of their old homesteads and chapels still stand. The road leads to **Ammarnäs** – 90km (56 miles) from Sorsele – a village of 300 people where the local Lapps tend Sweden's largest concentration of reindeer. Ammarnäs – a focal point for Lapps in the region – is the main settlement in **Vindelfjällen**, one of Europe's largest nature reserves covering 550,000 hectares (1,358,000 acres), and it is a base for treks/horse rides into the surrounding fells; local Lapps can serve as guides into this vast remoteness. Return to Sorsele via the same route.

ℹ Sorsele Railway Station

From Sorsele continue along road 45 to Slagnäs, about 35km

(22 miles), and then turn north for Arjeplog, 60km (37 miles).

Arjeplog, Lappland

2 Standing on the shores of two large lakes – the Hornavan and the Uddjaur – is Arjeplog, an old Lapp market town. With her missionary zeal to proselyise Lappland, Queen Kristina had Arjeplog church built in the 1640s.

Across the square is the **museum**. During his 43 years as district doctor in Arjeplog, Einar Wallquist amassed a large collection of Lappish silver and artefacts which he bequeathed, on his retirement in 1965, to the Silver Museum. With the profits from trading skins and furs the Lapps would commission silver goods (they never made their own silverware) such as decorative collars, spoons and bowls, which were regarded as symbols of wealth. The museum, which Wallquist had converted from an old school house, displays some of the finest Lapp silver as well as other treasures, including an atlas of Lappland by Mose Pit (Oxford 1680–82); furthermore, it provides an excellent insight into the Lappish history and culture.

ℹ Torget

From Arjeplog continue northwestwards on road 95 – the Silver Way – to the

SCENIC ROUTE

1 Road 45 – Inlandsvägen (the Inland Road) – runs from Göteborg northwards right through the interior of Sweden, including the heart of Lappland, to Karesuando (1,800km/1,118 miles) on the Finnish border, from where you can continue to the North Cape. Inlandsbanan (the Inland Railway) cuts through the same central regions between Mora and Gällivare.

SPECIAL TO...

2 The nomadic Lapps have long come together at huge annual markets. The 350-year-old Arjeplog market is still held every March, but most impressive is the February market at **Jokkmokk** – the Lapp 'capital', 100km (62 miles) northeast of Arjeplog – which dates from 1605.

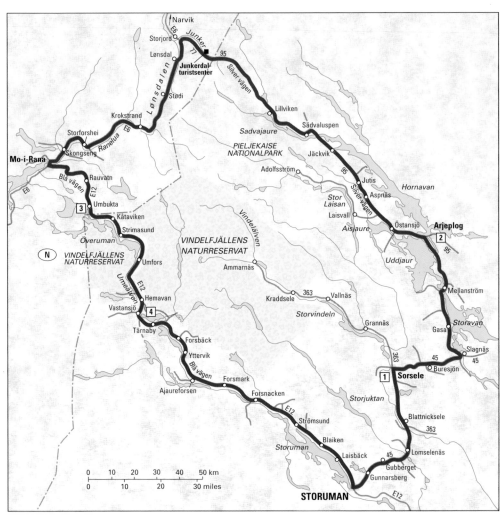

SPECIAL TO...

2 There are few settlements and even fewer sights along the Silver Way north of Arjeplog. Two places of note are on the same side-road, left off the 95: the **Laisvall mine** (38km/24 miles), opened in 1943, provided lead during World War II and became the largest lead mine in Europe; the village of **Adolfsström** (75km/47 miles) on the edge of **Pieljekaise National Park** has a house where silver was smelted in the 18th century. Further along road 95 is **Jackvik** (60km/37 miles), birthplace of Lars-Levi Laestadius who founded the 19th-century Laestadius Revivalist movement; the chapel here dates from the 1770s.

Norwegian border (139km/86 miles), where there is the Junkerdal Tourist Centre. The road becomes number **77**; follow it alongside the spectacular gorge of the River Junker to the junction with the **E6** (24km/15 miles). Turn south on the **E6** and cross the fells – and the Polar Circle – to Moi Rana (113km/70 miles); from here bear eastwards along the Blue Way to the border near Kåtaviken (40km/25 miles).

Border crossing near Kåtaviken

3 This crossing, like the others along the Swedish-Norwegian border, is rarely manned. This is fine high fell country; there are no settlements except for some summer cottages near the roadside. Lake Överuman to the right is a main source for the Umeälven (River Umeå), the course of which the Blue Way – so called because of the lakes and rivers it passes – follows through Sweden.

Continue downstream from the border to Tärnaby (73km/45 miles).

Hemavan and Tärnaby, Lapland

4 Hemavan and nearby Tärnaby are ski resorts in winter – Sweden's champion skiers Ingemar Stenmark and Stig Strand grew up and learnt their sport in Tärnaby; a **museum** houses some of their trophies. In the summer the two resorts become bases for various outdoor activities.

The region offers excellent fishing and invigorating fell and forest trekking. **Kungsleden**, the best-known trail, starts at Hamavan just to the north of Tärnaby and cuts east across Vindelfjällen nature reserve to Ammarnäs (79km/49 miles); there are huts for overnight stops. The trail continues to Adolfsström, across the Silver Way and beyond for a total of 500km (300 miles) to Abisko.

At Hemavan there is a **botanical garden** of mountain and fell flora, as well as the **Tärna Mountain Park** which has exhibitions introducing the beauty of this wild region.

Reindeer crossing a fjord

i V Strandvagen, Tärnaby

From Tärnaby it is 128km (80 miles) to Storuman.

Storuman – Sorele 75 (47)
Sorele – Arjeplog 95 (59)
Arjeplog – Kåtaviken 316 (196)
Kåtaviken – Tarnaby 73 (45)
Tarnaby – Storuman 128 (80)

Lappland: the far north is as close to a wilderness as you will find in Europe

NORWAY

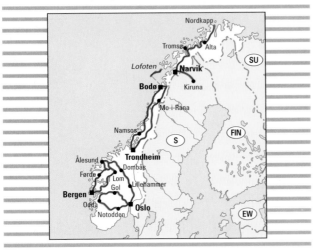

Norway's spectacular fjords and mountains cannot be matched anywhere in the world.

Two main routes (roads 7 and 11) lead westwards from Oslo, along valleys and over mountain passes in the direction of Bergen. A route north from Oslo (initially the E6) runs along the great Gudbrandsdalen and Romsdalen valleys and on to Ålesund.

The hinterland between the attractive west coast ports of Bergen and Ålesund is the heart of Norway's most stunning scenery. Highlights include the Hardanger and Sogne fjords which are at their most beautiful in June when the apple blossom is in bloom; follow the roads which hug their shores or take a break from the wheel and enjoy the surroundings from a ferry. Amidst this fjordland is Jostedalsbreen, a massive glacier with its arms of ice creeping down the valleys; it is a short walk beyond the road's end to the ice face and guides offer the chance to trek on the glacier. You ascend mountains by way of a succession of tight hairpin bends, crossing high passes with towering walls of snow long into June. Two routes are often singled out as the best in Norway: the road down to Geiranger from Dalsnibba and the famous Trollstigen which crosses mountains south of Åndalsnes. Thanks to the latest technology, new and very long tunnels are constantly being burrowed through mountains; this usually means the old roads up and over the mountains are now by-passed and are not in use: views are sometimes sacrificed for the sake of clipping distances.

North Norway is an extraordinary world. From Trondheim continue northwards and join the Royal Coast Road (road 17) and island-hop by local ferry along the jagged mountainous west coast. Just north of the Arctic Circle is Svartisen ('the Black Ice'), another impressive glacier, which is best reached by boat. The coastal journey can be continued by catching the ferry across the wide Vestfjorden to Lofoten, a cluster of wonderful islands known for their spiky peaks and dried cod. You can see the giant sperm whales off the coast of the neighbouring Vesterålen Islands.

At Narvik, back on the mainland, the choice is to return south through Norway, head east into Sweden or carry on northwards to Nordkapp, the northernmost tip of Europe. From Nordkapp the shortest route back south is through Finland.

Oslo

Founded in the 11th century by Harald Hardrade, Oslo was Norway's ecclesiastical base and later, around 1300, it became the country's capital. The city suffered bleak periods over the following centuries with a horrific plague, occupation by the Danes and a disastrous fire. Today, the city is the busy commercial and industrial hub of Norway. The pleasantest part of the downtown area is the walk along the main Karl Johansgate, past the old university and towards the palace. Bear left by the National Theatre to the huge, brown-brick, towered block of the Town Hall and quayside where there are bars, restaurants, shops and ferries to the outlying islands. The nearest island is Bygdøy (also accessible by road) with its extensive Folk Museum and collection of old buildings from around the country, the Viking Ship Museum with Viking vessels from the 9th century, and the Fram and Ship Museums with boats used by Nansen and Amundsen on their Arctic expeditions; Thor Heyerdahl's Kon-Tiki and Ra II are also here. Back in town there are many museums with notable art collections, the most celebrated being the Munch Museum with works by Norway's great artist Edvard Munch (1863–1944).

Bergen

Seat of medieval kings, Bergen is Norway's second city and the main west-coast port. A lively and attractive base for ventures northwards into the country's beautiful fjordlands, the city is something of a cultural centre, hosting many concerts and other events during the summer. There are bars and restaurants on the Vagen waterfront, with a popular promenade being along Bryggen, the wharf where the German merchants docked during Bergen's fruitful association with the Hanseatic League. On the hill behind the opposite quay of Strandkaien is a pleasant residential quarter of wooden houses and narrow cobbled lanes. Interesting exhibitions can be seen at the Hanseatic Museum, which gives an insight into the life of a Hanseatic mer-

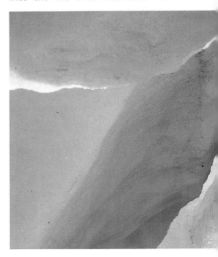

chant, the Leprosy Museum and the Fishery Museum. The Aquarium is one of the finest in Scandinavia. The best of the city's art is displayed at the Museum of Art and the nearby Rasmus Meyer Collection. Composer Edvard Grieg was from Bergen and his house, Troldhaugen, can be visited.

One of the main objectives for visitors in Bergen is to take the funicular to the top of Floyen (313m/1,027 feet), from where there are splendid views over the city and along the coast.

Trondheim

Known throughout the medieval period as Nidaros, Trondheim was founded by King Olof the Holy in 1016. He was buried here in 1030 and his shrine attracted a great number of pilgrims from all over Scandinavia until the destructive forces of the Reformation put an end to such idolatry. The great cathedral was built in honour of King Olof in the latter part of the 11th century in late Romanesque-early Gothic styles and, despite damage and renovation, it remains one of the great churches of Scandinavia.

The quarter around the cathedral and leading along Munkegata to the Olav Tryggvason Column is the downtown area. Museums

The dusk light of the midnight sun shines on a northern Norwegian village

here include the Archbishop's Palace and the Museum of Applied Art and the Art Union.

Trondheim is Norway's third city and its prime function is as an industrial base and a port; its seafaring role is recalled in the Maritime Museum near the harbour.

Bodø

The west-coast Arctic town of Bodø grew as a herring port in the 19th century, only to be destroyed during World War II. The whole city is modern, from the cathedral and Town Hall to the residences and factories. The past is remembered in the Norland County Museum. Bodø remains a significant port and a ferry point for services to Lofoten.

Narvik

The Arctic waters off Norway's west coast are kept ice free by the warm waters of the Gulf Stream. This made Narvik, lying in Ofotfjorden, a valuable year-round harbour for the export of iron ore transported by rail from the Swedish interior. During World War II the Germans secured this rail line and shipped the ore home for the manufacture of arms. The Allies attacked Narvik in their bid to stop the shipments. The Germans were driven back in May 1940, but Narvik had been destroyed in the process. The tale of the loss and recapture of Narvik is told in detail in the War Museum. Those who died – Germans, British and others fighting for the Allies' cause – are buried in the town's cemetery. The remains of some of the destroyed warships still lie visible in the fjords. A cableway leads high above the town, from where there are extensive views.

Jostedalbreen, the largest glacier on mainland Europe; its 24 arms of ice splay into narrow valleys

3 days – 756km (470 miles)

OSLO CIRCUIT

Oslo • Drammen • Kongsberg • Heddal • Røldal Odda • Kinsarvik • Eidfjord • Geilo • Gol • Oslo

This tour takes a route west from Oslo, passing the silver mines of Kongsberg and the stave church of Heddal before coming increasingly picturesque in its approach to the empty high Haukelifjell on the western borders of Telemark. Beyond the scenically situated village of Røldal, the road swings northwards to Odda and Sørfjorden to give the first taste of the fjords. The heart of the fjordlands is to the north, and ferries from Kinsarvik cross the beautiful Hardangerfjorden to join Tour 19 and the road to Bergen. To complete the circuit back to Oslo take road 7, the main route between the capital and Bergen; this way is through dramatic fell lands and it is all the more spectacular for its magnificent waterfalls. At the ski resort of Gol the road turns southwards to follow a gentler course along the Hallingdal Valley down to Oslo.

SPECIAL TO...

2 In summer you can catch a ride on the old mining train at **Saggrenda** (6km/4 miles west of Kongsberg) and travel deep into the now defunct silver mine of **Kongens Grube**. The guided tour is conducted 2.5km (1.5 miles) into the mountain and over 300m (980 feet) underground.

5 The region between Hardangar and Sogne is the heart of Norway's apple country and is at its most beautiful between May and June when the orchards on the slopes of the fjord's shores are in full blossom; magnificent snow-capped mountains serve as their backdrop.

6 From Brimnes, 18km (11 miles) beyond Kinsarvik, there is a 10-minute ferry ride to Bruravik and from here it is a short drive on road 572 to **Ulvik**, at the end of a small and distant tributary of the Hardangerfjorden. The village is one of Hardanger's main resorts.

ℹ Fylkeshuset, Oslo

Take the road southwest out of Oslo for 40km (25 miles) to Drammen.

Drammen, Buskerud

1 The industrial and port town of Drammen, comprising the Bragernes and Stromso districts, is mainly of interest for the **Spiral**, a 1,700m (5,577 feet) toll road which coils up through six spirals of tunnel to a high vantage point at the top of Bragernesasen (293m/961 feet). The **Drammen Museum**, with its 18th-century manor farmhouse of Marienlyst, concentrates on local history. Drammen's **Stromso church** of 1667 underwent an Empire-style facelift in 1840, whereas the **Town Hall** of 1872 was awarded the prestigious Europa Nostra Prize in 1986 for its accurate restoration.

Continue west on road 11 to Kongsberg (41km/26 miles).

Kongsberg, Buskerud

2 On 2 May 1624 King Christian IV opened Kongsberg's silver mines. Discovered here the year before,

A sculpture of bears at play, beside the fountains of downtown Oslo

the precious metal was to be the source of the town's fame and wealth for the next 300 years and the reason why it became Norway's second largest town (after Bergen) in the early 1800s. The mines were closed in 1957 and sections are now open to visitors.

The **Mining Museum** is housed in an old smelting hut and displays a fine collection of silver, including coins minted in Kongsberg's Royal Mint. The rich baroque interior of the large 18th-century **Kongsberg church** is a vestige of that golden age. Lagdals **open-air folk museum**, with its traditional cottages, offers memories of a more humble past.

From Kongsberg continue on road 11 to Heddal (37km/23 miles).

Heddal, Telemark

3 Built at the height of the settlement's importance, the splendid stave church at Heddal is one of the largest in Norway. Consecrated on the feast day of St Crispian (25 October) in 1147, its chancel was expanded and lavishly adorned with paintings over the next couple of centuries. The chair in the chancel is believed to be older than the church itself and is carved with tales from the ancient sagas, while the altarpiece dates from the 17th century.

Sadly, Heddal's importance declined and today it is no more

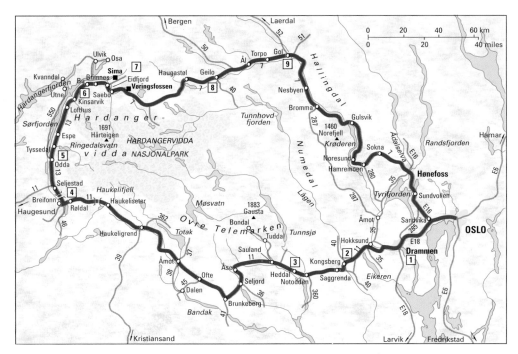

than a village. Although the church suffered neglect, a private donation in the 1950s enabled its restoration to the original medieval style. Near by is an **open-air museum** with a traditional farmstead.

From Heddal continue west on road 11 to Røldal (201km/125 miles).

The high fells of Telemark in June

Røldal, Hordaland

4 Road 11 travels through magnificent scenery as it climbs the fells of western Telemark, crosses the border into Hordaland and descends to pretty Røldal, a small lakeside enclave surrounded by steep mountains. Its 13th-century **stave church** used to draw pilgrims who believed its crucifix had miraculous powers.

From Røldal continue on road 11 through the Seljestad Gorge and

SCENIC ROUTES

3 At Sauland, 15km (9 miles) from Heddal, a road leads north to **Tuddal** and on to **Bondal**, two remote old farming communities where the traditional houses are now open for viewing.

Another pretty detour is from Ofte, 90km (56 miles) beyond Heddal on road 11, to the stave church at **Eidsborg** and on to **Dalen** on the western tip of Lake Bandak.

5 At Odda you can follow the quieter road 550 for 45km (28 miles) along the west shore of Sørfjorden to the pretty village of Utne where there are short ferry rides to Kinsarvik (back on this tour) and Kvanndal (on Tour 18).

then bear northwards on road 13 for Odda (44km/27 miles).

Odda, Hordaland

5 With its lovely situation at the southern tip of Sørfjorden, Odda was a fashionable resort at the turn of this century. However, after it built up a chemical industry, visitors gradually drifted elsewhere.

Energy for the chemical plants comes from the power stations at nearby Tyssedal, another centre for industry. From Tyssedal a road leads to Skjeggedal on man-made Ringedalsvatn (Lake Ringedals) and the cableway up to Magelitoppen (930m /2,735 feet). South of Odda a minor road goes to Buar, from where there is an approach to the Buar glacier.

From Odda continue north along road 13 to Kinsarvik (41km/26 miles).

Kinsarvik, Hordaland

6 Kinsarvik is the ferry point for the service across Hardangerfjorden via Utne to Kvanndal (45 minutes), a convenient point to join Tour 18 (see pages 76–80). Near Kinsarvik are the **Kinso falls**, a group of waterfalls of which Nykkjesøyfossen and Sotefossen have particularly impressive drops. Edvard Grieg used to retire to a cottage in **Lofthus**, 10km (6 miles) to the south, to compose his music. At **Bu**, 15km (9 miles)

beyond Kinsarvik, you can visit a museum of traditional costumes.

From Kinsarvik continue alongside the fjord, joining road 7 for Eidfjord (29km/18 miles).

Eidfjord, Hordaland

7 A minor road leads north from the resort of Eidfjord to **Sima**, one of Norway's largest power stations (guided tours available). The road from the Sima Valley snakes through tunnels up to **Kjeåsen** with its traditional farmstead. This is an area of plunging waterfalls, and further up the valley the mighty Skykkjefoss drops 600m/1,973 feet (half of which is vertical) to make it one of the main suppliers of hydroelectric energy to the local power stations. Five kilometres (3 miles) along route 7 from Eidfjord, a road from Saebo leads up into the mountains to the south, heading towards Hjølmo and waterfalls such as **Vedalsfoss**, one of the longest falls in Norway – 650m (2,138 feet), with a vertical drop of 200m (657 feet). **Vøringsfossen**, one of Norway's most spectacular falls, is further up road 7, and wonderful views of it plummeting 200m (656 feet) can be gained by ascending from Eidfjord to Isdola and turning left for Fossli (19km/12 miles).

From Eidfjord continue on road 7 to Geilo (90km/56 miles).

BACK TO NATURE

7 The tour encircles the Hardangervidda Nasjonalpark (**Hardangervidda National Park**) which covers an area of 3,422sq km (1,321 sq miles). It is centred on the huge Hardanger mountain plateau, which has a high point of 1,690m (5,545 feet) at Hårteigen, roughly 30km (19 miles) south of Eidfjord. The park is home to the largest herds of wild reindeer in Europe.

SPECIAL TO...

9 Twenty-one kilometres (13 miles) south of Gol on road 7, **Nesbyen** is one of the main tourist centres in Hallingdal. An impressive open-air heritage museum includes an early medieval loft house. Continue on road 7, and at Bromma the 287 to the right provides an alternative southbound journey along a minor route through mountains. Back on road 7 near Noresund, the island of Bjoroya on Lake Krøderen has the wooden 19th-century **Fridheim Villa**, with its exhibits and dramas about Norwegian fairytales and myths. South of Honefoss, at Sundvollen, you can see part of the old Oslo-Bergen royal road.

Geilo, Buskerud

8 Geilo is one of Scandinavia's top ski resorts, catering for both downhill and cross-country enthusiasts, and it remains the region's hub during the summer months. A cable car can be taken up to the top of 1,200m (3,937 feet) **Geilohogda** from where a magnificent path can be taken back downhill. This is splendid walking country and many other more demanding treks are found throughout the region. Three kilometres west of Geilo is **Fekjo** with its 9th–10th-century AD burial mounds.

From Geilo continue northwestwards for 50km (31 miles) on road 7 to Gol.

Gol, Buskerud

9 Gol, another popular skiing and trekking resort, has an **open-air museum** and a hydroelectric power station constructed within a mountain. Its stave church caught the eye of King Oscar II, who bought it in 1885 and had it erected near his summer palace on Bygdoy in Oslo, where it still stands today. There is a fine stave church at **Torpo**, 14km (9 miles) before Gol, which dates from the 12th century. It had its ceiling painted in the 13th century.

Fjord transport: The local car ferry approaches Kinsarvik on Sorfjord

From the high fells the road descends to the village of Røldal

From Gol bear southeastwards on road 7, initially along the Hallingdal valley, to Hønefoss (138km/86 miles). From Hønefoss take the E16 for the final stretch to Oslo.

Oslo – Drammen 40 (25)
Drammen – Kongsberg 41 (26)
Kongsberg – Heddal 37 (23)
Heddal – Roldal 201 (125)
Roldal – Odda 44 (27)
Odda – Kinsarvik 41 (26)
Kinsarvik – Eidfjord 29 (18)
Eidfjord – Geilo 90 (56)
Geilo – Gol 50 (31)
Gol – Oslo 200 (124)

SCENIC ROUTE

9 It is a lovely drive from Gol northwest along road 55, following the Hemsedal and Mørkedalen valleys to Laerdal (121km/75 miles), on the edge of Tour 18.

4 days – 815km (506 miles)

LILLEHAMMER-ÅLESUND

Oslo • Hamar and Lake Mjøsa • Lillehammer
Hunderfossen • Gudbrandsdalen • Horgheim
Trollstigen to Valldal and Tafjord • Ålesund
Langevatnet to Geiranger • Eagle Road

From Oslo and the gentle countryside of Lake Mjøsa, this tour follows Gudbrandsdalen, the river valley which serves as the route to the north. The surrounding landscape becomes increasing rugged and mountainous the further you push upstream. At Dombås you continue westwards along the Romsdalen Valley – another important avenue through Norway's mountainous lands – to the sheer grey rock face of Trollsveggen (the Troll Wall). Here the tour leaves the valleys and climbs Trollstigen, one of the world's great mountain passes. On descent the tour continues along fjords to the coast and the art nouveau town of Ålesund. The tour returns inland into the heart of magnificent high fells, mountains and fjords, reaching its climax with the dramatic snaking descent to the beautiful Geirangerfjorden.

FOR HISTORY BUFFS

2 In the winter of 1205/06 the Birkebeiners and the Baglers were on the verge of civil war. The heir apparent was 18-month-old Hakon Hakonsson who weighed in at 5.5kg (12lbs). His Birkebeiner (Birchlegger) supporters feared for his life and so two of the best skiers were chosen to carry the boy from Lillehammer across the snows to safety in Rena in Österdalen. They accomplished their mission and the lad grew up to become one of Norway's great kings. The hazardous 55km (34 mile) trek through the blizzard is remembered today by the annual Birkebeiner Ski Race, which follows the same historic route. Competitors carry 5.5kg (12lbs), the weight of baby Hakon. The event is held in March and draws about 5,000 entrants.

The troll is a common character in Norwegian folk tales

i Fylkeshuset, Oslo

From Oslo take the E6 to Lake Mjøsa, following its eastern shore to Hamar (120km/75 miles)

Hamar and Lake Mjøsa, Hedmark

1 Measuring 366sq km (141 sq miles) in area and 449m (1,473 feet) in depth, picturesque Lake Mjøsa is Norway's largest lake and the termination of the Gudbrandsdalen. Hamar, the main town on its shores, was an important medieval market and bishopric, but sadly very little of its ancient past remains. The oldest house, a two-storey wooden building called **Strandstuen**, was the birthplace of Kirsten Flagstad, the celebrated soprano. For other old memories visit the **Railway Museum** with its railway line and signalman's cottage; locomotive Number 16 is the oldest train in Norway.

The migration of Norwegians to America's Mid-West is remembered at the **Emigrant Museum** where a pioneer's cottage has been assembled. And at the **Hedmark Museum** there is a re-creation of a medieval monastic garden. But unique and most splendid of all is **Skibladner**, the world's oldest paddle steamer (1856) still in regular service. In summer it plies a course the length of Mjøsa, stopping at Hamar and Lillehammer; salmon and strawberries are served on board in keeping with tradition. As for the town's modern image, the 1994 **Hamar Olympia Hall**, known as the Viking Ship because its roof resembles an upturned boat, is now the symbol of the city.

i Gronnegatan

From Hamar continue to Lillehammer (58km/36 miles).

Winter brings its own beauty: a blanket of snow covers the countryside near Lillehammer

Lillehammer, Oppland

2 Lillehammer will long be remembered as the excellent venue of the 1994 Winter Olympics. The Olympic Park – with the Lysgardsbakkene ski jumps – is currently the most popular attraction. But Anders Sandvig's museum of old wooden buildings from the Gudbrandsdalen Valley is 90 years older. Sandvig, a dentist, was part of the Romantic movement which was so fashionable in Scandinavia at the start of this century. He responded to the fast trend of modernisation brought about by the industrial revolution by salvaging things traditional and saving them for posterity. **Maihaugen (The Sandvig Collections)** now comprises over 150 buildings and 40,000 items, and is one of Europe's largest open-air heritage museums. It provides a thorough introduction to the old life of the valley.

A new hall was opened at Maihaugen for the Olympics and houses a permanent exhibition entitled 'We won the land', tracing Norway's history. In the heart of town, a 10-minute stroll from Maihaugen, is the town's **art museum** with one of the country's main art collections covering the period from the 1830s to the present.

[i] Jernbanegate 2

From Lillehammer travel north on the E6 to Hunderfossen (13km/8 miles).

Hunderfossen, Oppland

3 One night, many thousands of years ago, a troll came down from his mountain home and out of the forests. He lingered too long, however, and when the sun suddenly rose he was turned to stone. Measuring 14m (46 feet) in height and weighing 70,000kg (154,000lbs), the old troll still stands, and around him has evolved the **Hunderfossen Family Park**. The trollish theme is continued with Ivo Caprino's troll grottoes depicting scenes from fairytales and in the Trollesalen restaurant serving troll dishes.

Equally educational are the imaginative and absorbing displays at the Experience Centre for Oil and Gas, and the Energy Centre, where you are introduced to the elements so significant to Norwegians' well-being. Also fun is the helicopter ride over Norway's mountains as experienced on the five-screen super-videograph. More conventional attractions include the circus, waxworks, swimming pools and many different funparks which number about 50 activities in total. The price of entry includes admission to all these events.

The **Norwegian Road Museum** is also at Hunderfossen and while this may not seem the most enticing of subject matters, it does not require too much driving in Norway to appreciate the extraordinary feats of engineering and labour involved in building the country's roads, tunnels and bridges. The workers deserve recognition.

The Hunderfossen power station below the impressive Hunder dam is a main source of energy for the valley.

Waterfalls cut glistening swathes through the forests of Gudbrandsdalen

From Hunderfossen continue on the E6 up the Gudbrandsdalen to Dombas (146km/91 miles).

Gudbrandsdalen, Oppland

4 Legend has it that a king of this *dal* (valley) sacrificed his son, Brand, to God to save his people, and the grateful locals dutifully named the valley Gudbrandsdalen. Norway's longest valley, it stretches 203km (126 miles) between Bjorli and Lake Mjøsa. The valley has always been the main route between the north and south of the country, serving as a path of trade, pilgrimage and conquest. The evidence of that history is scattered along the way. Travelling north on the E6 from Hunderfossen, the settlements of **Tretten**, **Fåvang**, **Ringebu** and **Kvam** all have notable churches. The **Ringebu stave church** dates from around 1200 (restored in 1980), while the cemetery at the modern **Kvam church** contains the graves of 54 British soldiers who died trying to hold the valley against German troops in World War II. Germany invaded Norway on 9 April 1940 and advanced quite smoothly until they arrived in the Gudbrandsdalen, where they met with stout Norwegian and Allied opposition. Among the casualities in the clash at Dovre on 21 April was Captain Robert Losey, who was the first American fatality of World War II. The Germans had their main base at Dombås where, at one time, they stationed 10,000 men and even built

SCENIC ROUTE

3 There are several scenic alternatives to the E6. Best known is the Peer Gyntveien **(Peer Gynt Trail)** which runs through the homelands of Peder Olsen, who lived here in the 18th century and was the inspiration for Henrik Ibsen's Peer Gynt. From Lillehammer take road 253 and follow it north, soon bearing left on the 255 for **Follebu** (with its medieval stone church). The 'Trail' is signposted and follows road 254 northwards, but bears left at Svingvoll, continuing north along the fell and reaching the highest point of 1,053m (3,455 feet) just after Fagerhoi, from where the Rondane range is visible to the north. The road descends: bear left, then right on to road 256 and rejoin E6 to Vinstra. The distance of this detour is about 90km (56 miles).

An extension continues on the other side of the E6; information can be obtained from the tourist office in Vinstra which is housed in a cottage brought from Haga, Peder Olsen's village. The 117km (73 miles) Espedalenveien **(Espedalen route)** to the west of the Peer Gynt Trail, along road 255, is an alternative, but longer, scenic detour.

SCENIC ROUTES

5 Opened in 1924, the
Rauma Rail Line leaves
from Dombas and follows the
Romsdalen (valley), becoming
increasingly spectacular after
Bjorli. There are snow-capped
mountains and magnificent
waterfalls along the line.
From a height of around
518m (1,700 feet) the train
takes a steep spiralling
descent which involves passing through U-shaped tunnels.
In the 1,340m (4,396 feet) -
long Stavens Tunnel the train
turns 180 degrees inside the
mountain and reappears
under the point of entry, fac-
ing the opposite direction.
The railway continues via the
Trolls' Wall to Andalsnes. The
River Rauma is crossed several times and the 56m (184
feet) -high, 76m (249 feet) -
long Kylling bridge is the most
spectacular span; it can be
seen from the road at Verma.

a cinema (still standing) for their
entertainment.

ⓘ Dombås

*From Dombås take road **9** northwestwards into the Romsdalen
(valley) to Horgheim (90km/56
miles). Note the richly decorated
18th-century church at Lesja.*

Horgheim, Møre og Romsdal

5 The scenery becomes increasingly dramatic as you drive up the
Romsdalen. The mountains are
higher and the waterfalls – such as
Slettafoss and Vermafoss – are bigger and more impressive. Although
there is an ancient burial ground at
Horgheim of some importance, the
main reason for stopping here is to
view the **Trollsveggen** (the Troll
Wall), a sheer 1,000m (3,281 feet)
rockface accounting for over half
the total height of the mountain. It
is one of the world's great rock
climbs and the vertical wall was
first conquered by a joint
Norwegian and English team in
1967. The fastest way down
Trollsveggen is by parachute, and
cliff diving was in vogue here in the
early 1980s; almost 400 people
took the jump before the sport was
banned in 1986 due to the increasing number of accidents.

*From Horgheim it is 14km (9
miles) to Åndalsnes, the small
tourist town where the Romsdal
fjord meets its valley. Five
kilometres (3 miles) before
Åndalsnes at Sogge bridge, a
turning to the left (road **63**) leads
to the Trollstigen and Valldal
(55km/34 miles).*

Trollstigen to Valldal and Tafjord, Møre og Romsdal

6 In a land of countless dramatic
mountain passes, Trollstigen is
probably the most spectacular.
Opened in 1936, it has an incline
ratio of 1 to 12 and coils up the
mountainside by way of 11 hairpin
curves. The collection of summits
include **Bispen** (the Bishop) at
1,475m (4,839 feet), **Kongen** (the
King) at 1,536m (5,039 feet),
Dronningen (the Queen) at 1,568m
(5,144 feet) and **Karitind** at 1,589m
(5,213 feet). The road crosses the
dramatic 180m (591 feet) **Stigfoss
waterfall**, and passes close to the
even bigger **Tverrdalsfoss**. A white
line on the opposite slope indicates
the old horse trail.

The road's highest point is at
850m (2,789 feet), after which it
descends to **Slettvikane**, where a
pillar commemorates King Olof's
expedition of 1028, and crosses the

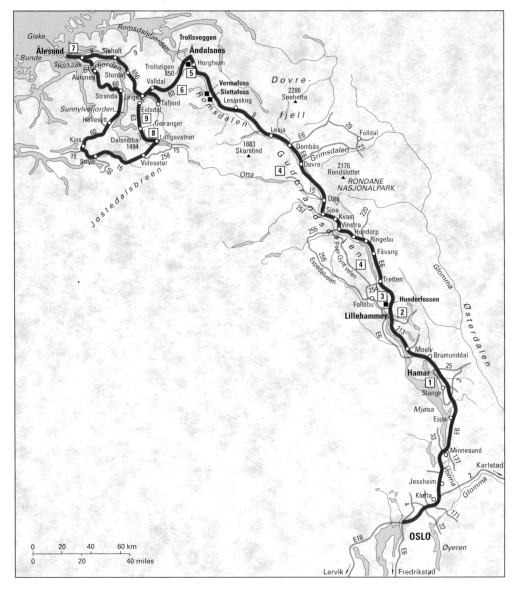

Ålesund and its neighbouring islands, seen from Aksla Lodge

Gudbrands gorge before the final stetch down to Valldal. The village of **Valldal** is famed for its strawberries and its serpent; the white stripe on the rockface is believed to be the snake King Olof hurled at the mountain on his arrival here ın 1028, at the time when he was in conflict with his **jarls** (local lords).

From here a scenic road leads eastwards to Tafjord (14km/9 miles) and a region of more waterfalls and dramatic landscapes. **Tafjord** is known for its power stations but it is also remembered for the tragedy of 1934 when a cliff crashed into the fjord, creating immense waves in both directions and killing over 40 people. A memorial and photo exhibition near the boathouse commemorate the disaster. Typical dalesmen's cottages can be found in Funder Street.

From Valldal drive west via Linge and Stordal to Sjøholt (41km/26 miles). Continue west on road 9 for Ålesund (39km/24 miles).

Ålesund, Møre og Romsdal

7 A fire on the night of 23 January 1904 destroyed the fishing port of Ålesund and left 10,000 people homeless. Fortunately Europe came to the rescue by donating building materials and Ålesund re-emerged as a very modern art nouveau-style town. It remains one of the best examples of its kind and holds the Houens National Memorial Prize for being so well preserved.

Ålesund is built on islands and to best appreciate its lovely situation go to the **Aksla Lodge**, on the hill to the east, from where there is a splendid panorama over the town and the more distant islands. A network of bridges and tunnels links Ålesund with the neighbouring islands of **Giske** where, besides the natural scenery, the attraction is the 12th-century 'marble' church – the starting point of the first Scandinavian pilgrims travelling to Jerusalem in 1102. The Viking Gange-Rolv, better known as Rollo, was born in Ålesund. After one of his raids on France he was granted the whole of Normandy as a prize, and now lies buried in Rouen cathedral. His line produced William the Conqueror and therein lies England's Giske heritage. A statue of Rollo stands in Ålesund park. Replicas of Viking boats and archaeological finds at the **Medieval Age Museum** add light to this, Ålesund's most interesting period before its art nouveau phase. Ålesund also lays claim to fame as one of the biggest Norwegian exporters of *klippfisk* (split, dried and salted cod). A few fishermen sell their catch at the downtown harbour, but the main commercial port is on the outskirts of the town.

ℹ Radhuset

From Ålesund head east on road 9 and bear right at Spjelkavik, taking road 60 to Magerholm, from where it is a 15-minute ferry ride to Aursnes. Continue on road 60 via Hellesylt (there is a ferry from here to Geiranger) to Kjos. Bear left on road 15, following it via Stryn to Videseter and ascend through tunnels to Langevatnet on road 63, a total distance of 190km/118 miles.

Langevatnet to Geiranger, Møre og Romsdal

8 In the whole of this region the surrounding valley, fell and mountain landscape is dramatic and scenic, but the best is to come. From Langevatnet it is 2km (1 mile) to the road's highest point at 1,038m (3,406 feet), and a further 5km (3 miles) to reach the **Nibbeveien** (Nibbe Road) which ascends through hairpin bends to the top of **Dalsnibba** (1,494m/4,902 feet). From here there are splendid views over mountains and the Geiranger

Cruise ships in Geiranger fjord

fjord. Returning to road 63 continue to the right and make the 15km (9 mile) serpentine descent to Geiranger. This drive offers some of the most picturesque fjord scenery in Norway. From Geiranger village there are car ferries to **Hellesylt**, as well as shorter boat excursions along the narrow fjord where waterfalls, with names like the Bridal Veil and the Seven Sisters, fall over the sheer cliff faces. Ocean cruise ships also venture this deep inland and, if the view from the road was not good enough, you can take a special trip in a plane or helicopter. There are good walking routes from Geiranger, and other points along the fjord, to the old farmsteads and mountainside pastures.

ℹ The ferry point, Geiranger

From Geiranger continue on road 63 over Eagle Pass to Eidsdal (25km/16 miles).

Eagle Road, Møre og Romsdal

9 Climbing out of the Geiranger fjord, there are 11 hairpin bends along the first section of Eagle Road to Korsmyra (9km/6 miles) at the highest point (624m/2,052 feet). From Geiranger it is 5km (3 miles) to Eagle Bend, with a fine view along the fjord.

From Eidsdal there is a 15-minute ferry ride to Linge. Valldal is 5km (3 miles) to the north.

Oslo – Hamar 120 (75)
Hamar – Lillehammer 58 (36)
Lillehammer – Hunderfossen 13 (8)
Hunderfossen – Dombås 146 (91)
Dombås – Horgheim 97 (60)
Horgheim – Valldal 55 (34)
Valldal – Ålesund 108 (67)
Ålesund – Langevatnet 190 (118)
Langevatnet – Eidsdal 46 (29)

FOR HISTORY BUFFS

Snorre Sturlason's 13th-century saga about the Norwegian kings dramatically describes how King Olof the Holy encountered Dale-Gudbrand, the powerful pagan lord of the valley, at Hundorp (between Ringebu and Vinstra) in 1021 and inspired him to see the beauty of Christianity; the church built by Dale-Gudbrand to commemorate his conversion was one of the first churches in the valley.

FOR HISTORY BUFFS

Prillaguri, sighting Sinclair and his band of Scots' mercenaries coming down the valley, sounded her birch-bark horn. This enabled the farmers to brace themselves for battle and gain victory in the ensuing clash, effectively stopping Sinclair's march to Sweden. A memorial to this event of 1612 is at **Kringen**. **Prillagurikamp**, accessible by road from Otta, is where Prillaguri spotted the Scots. She had a splendid vantage point.

The famous row of old wooden houses on Bryggen, Bergen's popular waterfront

ⓘ Bryggen, Bergen

From Bergen take road 1 northwards to Steinestø (24km/15 miles) and catch the ferry to Knarvik (10 minutes). Continue on road 1 along a picturesque route through mountain valleys to Oppedal (77km/48 miles) and take the ferry to Lavik (20 minutes). Keep on road 1 for a further 28km (17 miles) along Sognefjorden to Vadheim.

Vadheim and Sognefjorden, Sogn og Fjordane

1 The pretty stretch of shoreline road between the village of Lavik and the small factory community at Vadheim gives you a taste of Sognefjorden, the longest and deepest fjord in the world, with a length of 200km (124 miles) and a depth of 1,308m (4,291 feet). Road 1, the course followed by this section of the tour, runs north from Vadheim; the alternative route is road 55, which continues along the northern banks of Sognefjorden to Høyanger and Balestrand.

In the 1800s a succession of artists were attracted by the beauty of Sognefjorden; some settled in **Balestrand** and their old wooden villas are now mainly holiday homes. Balestrand's Swiss-style Kvikne Hotel, mostly constructed between 1894 and 1913, is Europe's largest wooden building. Margaret, daughter of an English clergyman and the wife of Knut Kvikne, whose name the hotel bears, built the Norwegian medieval-styled **St Olof's church** in 1897. Her intent was to provide a place where British tourists could worship, but sadly she died before this wish was realised. Today, the church comes under the auspices of the Bishop of Gibraltar, and Sunday services in summer are conducted by British vicars. From Balestrand there is a ferry to Hella and Sogndals (106km/66 miles), the latter being on this tour's southbound section.

ⓘ Harbour, Balestrand

From Vadheim continue north on road 1 for 38km (24 miles) to Førde.

Førde, Sogn og Fjordane

2 Situated at the end of Førdefjorden, with a population of around 5,000, Førde is the largest community on this stretch of the tour. Its church dates from 1885 and there are older buildings further along the road: a tax collector's farm from the 1700s at **Bruland** (7km/4 miles) and farm buildings from the 16th to 19th centuries at **Sunnfjordtunet** (8km/5 miles). The 90m (295 feet) **Huldrefossen**, one of the great falls of Norway, is 2km (1 mile) beyond Sunnfjordtunet, near Moskog.

From Førde continue on road 1, branching right on to road 60 at Byrkjelo for Olden (104km/65 miles).

BERGEN CIRCUIT

Bergen • Vadheim and Sognefjorden • Førde
Olden and Nordfjord • Lom • Luster • Kaupanger
Flam • Voss • Bergen

From the splendid west coast city of Bergen road 1 leads northwards into quintessential Norway. This is a tour of great fjords and glaciers, of spectacular high mountain passes and dramatic waterfalls; of medieval stave churches, traditional farmsteads and of Norway's best-loved railway journey. You can walk on blue ice, ski in mid-summer or trek across remote fells where the rains are as scarce as in the Sahara; you can take boats to the ends of the narrowest fjords or fly-fish in the most excellent salmon and trout waters. This is Norway at its best and most picturesque.

The springtime thaw

Olden and Nordfjord, Sogn og Fjordane

3 Three valleys lead down from the Jostedalsbreen (Jostedal glacier) to the village-resorts of Olden, Leon and Stryn on the innermost branches of the lovely Nordfjord. From Olden, with its 18th-century church, there is a minor road up the valley and beside Lake Olde to Oldedalen, with its old stone bridge. This minor road continues to **Briksdal** (23km/14 miles), from where there is pony-

SCENIC ROUTE

2 From Vassenden, 20km (12 miles) after Forde, a minor road leads right along the southern shore of Jølstravatnet to **Astruptunet**, home of artist Nikolai Astrup (1880–1928). Astrup spent his early life at the vicarage at **Ålhus**, on the opposite side of the excellent fishing lake of Jølstravatnet, and his remains are buried in the cemetery of the late 18th-century church.

and-trap transport to Briksdalsbreen, a spectacular arm of the Jostedal glacier.

Leon, 6km (4 miles) further along road 1 from Olden, also has an interesting church (1837) and a road running up its valley and by its lake, but this time to Kjenndalsbreen, another branch of the Jostedal glacier. **Stryn**, 11km (7 miles) beyond Leon on road 1, is the largest centre of the three communities, with the Walhalla Inn and the Central Hotel among several old hotels which served as lodgings for early tourists. The **Jostedalsbreen National Park Centre** at Stryn provides a graphic account of the 1,230 sq km (475 sq mile) national park. Stryn lies at the heart of scenic fjordland, and the spectacular path along its valley and lake is the route followed by road 15, which eventually crosses the fells and the 'desert' of Skjak to Lom.

*From Olden continue on road **60** to Stryn and then take road **15** eastwards to Grotli and then Lom (140km/84 miles).*

Lom, Oppland

4 Lom is the main centre at the heart of the fell country. To the south spreads **Jotunheimen National Park**, covering an area of 1,145 sq km (442 sq miles). Within the park's boundaries are Bøverdal, Scandinavia's highest road pass (1,440m/4,724 feet, on road 55), and Norway's loftiest mountains, with several, such as Galdhøpiggen, rising to over 2,250m (7,382 feet). Lom is a base for trekking and mountaineering expeditions into the

BACK TO NATURE

3 Jostedalsbreen (Jostedal glacier), the largest glacier on mainland Europe, covers 480sq km (185 sq miles) and is up to 400m (1,312 feet) in depth. There are 24 arms or branches of ice splaying into narrow valleys from its main high plateau. It is possible to travel up some of these valleys and walk on to the glacier offshoots.

SPECIAL TO...

3 Before the building of modern roads the fjord horse (Fjordingen) used to be the main means of transport through this difficult terrain of fjord and glacier. This tiny, sturdy animal has once again become fashionable, carrying visitors along the well-trodden and remote paths of the region.

BACK TO NATURE

1 The long, narrow, deep fjords which dent the Norwegian coast were created during the Ice Age by huge, powerful glaciers. They can be 200km (124 miles) in length and are sometimes over 1,000m (3,281 feet) deep far inland where the weight of the ice was greatest. The shallowest section is at the mouth, where the depth may be only 10m (32 feet). When the ice receded the sea level rose sufficiently to spill over the lip of the mouth to fill the fjord with water.

*Above: the stave church and the graveyard at Lom
Below: the view across Lustrafjord from Luster*

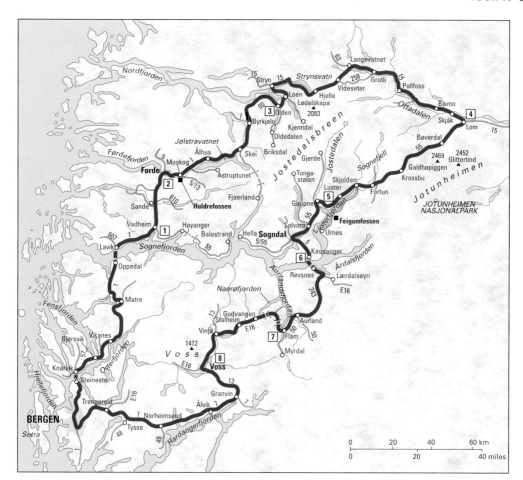

park as well as less ambitious hikes into the surrounding fells; the tourist office has maps and information about walking and routes (guides are available). The 12th-century **stave church** at Lom is one of the finest in Norway; refurbished during the 17th century, it was restored in the 1930s and has an impressive collection of art, mostly painted in the early 1600s by Eggert Munch, the son of a vicar from Vaga and possibly of the same stock as the later artist Edvard Munch. Also of interest is the collection of rocks at the **Fossheim Steinsenter**, and the **Lomsgarden open-air museum** with 21 old buildings, mainly from the Ottadalen (Otta Valley), including a cottage where King Olof the Holy once spent a night. For more about the wildlife and peoples of the fells visit the **Norsk Fjell Museum**. The southbound road 55 nudges the western part of the Jotunheimen National Park; it is one of the most dramatic stretches of road in this part of Norway and, along the way, there are opportunities for walks to glaciers and waterfalls.

From Lom take road **55** *southwestwards to Luster (93km/58 miles).*

Luster, Sogn og Fjordane

5 Luster is one of a cluster of small village resorts spread along the lovely shores of Lusterfjorden. It has a famous medieval Dale church, a cable car running up the side of the cliff to its nursing home and easy access to the Nigardsbreen (Nigard glacier), another arm of the Jostedalsbreen. For an excursion from Luster, continue on road 55 and at Gaupne bear right to follow the Jostedal river upstream to **Gjerde** (about 50km/31 miles) and

SPECIAL TO...

5 For many years the waters of the beautiful valleys of Norway have been harnessed to create hydroelectric energy. The Fortun and Jostedal power stations, to the north and south of Luster respectively, are among several in the vicinity of this tour that can be visited by the public.

5 Ludwig Wittgenstein, the Austrian philosopher, spent time writing in a cottage near Skjolden, north of Luster; the locals call this district 'Austria' in his memory.

5 The greatest concentration of Norway's splendid medieval stave churches is in the central southern part of the country. They are unusual because the wooden planks, or staves, used in their construction are laid vertically, rather than horizontally as in most buildings. At the turn of the 14th century there were about 850 stave churches in Norway. Today, only 32 survive. One of the finest is at **Urnes**, included on the Unesco Heritage List. It is situated on the remote east side of Lusterfjorden and can be reached by taking the turning near Skjolden, before Luster, off road 55; alternatively, continue on road 55 to Solvorn from where there is a boat directly across the fjord to Urnes.

6 Instead of driving you can take a ferry from Kaupanger across Sognefjorden and along the Aurlandsfjorden, continuing up its spectacular 'tributary', the narrow Naerøyfjord, to Gudvangen. The trip takes about 2 hours 20 minutes and is one of the classic fjord boat trips.

5 Another approach to Jostedalsbreen is on road 55 via Hafslo (29km/18 miles), south of Luster, where a road to the right leads to Tungestølen (35km/22 miles). Here visitors can walk across the Austerdalsbreen glacier.

7 The section of road between Gudvangen and Voss is not untypical of the region. Travelling through long tunnels and encountering hairpin bends, you will see high waterfalls, old churches and open-air museums with traditional farmsteads. New roads have left some of the interesting old roads redundant. For example, the 2km (1 mile) stretch between Glashamaren and Stalheim, known as the Stalheimskleiva, was built in the 1840s and is now by-passed. But it is still possible to follow its sharp old curves, and with a 1 in 5 gradient it is probably the steepest road in Norway.

the Glacier Centre Jostedal (Breheimseteret). Here there is an exhibition about glaciers, and guides lead excursions across the blue ice of the nearby Nigard glacier. From Ness, just to the south of Luster on road 55, you can see and hear the 200m (656 feet) high falls of **Feigumfossen** across the fjord.

From Luster continue on road 55 to Sogndal, then turn left to Kaupanger (57km/35 miles).

Kaupanger, Sogn og Fjordane

6 Eleven kilometres (7 miles) south of Sogndal, Kaupanger is the region's main centre. The large 12th-century **stave church** underwent drastic renovation in 1862, but recent refurbishing restored something of its old style. The **Sognefjord Boat Museum** near the quay has a varied collection of Norwegian boats and exhibitions about boatbuilding and local fjord transport through the ages. Just outside Kaupanger, the **Sogn Folkmuseum** comprises the Heibergske Collection of 200- to 300-year-old farms and houses; traditional rural life from those times is re-enacted. There are several other old farms and homes in the region which are open to visitors; the local tourist office has details.

ⓘ Sogndal

From Kaupanger take the ferry to Revsnes (15 minutes) and continue in the direction of Laerdalsøyri. Bear right after 12km (7 miles) on road 243 for Aurland and Flam (53km/33 miles).

Flam, Sogn og Fjordane

7 The train descends 865m (2,838 feet) on its dramatic 20km (12 mile) course from Myrdal to Flam at the end of Aulandsfjorden. Short but spectacular, this is one of the great train rides of Europe. Bikes can be hired at Flam and taken to Myrdal, or

Small planes land on still waters in Norway's more remote mountainous regions

even further to Hallingskeid or to Finse (only possible in the middle of summer), and then cycled back to Flam on the old railroad. The highest point is 1,300m (4,265 feet).

From Flam continue to Gudvangen and join the E16 to Voss (66km/41 miles).

Voss, Hordaland

8 Voss is one of Norway's top ski resorts and in summer it is a popular centre for treks far into the surrounding countryside. The **Hangursbanen cable car** is Voss' prime attraction, travelling 1,200m (3,937 feet) in distance and 750m (2,461 feet) in altitude, and providing magnificent views from the top.

Several old buildings are of interest in the town: **Finneloftet**, the nobles' meeting place, dates from around 1200 and is said to be Norway's oldest secular building; and the local medieval **church** was built at least 50 years later. **Molstertunet**, the folk museum, has a preserved old farm and other traditional buildings. About 25km (15 miles) south of Voss you reach the beautiful Hardangerfjorden.

ⓘ Voss

From Voss take road 13 to Granvin and continue along the Hardangerfjorden, bearing inland at Norheimsund for Kvamskogen and Bergen (159km/99 miles).

Bergen – Vadheim 129 (80)
Vadheim – Førde 38 (24)
Førde – Olden 104 (65)
Olden – Lom 140 (87)
Lom – Luster 81 (50)
Luster – Kaupanger 57 (35)
Kaupanger – Flam 65 (40)
Flam – Voss 66 (41)
Voss – Bergen 159 (99)

WEST COAST NORWAY

Lapp woman in traditional costume

ⓘ Kongensgate 7C, Trondheim

From Trondheim take road 715 to Flak (13km/8 miles) then take the 15-minute ferry ride to Rørvik, in Fosna county.

Fosna, Sor-Trøndelag

1 As most people choose the E6 as their route through Norway, the peninsula of Fosna remains off the beaten track. Road 715 has been picked as a quieter, more pleasant – albeit longer – route north to the 'Coast Road'. It passes through farming country, where the rivers are famous for their salmon. From Rørvik take the 715 to Rissa, then Olsøy, Rødsjø, Åfjord, Reppkleiv, Osen and finally turn inland to Fossli on the 'Coast Road' (road 17). This stretch of the 715 between Rørvik and Fossli is 182km (113 miles).

From Fossli drive north on 17 for 34km (21 miles) to Namsos.

Namsos, Nord-Trøndelag

2 With a population of 12,000 Namsos is the largest town along this tour before reaching Bodø and an important centre for the outlying settlements. It dates from the mid-19th century, though it had to be largely rebuilt after it was badly bombed in 1940. Namsos' two main attractions are its fine salmon in the Namsen and its sawmills, the workings of which are explained in a **museum for steam-operated sawmills** (Spillum Dampsag og hovleri). The town's **Namdalen Museum** concentrates on the local culture and has an old, well-preserved *femboring*. This traditional boat with five pairs of oars measures 13m (44 feet). The museum also contains an exhibition about Lapps. A recent curiosity is the huge public swimming pool built into the side of the mountain. Bikes and boats can be hired for expeditions.

The Royal Coast Road, the most interesting northbound route

Trondheim • Fosna • Namsos • Brønnøysund Tjøtta and Alstahaug • Nesna to Kilboghamn Engabreen • Glomfjord to Saltstraumen • Bodø Stiklestad • Trondheim

This tour starts in Trondheim, the city where pilgrims once came to pay homage at the tomb of King Olof. It proceeds north to join Road 17 (Kystriksveien, the Royal Coast Road) near Namsos. This is the best route northwards through this part of Norway. Avoid it, and you miss out on the most spectacular stretch of coast in Scandinavia. Take it, and you will progress up the jagged coast along a serpentine path, driving alongside fjords and hopping by ferry from islands to peninsulas. It may not be the quickest way of getting to the north, but the purpose, and pleasure, of travelling the Coast Road is not so much to reach the destination, as to enjoy the journey itself. The return to Trondheim is along the E6, Norway's main north–south artery, and it passes Stiklestad, the battlefield where King Olof was killed and rose to become a martyr and saint.

SCENIC ROUTE

2 While road 17 passes through fells from Namsos, an alternative route north is road 769 which is, at this point, more of a coast road than the 'Coast Road'. At Lund (Haraneset) there is a ferry to Geisnes and Hofles (20 minutes), from where you join the 770 which meets road 17 at Nordlandskorsen near Foldereid. Namsos to Lund is 130km (81 miles) and Hofles to Foldereid is 123km (76 miles).

SPECIAL TO...

The ferries provide an excellent service between the coastal settlements. A discount card can be purchased from tourist offices, reducing the normal fare on certain crossings along the Coastal Route (road 17) by a third.

SPECIAL TO...

2 From Årsandøy, 32km (20 miles) before Holm, road 801 leads to **Terråk**. This village of 700 people is the centre of the Bindel district and still famous for its traditional boat building; a regatta of locally made boats is held in July. Across the bay is **Vassås church** (1733) and a path to **Viking graves** and **Bygdetum**, the Bindel Farm Museum. The tidal current is very strong here and this makes for good sea fishing.

SPECIAL TO...

3 Norway's Arctic coast remains ice-free and its climate relatively clement thanks to the Gulf Stream which swings across the Atlantic from Mexico to warm these Nordic waters.

3 Prehistoric man carved rocks along this coast. Near Forvik there are two reindeer engraved in rock, while on the island of Tro (passed on the ferry from Forvik) there is a man on skis, unquestionable evidence that our ancestors skied 4,000 years ago. It was this man that became the inspiration for the graphic sports figures used as symbols in the 1994 Winter Olympics.

From Namsos, road 17 follows the Namsen upstream to where the Bjora bridge is the geographical centre of Norway. The road then bears north, skirting the hills of the fells, and eventually passes Mount Heilhorn (1,064m/3,491 feet) on the right before leading to Holm (217km/135 miles). Catch the ferry from Holm to Vennesund (20 minutes) and continue on road 17 to Brønnøysund (64km/40 miles).

Brønnøysund, Nordland

3 This is the main port and centre along the south Helgeland coast. Twelve kilometres (7 miles) beyond the Brønnøysund Bridge is Torghatten, a hat-shaped mountain which is not particularly impressive, save for the fact that it has a 35m (115 feet) high, 15–20m (49–66 feet) wide and 160m (525 feet) - long hole through the middle. You can climb up to and into the hole, and to walk right through the mountain is quite extraordinary. The hole is not visible from the foot of the mountain, you must stand back and view it face-on from afar. It looks like a cyclopic eye in a grey, sad forehead. The Sagas explain it thus: the Horseman was in pursuit of Lekamoyen, the princess he desired. Frustrated that she was outpacing his steed, he shot an arrow at her before she disappeared over the horizon, but a bystander, King Sømna of the mountains, threw his hat in the way. As the arrow pierced the hat, the sun rose and turned it to stone. A more likely explanation, however, is that the hole was formed by frost and wave action during the Ice Age when the mountain was totally submerged.

After a while in Norway you get used to the weird and wonderful in the mountainscapes. As remarkable, considering the latitude, as a mountain with a hole is the herbivarium near Tilrem (*en route* to Horn). **Hildur's Urterarium** grows over 400 types of herbs and spices, and many different roses grow outside in gardens.

A colourful patterned door is welcome decoration on the bland red wall of a typical west coast house

From Brønnøysund continue to Horn and catch the ferry to Anndalsvågen (20 minutes). On disembarkation continue on road 17 to Forvik (17km/11 miles) and take the ferry to Tjøtta (60 minutes).

Tjøtta and Alstahaug, Nordland

4 Situated 2km (1 mile) inland from the harbour on road 17, the **War Cemetery** at Tjøtta is a simple graveyard. Of the 10,000 soldiers that lie here, the vast majority were Russian prisoners of war captured by the Germans in World War II. One thousand of the graves are occupied by prisoners of war of various nationalities who were on board the German transport carrier *Reigel* when Allied planes sank it in Tjøtta's waters in 1945, killing 3,000 men.

A further 17km (11 miles) along road 17 is the medieval church Alstahaug. The great Norwegian poet-priest Petter Dass lived beside the waters here from 1689; a **museum** has been established in his memory. Continuing on road 17 you pass the Seven Sisters which rise like teeth, the gaps between them having been formed by the receding glaciers. The highest peak is Botnkrona at 1,074m (3,524 feet). Every couple of years a race is run incorporating all the summits; the present record is 3 hours 54 minutes.

Some 20km (12 miles) beyond Alstahaug, on road 17, is Sandnessjøen, the main town and port on the island. Road 17 then crosses the elegant Helgelandsbrua suspension bridge (toll), completed in 1991, and continues to Levang (33km/21 miles).

Catch the ferry from Levang to Nesna (25 minutes).

Nesna to Kilboghamn, Nordland

5 From Nesna, road 17 follows the coastline of the deep Sonja inlet and the waters opposite Aldra before cutting across the peninsula to Kilboghamn (91km/57 miles). It is a scenic drive along shore and over hill, through a landscape reminiscent of the Scottish Highlands. There are no towns, only small fishing settlements. Between 1942 and 1945 the Germans defended the Sonja stretch of coast from their high vantage base at Gronsvik. The battery was built by 100 Russian and Polish prisoners of war, and has now been partly restored.

Catch the ferry from Kilboghamn to Jektvik (60 minutes) to cross the Arctic Circle. The mountains become increasingly dramatic. From Jektvik it is a 28km (17 mile) drive around Tjongsfjord to Ågskaret. Take the ferry from here to Forøy (10 minutes), and follow the coast to the jetty at Braset (9km/6 miles) or nearby Holand, for the boat to Engabreen glacier (10 minutes).

Engabreen, Nordland

6 Engabreen is part of the 375 sq km (145 sq mile) Svartisen, Norway's second largest glacier. From the road it can be seen in the

A charter ferry docks near Engabreen

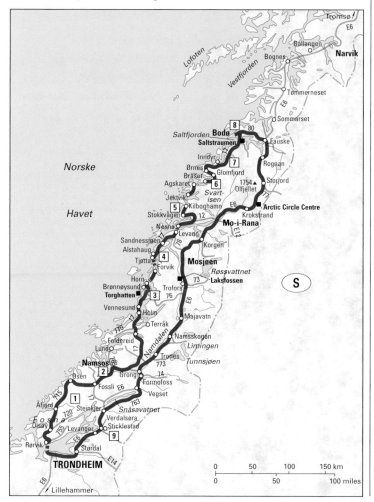

SPECIAL TO...

7 Occurring in a 3km (2 mile) long, 150m (493 feet) wide stretch of water between the Skjerstad and Salt fjords, the Saltstraumen is the world's largest tidal current. The maelstrom reaches speeds of 20 knots and forms whirlpools 10m (33 feet) in diameter.

SPECIAL TO...

8 Located at the point where the E6 crosses the Arctic Circle, the **Arctic Circle Centre** is an information and exhibition centre for northern Norway. In addition to its displays there is a short film giving a panoramic view of Norwegian nature. Outside are monuments dedicated to various peoples, including one to Yugoslavian prisoners of war who died working in terrible conditions on the fells during World War II.

distance across Holand fjord. Take the passenger boat across the fjord and then walk to the small lake, following its shore around to the ice face. It is a particularly picturesque glacial scene, with the tongue of ice reaching down the mountain slope almost to the water's edge; with the boat ride and walk it makes a very enjoyable two- to three-hour excursion.

From the Braset/Holand jetty continue on road 17 along Nordfjord and through the 7.6km (4.7 mile) Svartis Tunnel to Glomfjord (26km/16 miles), a town famous for its power station.

Glomfjord to Saltstraumen, Nordland

7 Road 17 continues to follow the coast via the small district capital and port of **Ørnes** and the town of **Reipa** with its heritage museum. It passes the Kunna peninsula where many a ship has foundered; a Dutch wreck from the 1920s is still visible. The submarine *Udea* was sunk here during World War II, but was only discovered in 1985; a statue of a swordfish by the road at Gransen commemorates its Norwegian and British crew. The road climbs to 188m (617 feet) at Storvikskaret and continues for 70km (42 miles) to Saltstraumen. From Glomfjord the distance to Saltstraumen is 116km (72 miles).

From Saltstraumen road 17 crosses the Saltfjorden to Loding, where it joins road 80 for Bodø (32km/20 miles).

Brooks, forests and mountains constitute the inland scenery of the west coast

Bodø, Nordland

8 German bombers destroyed the city of Bodø in 1940, leaving little of the past, although one survivor of the war is the 13th-century **Bodin church**. The **Norland County Museum** gives an account of the more ancient history and the important local fishing industry. The **cathedral** dates from 1956. A popular viewpoint for the midnight sun is 155m (509 feet) **Mount Rønvikfjell**. Bodø is rather out on a limb and the main purpose for coming here is to catch a ferry to Lofoten (see Tour 21).

From Bodø take road 80 to Fauske. (From here it is about 244km/152 miles north on the E6 to Narvik.) For the shortest return to Trondheim turn south on the E6 and follow it along river valleys and over high fells to the industrial town and port of Mo i Rana (179km/111 miles). From Mo i Rana continue on the E6 for 90km (56 miles) to Mosjøen, famous for its wooden 18th-century Dolstad church. From Mosjøen it is 27km (17 miles) to the Laksfossen waterfalls and a further 172km (107 miles) to the Formofoss falls. An additional 89km (55 miles) reaches Vegset, where a detour from the E6 along the 763 takes you to the Reindeer of Bolo, Norway's most famous rock carving dating from about 6,000 years ago. Continue on the 763 through Steinkjer to join the E6 and on to Verdalsøra, 94km (58 miles) from Vegset. Turn left for 4km (3 miles) up to Stiklestad. From Fauske to Stiklestad the distance is about 560km (348 miles).

Stiklestad, Nord-Trøndelag

9 King Olof the Holy was killed at Stiklestad on 29 July 1030 while fighting against the large army of local pagan chiefs from the Trondheim region. Ironically, his opposition weakened after his death, and Norway united as one country under his heirs. Many saw Olof as a martyr who had fought and died for Christianity. On death he developed a huge cult following and many travelled to his tomb in Trondheim Cathedral. The old pilgrim routes and churches in his name can still be seen throughout Scandinavia. The **Cultural Centre** at Stiklestad recounts the history, and near by is the medieval **chapel of St Olof**. The centre also commemorates the landslide at Verdal (just to the east), when 55cu m (1,941cu ft) of earth fell in 1893 destroying 100 farms and killing 112 people.

From Stiklestad rejoin the E6 and head south, bearing west at Hell for Trondheim (96km/60 miles).

Arctic cod is hung up to dry from nails on wooden rafters

> *Take the 4-hour ferry journey from Bodø to Moskenes on Moskenesøya.*

Moskenes, Lofoten

1 The ferry docks in the bay at Moskenes. A few minutes' drive southwards along the coast are the two fishing villages of **Sørvågen**, where the world's second wireless telegraph office was opened in 1906, and **Å**, the southernmost village on the island. The **Norwegian Fishing Village Museum** at Å comprises nine buildings typical of an old Lofoten fishing community, including fishermen's huts, a bakery, a forge and a cod-liver oil processing plant. Also in the village is an exhibition about stockfish, the product that has been so central to Lofoten life for over 1,000 years.

Locals talk about 'Outside' and 'Inside' Lofoten, referring respectively to the open seas and the more sheltered waters within its cluster of islands. Excursions are offered to 'Outside' Lofoten, beyond the southern tip of Moskenesøya and to the scene of the Moskenes Maelstroem, one of the world's fiercest ocean currents, which churns the seas with 'part scream, part roar, and so powerful that not even the Niagara Falls can raise their voice higher to the heavens' (Edgar Allan Poe). From **Reine**, on the E10 north of Moskenes, there are boat journeys into 'Inside' Lofoten, along the scenic Reine fjord. Near Reine is the equally picturesque fishing village of **Hamnøy**, where birds nest on the rock face.

ⓘ Moskenes

> *From Moskenes follow the E10 northwards via Reine and Hamnøy to Ramberg, on the island of Flakstadøya (30km/19 miles).*

Ramberg, Lofoten

2 On the ocean side of the island and with a white sand beach, the fishing village of Ramberg is the administrative centre on Flakstadøya. Just to its north is the wooden **Flakstad church**, topped by an onion-shaped cupola and dating from 1780; the altarpiece, older than the church, was painted by Godtfred Ezechiel, a master painter from Bergen. Beyond is Vikten, where there is a glass workshop with glass-blowing on view. Minor roads lead from the E10 to villages on the other side of the island. A turning to the right, just after crossing on to Flakstadøya, brings you to **Sund**, where the workshop of a blacksmith has become one of the most visited attractions on Lofoten; he specialises in making steel cormorants. Further along this inner coast is the abandoned fishing and farming village of Ostre Nesland and the thriving **Nusland**, the quaintest of all Lofoten's fishing villages and, since 1975, a preserved village listed by Unesco.

ⓘ Ramberg

> *From Ramberg it is about 30km*

Bodø • Lofoten • Moskenes • Ramberg
Leknes • Svolvær • Narvik

Lofoten is the reward for coming this far north. Of all the many dramatic and picturesque islands off the west coast of Norway, those of Lofoten are the most magnificent. Beneath the extraordinary mountainscape of sharp pinnacled summits cluster the red-painted fishermen's cottages, affording what shelter is possible from the bracing winds. Lofoten's fame, wealth and sustenance is its fish and, in particular, its cod. Hauled ashore and hung to dry, the cod is auctioned to merchants and sold as a delicacy in Italy.

The tour begins at Bodø on the mainland, from where there are two ferries daily during the summer across the waters of Vestfjorden to Moskenes at the southern end of Lofoten. By taking the night boat the islands are approached in the gentle glow of the midnight twilight; come in the day and the scene will be similar to that described by Nobel Laureate for literature, Bjornstjerne Bjornson, who sailed towards Lofoten in 1869:

'The mountains of Lofoten are turning blue. I don't know what stirs me the most, seeing them from far away, a dark blue wall crowned by thousands of towers... shimmering in the sun for as far as you can see, or fenced in by mirages of upside-down mountains hovering in the air ahead of you and behind you, while whales are playing, birds are clamouring and diving, or to draw near them and behold how the wall opens, how each and every peak becomes a separate mountain, each wilder than the next.'

The tour continues along road E10 (the King's Road), which was opened on Lofoten by King Olav in 1963. It runs the length of the four main islands – Moskenesøya, Flakstadøya, Vestvågøy and Vågan (all linked by bridge or tunnel) – and then crosses by ferry to the Vesterålen islands, from where it continues alongside fjords and over hills to the mainland and the city of Narvik.

> *(19 miles) along the E10 and through the Nappstraumen tunnel (toll) to Leknes.*

Leknes, Lofoten

3 Leknes is the administrative centre on Vestvågøy. The peninsulas to the town's south are tipped with fishing villages, among them **Ballstad**; with 1,000 inhabitants, this village is one of the largest fishing communities in Lofoten. A huge

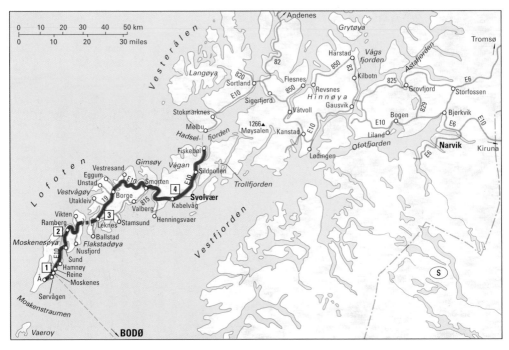

mural – some say the largest in the world – covers the walls of one of its shipyards. *En route* to Ballstad, Gravdel is passed with its 1905 Buksnes church. Smaller fishing villages include Mortsund and Ure.

The wide valley to the east of Leknes is the most fertile farmland on the island, and it is here that you can see the new **church of Borge** (1987), nicknamed the 'ski jump' because of the shape of its roof. The north coast has a sand beach at **Utakleiv**, a pebble-boulder beach at **Eggum** (where the Germans had a radar station during World War II) and, in between them, a popular viewpoint for the midnight sun at **Unstad**. Further along, at the end of another headland, is the typical fishing village of **Vestresand**.

☐ Leknes

From Leknes follow the E10 through Vestvågøy and cross via Gimsøy to Vågan and the port of Svolvær (70km/43 miles).

Svolvær, Lofoten

4 With a population of around 4,000, Svolvær is the largest town and 'capital' of Lofoten. Ferry services operate from here to Bodø (via Skutvik) and to Narvik (via Lødingen). Paintings by the local artist, Gunnar Berg, are at the **County Hall**; works by other regional artists are displayed at the **North Norwegian Art Centre**. Archaeological digs at **Storvagan** (5km/3 miles southwest of Svolvær) have uncovered evidence of a sizeable medieval fishing community, probably the largest at that time in northern Norway. The history of the site is documented at the local **Lofoten Museum**. Other attractions in the town are the exhibition of **Kaare Espolin Johnson** paintings and the **Lofoten Aquarium**, with its wide variety of marine life and a seal pool.

The old wooden town of **Kabelvåg**

Left: the picturesque village of Hamnøy is typical of the small fishing communities on Lofoten

The preparation of a delicacy: cod hangs high and dry near Stamsund

was the busiest of all the Lofoten fishing ports in the 19th century. A statue commemorates King Oystein, who was responsible for the building of the first *rorbuer* (fisherman's hut) here in 1120. He even constructed a church here in 1103. Today's **Vågan church** dates from 1898 and is the second largest wooden church in Norway, with a capacity for 1,200 worshippers.

☐ Svolvær

From Svolvær head north on E10 along the Austnesfjorden to Fiskebøl (34km/21 miles). From here catch a ferry to Melbu (25 minutes). The E10 continues across the Vesterålen islands to Narvik (246km/153 miles).

Moskenes – Ramberg 30 (19)
Ramberg – Leknes 24 (15)
Leknes – Svolvær 70 (43)
Svolvær – Narvik 280 (174)

Buksnes church rises above Gravdel

3 days – 819km (509 miles)

BEYOND NARVIK

Narvik • Tromsø • Alta • Nordkapp
Riksgransen • Kiruna

Although Narvik may be well inside the Arctic Circle, it is still a further 819km (509 miles) along the E6–E69 to the Nordkapp (North Cape). The route follows the coastline to the town of Alta, from where it cuts across the empty region of Finnmark before the final stretch to Nordkapp. If a journey of such a distance appears rather daunting and reaching Nordkapp is not a goal, then do consider bearing east from Narvik and crossing the high fells into Sweden to the city of Kiruna, from where roads lead southwards and eastwards to Finland.

FOR HISTORY BUFFS

1 The German battleship *Tirpitz* was sunk by British fighter planes in the waters off Tromsø in 1944.

SCENIC ROUTE

3 The most leisurely way to see the Nordkapp – and indeed the Norwegian coast – is from *Hurtigruten*, Norway's coastal steamer. Every day a boat departs from Bergen and heads northwards, making 34 stops *en route* to Kirkenes. The warm waters of the Gulf Stream keep the coast ice free, making it possible to operate the service through the winter. A lifeline for the locals, *Hurtigruten* has become increasingly popular with visitors. The round trip takes 11 days.

[i] Kongens Gate, Narvik

From Narvik take the E6 northwards to Vollan (180km/112 miles). Bear left here and follow the E8 to Tromsø (73km/45 miles).

Tromsø, Troms

1 Thirteenth-century Tromsø is the traditional starting point for polar expeditions, a fact confirmed by the presence of a monument to the great Norwegian explorer, Roald Amundsen (1872–1928). The **Skansen Museum**, which features displays on local history, exhibits some of Amundsen's South Pole equipment. The town's second museum, the Tromsø Museum, concentrates on the region's nature and ethnography. Tromsø is a young and lively town with much drinking and dancing in its 70 bars and 17 night-clubs. Symbolising this youthful vivacity is the striking modernity of the **Tromsdal church**, the 'Cathedral of the Arctic', built by Jan Inge Hovig in 1965.

[i] Kirkegate 2, Tromsø

From Tromsø return on the E8 as far as Fagernes (25km/16 miles).

A traditional Lapp granary, built high to avoid raids by vermin

Bear left here on road 91 for 24km (15 miles) to Breivikeidet, from where there is a ferry to Svensby. Continue along the 91 for 22km (14 miles) to Lyngseidet and catch another ferry to Kåfjord (Olderdalen). From here it is 224km (139 miles) on the E6 to Alta.

Alta, Finnmark

2 A port with a population of 12,000, Alta is the most significant settlement in Norway's county of Finnmark. Prehistoric man lived here and left his mark etched in rock. There are around 5,000 **rock carvings** in the region, dating from 2,500 to 6,200 years ago; this early art is now protected by the Unesco World Heritage List. In more recent times the locals have dug into the rock, and the old copper mines at Kåfjord can be visited on the way north.
The skies up here are as rich as the earth and Alta is the home of the first observatory built to study the Northern Lights. However, Finnmark is probably best remembered for the disaster inflicted upon it in 1944 during World War II when the Germans withdrew, burning buildings and scorching the earth. The local history of this northernmost quarter of Europe – from prehistoric man to the modern means of generating hydro-electricity on the Altaelva (River Alta) – is well documented in the **Alta Museum**.

[i] Alta

From Alta continue on the E6 and at Olderfjord bear left on the E69 for Kåfjord (180km/112 miles). Here catch the ferry to Honningsvåg, from where it is 33km (21 miles) to Nordkapp.

Nordkapp (North Cape), Finnmark

3 Every year around 250,000 people make the pilgrimage north to the 307m (1,007 feet) high cliff of Nordkapp. At a latitude of 71° 10' 21", this craggy grey rock at the end of Magerøya is traditionally regarded as the most northerly point of mainland Europe. In fact this honour should go to Kinnarodden, the point on the Nordkinn peninsula, 68km (42 miles) further east, which is marginally further north. The **viewing plateau** at Nordkapp is where most people aim for. The **North Cape Hall**, a souvenir and service centre, has been cut into the rock; from its window visitors have a wide outlook over the Arctic Ocean. There are admission charges to both plateau and hall. From Nordkapp you turn southwards and, as the Norwegians say, travel ever closer to the South Pole.

Journey into Sweden

Return to Narvik and take the E6. After 14km (9 miles) bear right on the E10 for 30km (19 miles) to Riksgränsen.

Riksgränsen, Lappland

4 The border ski resort of Riksgränsen (which means 'the royal border') evolved with the

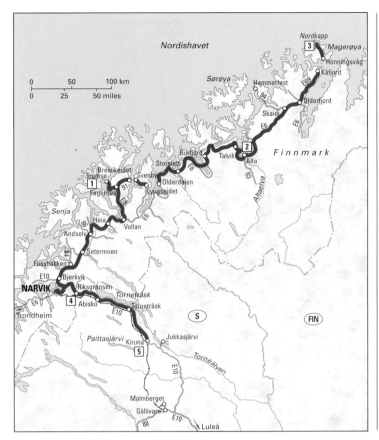

SPECIAL TO...

3 At Nordkapp the midnight sun can be seen between 11 May and 31 July. The Polar Nights – 24 hours of darkness – are between 21 November and 23 January. The Northern Lights (Aurora Borealis) are most likely to be seen on the cold clear nights of mid-winter.

SPECIAL TO...

4 In 1903 the **Ofoten railway** line was opened between the port of Narvik and the Swedish Lappland iron-ore mines of Kiruna and Malmberget. Running along fjord and ascending steep valley slopes, the track frequently passes through tunnels as it reaches and then traverses the high fells. Much folklore surrounds this railway, especially with regard to the hardened men (known as *rallar*) who built it; the remains of their burnt-down village of Rombaksbotn can be visited, and the Ofoten Museum in Narvik recounts the history of the *rallar* and his railway. Today, the Ofoten line is linked to the Swedish rail network and it takes a little under 24 hours by train from Stockholm to Narvik.

creation of the Ofoten railway. With 60 peaks over 1,300m (4,265 feet), the surrounding high fell country remains popular skiing territory, providing both downhill and cross-country courses. In summer (mid-May to July) there is midnight skiing.

From Riksgränsen continue on the E10 for 120km (75 miles) to Kiruna.

Kiruna, Lappland

5 Sweden's most northerly town, Kiruna was a small Lapp settlement until the mining of iron ore commenced in the 1900s. Thereafter it grew rapidly, becoming – according to the local people – the largest city in the world. The population today is around 27,000 and the huge ore mountain of Kirunavaara continues to dominate the town both visually and economically. Open-cast

Christ at the altar, *Jukkasjärvi*

A magnificent bridge links the island city of Tromsø to the Norwegian mainland

mining is now the favoured method of extracting the ore, but the old **underground pits** are the most extensive in the world and can be visited. Kiruna's other landmark is its large wooden **church** built in 1912 in the style of a Lapp hut.

ⓘ Folkets Hus

SPECIAL TO...

5 Situated on the banks of the River Torne east of Kiruna, the 17th-century village of **Jukkasjärvi** has Lapland's oldest wooden church, dating from 1609. The extraordinarily vivid altarpiece depicts earnest Lutheran pastors amidst hedonistic Lapps. A heritage village has been assembled here on the river bank.

Narvik – Tromsø 253 (157)
Tromsø – Alta 295 (183)
Alta – Nordkapp 213 (132)
Nordkapp – Riksgransen 805 (500)
Riksgransen – Kiruna 120 (75)

FINLAND

Most people approach Finland by sea from the southwest. The Swedes certainly did, arriving in medieval times and occupying the country as a province, with the capital at Turku (Åbo). They were ousted by the Russians in 1808, who in 1809 made it a Grand Duchy and then shifted the seat of power to Helsinki. Finland declared itself independent in 1917 following the Russian revolution.

From mid-way along the Gulf of Bothnia to the borders of Russia, the coast and its immediate hinterland bear the marks of this past; most of the towns were built by the Swedes, though some were later redesigned by the Russians; the majority of castles and churches have Swedish origins; and even today many communities are bilingual, with towns and streets often having both Finnish and Swedish names. With its splendid archipelago of countless islands and charming old towns, this coast has evolved into Finland's commercial and industrial heartland. Although the Swedes ventured inland and built their outposts, they did not really develop the interior. Even now, when you push beyond the coast, you soon appreciate the emptiness of the country.

The central southern region is covered by an enormous and beautiful lakeland which is more water than land. The lakes stretch east into Karelia, a territory now torn in two by an international border. Elias Lonnrot travelled the region in the early part of the last century and came across bards who recounted old folk poetry to him. He compiled these into the epic poem *Kalevala*, which was heralded as the discovery of Finnish roots. At last the Finns could trace an identity of their own which was divorced from their intimate past with the Swedes.

Pushing north you continue through the same kind of beauty, though here the forests are larger and the lakes fewer. Along the quiet, sparsely populated borderlands near Kuhmo and Suomussalmi are memorials to the thousands who died fighting in the bitter Winter War (against the USSR) of 1939–40. From Rovaniemi, gateway to the north, highway E75 cuts through the forested heart of Arctic Finland to magnificent Lake Inari, the vast and remote lake of Scandinavia's far north. Up here in this wilderness the Lapps tend their reindeer herds and the ever hopeful oldtimers prospect for gold. The road from Inari continues northwards into Norway and to the Nordkapp.

Helsinki (Helsingfors)

Helsinki was founded by the Swedes in 1550 and made capital by the Russians in 1812. After a damaging fire, C L Engel was assigned in 1816 to design the reconstruction in the grand neo-classical Empire style, and his work still dominates the heart of Helsinki.

The ferries from Stockholm dock fairly near to the city's centre and the hub of activity is the waterfront Market Square. To its north is the President's Palace, the Town Hall and then the Senate Square with the university, various government buildings and the high-domed Lutheran Cathedral of St Nicolas atop an impressive flight of steps.

East from the market leads the elegant Esplanade, a boulevard of shops that constitutes the focus of the downtown area. Finns are famous for their architecture, and besides Engel's Empire buildings there is Saarinen's sombre Central Station (1919) and a conspicuous art nouveau presence in the city. But best of all is Timo and Tuomo Suomalainen's beautiful Rock Church (1969), Alvar Aalto's Finlandia Hall (1971) and the new Opera House (1993). Museums of note are the National Museum, with its Finno-Ugrian collection and exhibitions about the history and culture of the country, the National Museum of Art (Ateneum) and the Amos Andersen Museum of Art. The Swedes fortified the island of Svaeborg (Suomenlinna) with a castle, which fell to the Russians in 1808; this Unesco-protected monument is reached by ferry (20 minutes). For children there is the Linnanmaki amusement park.

Tampere

Finland's three big centres – Helsinki, Turku and Tampere – form a triangle, with Tampere as the inland point. Founded in the late 18th century, Tampere was developed by the Russians as an industrial base, a function still fulfilled by the city. Its attractive waterside setting is enhanced by an art nouveau cathedral, long, wide, straight avenues, a university, modern concert halls and some fine art museums, notably the Sara Hilden Museum of Art next to the observation tower and Sarkanniemi amusement park. A block away from the Alexander church in Downtown is one of the few remaining Lenin Museums in the world.

Vaasa

Destroyed by fire in the mid-1800s, there arose from the dying embers of Old Vaasa the present wide-avenued town of Vaasa. It is the main ferry point for services from Sundsvall, the Swedish port across the Gulf of Bothnia. For a brief moment in December 1917 Vaasa served Finland as its capital, when the Senate retreated here after Helsinki was taken by socialist militia. Local history and culture is displayed at the Osterbotten Museum.

Kuopio

Kuopio has a beautiful waterside location in Finland's northern lakeland region. Its position is best appreciated from the watch tower on Puijo Hill, from where there is a splendid view over the spacious modern city and the lakes dotted with numerous islands. Kuopio has a large Finnish Orthodox community with St Nicolas church as the seat of its archbishop. North of the centre, at the archbishop's residence, is the Orthodox Church Museum, which includes priceless works of religious art salvaged from the original Valamo monastery. Kuopio's Lutheran cathedral is in the centre of this city of straight, leafy avenues, together with a university (1972), a modern concert hall and a museum recalling the background of the region.

Kajaani

In 1605 King Charles IX of Sweden built a castle on an island in the River Kajaani. Later that same century Governor Per Brahe authorised the construction of a town on the opposite banks. With waterways linking the new settlement of Kajaani with the forested interior and the Gulf of Bothnia, it became a centre on the tar trail, for which these northern parts of Finland were once famous. The history of the town is told in the Kainuu Museum, which also houses an exhibition about the *Kalevala*. Elias Lonnrot, the compiler of this national epic, was stationed in Kajaani as a doctor. Urho

Helsinki was founded by Gustavus I Vasa of Sweden in 1550. Its spacious, but ordered layout was introduced after fire damage in the 18th century

Kekkonen (1900–86), the President of Finland between 1956 and 1981, also lived in Kajaani as a youngster.

Rovaniemi

A few kilometres below the Arctic Circle, Rovaniemi was originally a Swedish administrative outpost in this remote region of Finnish Lappland. When the forests were exploited it became a centre for the timber trade. The town itself was built of wood and was burnt to the ground by the Germans in 1944–5; it was rebuilt in stone on a street plan designed by Alva Aalto in the shape of a reindeer's antlers. As the gateway to Lappland, the Arctic and the road to Nordkapp, tourism is big business in Rovaniemi. Not to be missed is the town's excellent Arktikum, one of the best museums in Scandinavia; it displays thorough and imaginative exhibitions about the Arctic and, in particular, Finnish Lappland.

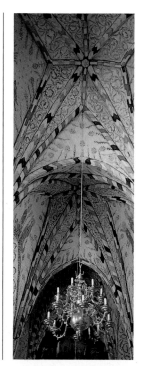

Right: Jaivassalo church
Below: Lapp baggage, Inari village

4 days – 602km (374 miles)

HELSINKI (HELSINGFORS) CIRCUIT

Helsinki • Riihimäki • Hämeenlinna • Iittala • Pori
Rauma • Uusikaupunki • Luohisaari • Naantali
Turku (Åbo) • Hanko (Hangö) and the road to
Helsinki • Porvoo (Borgå) • Lovisa (Loviisa)
Kotka • Hamina (Fredrikshamn) • Helsinki

Finland's southwest corner, the closest point to Europe, is the traditional gateway into the country. The colonising Swedes arrived by this route and set up their capital in Turku (Åbo). The region developed as the commercial hinterland of Finland and today it has the greatest concentration of industry and peoples – especially within the triangle of the three big cities of Helsinki, Turku and Tampere. Beyond this gateway lies a vast interior which becomes increasingly remote and empty the deeper you venture.

The tour heads inland from Helsinki, travels to Pori on the Gulf of Bothnia and then follows the beautiful coast, via Turku, back to Helsinki. There is an extension eastwards to the Russian border, passing the spas once favoured by the tsars.

SCENIC ROUTE...

The world's finest ferries are in service across the Baltic between Stockholm and Helsinki or Turku. The start and finish of the journey is through beautiful archipelagoes; on board there is live music, cabaret, shopping arcades and restaurants. It is more like a cruise than a ferry crossing, and it is an excellent way of travelling between Sweden and Finland. (See page 5 for details.)

From Helsinki take the E12 north for 67km (42 miles) to Riihimäki.

Riihimäki

1 Riihimäki developed as a railway junction after the laying of the Helsinki-Hämeenlinna line in the mid-19th century, and later became a garrison town when the tsar stationed his Russian defence here in the early 1900s; memories of that past can still be found in the downtown area.

This region is Finland's traditional glassmaking heartland and the making of glass gave Riihimäki an artistic dimension. The **Glass Museum** (directions are given from the E12) presents a history of glass and also displays examples of exquisite local glassware through the ages. A small, one-room gallery includes works by Picasso, Miro and Dali, who were all fans of Finnish glass, and sculptures by Wäinö Aaltonen; the town library exhibits paintings by other modern Finnish artists. Next to the Glass Museum is the **Hunting Museum of Finland**, an attractively displayed account of the evolution of man the hunter.

ⓘ Kalevankatu 1

From Riihimäki continue on the E12 northwards for 33km (21 miles) to Hämeenlinna.

Hämeenlinna

2 Situated on the medieval oxen route from Turku into the interior – the only such road of the day –

The pipes of Sibelius in Helsinki serve as a monument to Finland's great composer

Hämeenlinna was built by Swedish governor Per Brahe in 1639 and became Finland's first inland town. The original site was near the 13th-century castle but was shifted a short distance south to its present location in 1777. The large solid **fort** founded by the Swedish ruler, Birger Jarl, and greatly developed by Governor Brahe, has a fine waterfront setting and is Hämeenlinna's main attraction; interesting tales of castle, kings and country are related by guides suitably attired in medieval costume. Behind the castle stands the old prison, which in 1871 became the first in Finland to have cells. The last prisoner departed in 1993, and the building is now a youth hostel, with cells as rooms. Across the water are the **Aulanko parklands and nature reserve**, Hämeenlinna's pleasant recreational area established by Colonel Hugo Standertskjöld, a local man who made his fortune as an arms dealer in Russia at the turn of the century. A junior contemporary of a different disposition was Jean Sibelius, the composer, who was born in the downtown area at **Hallituskatu 11** on 8 December 1865. Three rooms of the house are now set aside as a museum and include two of his pianos; the Sibelius music of your choice is played during your visit. Like other Finnish artists he drew his inspiration from the power of nature and his tone poem *Tapiola* is a musical interpretation of the vast forests.

The brick church of the Holy Cross at Hattula, 6km (4 miles) north of Hämeenlinna, dates from the 14th century and has fine frescos dating from the 16th century.

ⓘ Sibeliuksenkatu 5A

From Hämeenlinna follow road 3 for 22km (14 miles) to Iittala.

Iittala

3 'A work that isn't startling is not a work worth making', states the Iittala glassmakers' motto. Iittala, the best-known name in Finnish glass, does indeed produce 'startling work'. Here in the village their museum relates the history of the company through exhibits of its famous 'i-glass'; there are guided tours of the factory. The great crowd puller, however, is the shop, where old stock and slightly flawed seconds (very often of favourite classic designs) are sold at a fraction of the retail price. Other manufacturers have similar outlets, which are usually signposted on the main road.

From Iittala continue north on road 3 for 53km (33 miles) to Tampere; see Tour 24. From Tampere take road 11 west for 114km (71 miles) to Pori.

Pori

4 Created as a port on the Gulf of Bothnia in 1558, Pori saw the sea slip away as the land rose, gradually transforming it into an inland port on a river. As sail gave way to steam Kristinestad – the great port of the

19th century – declined in favour of Pori which, thanks to its deep-water harbour, was able to cope with the modern trans-Atlantic vessels. Pori is primarily an industrial town, but it is internationally renowned for its excellent Jazz Festival, held every summer on the river island of Kirjurinluoto.

Twenty kilometres (12 miles) out of town, beyond the resort of Meri-Pori, on a narrow spit of land, is the long sand beach of Yyteri.

ⓘ Court House, Hallituskatu 9A

From Pori follow road 8 south for 47km (29 miles) to Rauma.

Rauma

5 In 1991 the wooden town of Old Rauma was the first Finnish site to be placed on the Unesco World Heritage list of important cultural monuments. It is an honour Old Rauma wears proudly, and its 600 residents – Rauma as a whole has a population of around 40,000 – lovingly care for their charming wooden town. Old Rauma's last major fire was in 1682 and many of the buildings date from the late 17th century. During the 18th century a toll barrier surrounded the town, virtually preventing outward construction; when restrictions eased in the 19th century the town expanded by several blocks and today Old Rauma covers 30 hectares (74 acres), making it the largest 'living' wooden town in Scandinavia.

The town centres around the busy market square, and the tourist office located here provides a map with a suggested walk route incorporating the main sights along the quaint lanes. Also found in the market square is the **local museum**, housed in the old Town Hall; exhibits

The Garum Superb masher ordered by Lenin is displayed at the Bonk Museum

include models of old ships and bobbin lace, reminders of the activities for which Rauma was famed. The pretty **cottage of Kirsti** (Pohjankatu 3) shows the living conditions of an ordinary 18th/19th-century sailor and his family.

ⓘ Market Place, Old Rauma; Valtakatu 2

Leave Rauma on road 8, but then bear right on the coastal road (196) through Reila and Pyhäranta to Uusikaupunki (47km/29 miles).

Uusikaupunki

6 Founded in 1617, Uusikaupunki is one of Finland's oldest towns – the tenth oldest to be precise – but it is probably better known by its Swedish name of Nystad (New Town). In 1721 the Treaty of Nystad was signed here, concluding the Northern War and gaving Russia prize Baltic possessions. The town, with its mixture of old and new, has a pleasant feel. Its main attractions are the cluster of old red **windmills**, the 17th-century **church**, the modest **maritime museum** and the waterfront **promenade** alongside the old wooden salt-houses – which are now small shops selling nautical bric-à-brac. The nearby **Bonk Museum** displays some of the extraordinary machines invented by the Bonk Business Inc over the past 100 years. The success of the company was based on the discovery by Per Bonk – an adopted son of a boatbuilder from Uusikaupunki's archipelago – that the anchovy oils he was using in Garum Superb, the highly popular and potent brand of relish he was producing from the marinated flesh and fins of the Baltic anchovy (*Engraulis baltica*), could also serve as a lubricant for machines. After exploiting the native anchovy species to virtual extinction, Bonk began to import the giant Peruvian anchovy (*Engraulis Ringens*

SCENIC ROUTE

6 Heading north from Uusikaupunki, the coast road 1974 runs along the ring of islands to **Pyhämaa**. Ruotsinvesi, the expanse of water to the right, was where Per Bonk used to catch his Baltic anchovies. Today it is cordoned from the open sea and provides sweet water. Merchants from Europe traded here in medieval times and brought their religion with them; Christianity is thought to have entered Finland through these islands, hence the name Pyhämaa, or Helgoland (Swedish), meaning Holy Land. The wooden church, with its painted walls and ceiling, replaced the more modest place of worship around 1650. You can return to the mainland on road 1973 which meets the 196, the road back to Uusikaupunki.

gig) to oil the wheels of his fast-expanding industry. Exhibits at the museum include a Garum Superb masher ordered by Lenin and the original 1893 Anchovy Feeding Barrow, which would dispense into the anchovy pools a special mixture of krill, lava dust and sea cucumber; the fish were trained to start feeding on hearing the sound of the barrow's bell. In addition to Bonk, Uusikaupunki is home to a Saab car factory, where a collection of old Saab automobiles can be visited.

The composer Berndt Henric Crusell was born in the town in 1775 and the Crusell Week music festival is held every summer in his memory.

[i] Rauhanpuisto Park (summertime location)

From Uusikaupunki continue on road 196 through Taivassalo (noted for its church with frescoed interior) and around the bay on roads 192 and 193 to Askainen and the manor house of Luohisaari (65km/40 miles).

Luohisaari, Askainen

7 The mid-17th-century manor of Luohisaari, beautifully set in meadows and parklands, was the birthplace of Carl Gustav Mannerheim (1867–1951). Marshall Mannerheim was the country's great soldier and leader at a time when Finland had to stand firm – on both the battlefield and at the negotiating table – in order to maintain its independence and democracy against powerful Russian neighbours. Mannerheim became president of Finland in 1944, relinquishing the post two years later due to illness. There are guided tours around the manor and visitors are free to wander the estate.

From Luohisaari continue southwards for 11km (7 miles) to Merimasku and take the short free ferry trip. Continue ahead for 4km (2 miles) and then bear left for Naantali (7km/4 miles).

FOR CHILDREN

8 In 1993 the Moomin family moved to the small island of **Kailo**. Here these very popular polar hippo-like characters – the creation of Finnish writer, Tove Jansson – set up a village, and children are invited to visit them in Moomin Valley and to join them in their adventures around their island. There is a children's theatre and various organised activities, including a raft trip to the nearby pirate island of Vaskin. The world of the Moomins is reached on foot by bridge from Naantali.

Naantali

8 The building of the Convent of the Order of St Birgitta on this lovely spot in southwest Finland was completed in 1462. Pilgrims flocked here and around it grew the town of 'Valley of the Grace' ('Nadhendal' in old Swedish and thus 'Naantali'). As the convent began to decay after the Reformation so, too, did the town. Previously the citizens had prospered through business with the pilgrims; now they relied on making socks, the only skill they had learnt from the nuns. At one time Naantali exported 30,000 pairs of socks a year, with both sexes and all ages involved in the production process. The preoccupation with production was total and a law had to be passed to stop groups of more than six people forming their knitting groups in the lanes, a practice that had hitherto caused obstruction and traffic congestion. Despite the brisk trade, time in Naantali stood still; the clock on the old tower was painted with the hands set at 11.30 because of a superstition that the world would come to an end at 12. That idiosyncracy has gone, but the new custom of playing a trumpet rendition of Vespers – a Protestant habit imported from Germany – has been introduced and is played at 8pm every summer's evening.

The **convent** building was restored in 1963 and is once again the focal point of Naantali. Business has returned to the old lanes as tourists have replaced the pilgrims. The wooden houses, dating from the 18th and 19th centuries, replaced those destroyed by the fire in 1628; the street layout, however, is original, preferred by the citizens to the new plans on offer. With its attractive waterside location so close to Turku, Naantali developed into a spa resort and today it is a fashionable weekend retreat – the president has his summer residence here at **Kultaranta**, a 56 hectare (138 acre) estate with a fine rose garden (guided tours).

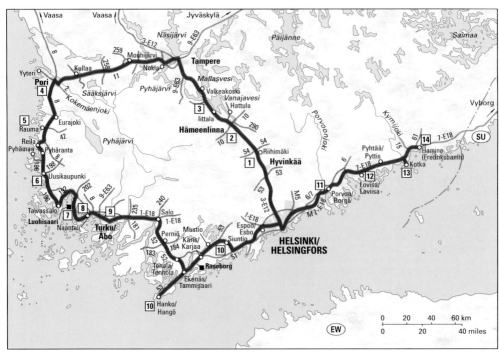

A Moomin couple at home on the small island of Kailo, reached on foot by a bridge from Naantali

ℹ️ Kaivotori 2

From Naantali it is 10km (6 miles) to downtown Turku.

Turku (Åbo)

9 Turku was the gateway for the Swedish conquest of Finland. The city was given its charter in 1525, making it the country's oldest town, and it served as the capital until 1809; a year later Sweden signed Finland over to the Russians and the seat of power was shifted to Helsinki.

Turku is the country's second largest city and continues to function as a major port (including several daily ferry crossings to Stockholm). The Swedish legacy is all around and this is the only place in Finland with a Swedish-speaking university.

The huge 13th-century brick **cathedral** – the most significant medieval building in the country – is surrounded by the old town, the greater part of which post-dates 1827, the year the Great Fire destroyed most of the city; small parks were subsequently planted to prevent the spread of future fires. Among the buildings of this district is the **Sibelius Museum**, with a large collection of musical instruments. A 10-minute walk downstream is the **Wäinö Aaltonen Museum** with works by that sculptor; the **Turku Art Museum**, at the top of Aurakatu, exhibits a comprehensive collection of Finnish art. Moored near by are the **Sigyn**, a barque from 1887, and the **Suomen Joutsen**, a 1902 French cargo vessel; both ships are museums.

Three kilometres (2 miles) downstream from the old town, the **castle** dates from the 1280s and is the largest in Finland; it has been superbly restored and the history of the city – indeed the country – is effectively displayed in a maze of rooms on many floors. The district of Vartiovuori Hill survived the Great Fire and 30 houses here have been converted into the **Luostarinmaki heritage craft centre**.

ℹ️ Aurakatu 4

From Turku take the E18 east for 52km (32 miles) to Salo and bear southeast on road 52, via Perniö and Tenala (Tenhola) – both with medieval churches of note – to Ekenäs (Tammisaari) (45km/28 miles). From here continue southwest on road 53 for 35km (22 miles) to Hanko (Hangö).

Hanko (Hangö) and the road to Helsinki

10 Hanko Cape, a long narrow peninsula protruding into the Baltic, is Finland's most southerly point. It has long been valued for its strategic location – forts have been built here and they have suffered bombardment many times, including once at the hands of the British Royal Navy in 1854, during the Crimean War. Hanko's role as a port developed with the laying of the railway from Helsinki in 1874 and it served as the main point of exit for

Finns emigrating to America up until the late 1920s. During the Winter War, Hanko was ceded to the Russians, though the following year, 1941, it was won back with great loss of Russian life.

Today, Hanko is as popular with tourists as it had been with the tsars – and it has sand beaches and the largest yacht marina in Finland. This stretch of coast, with its islands and inlets, is very scenic and a favorite place for the people of Helsinki to escape to at weekends.

Return to **Ekenäs**, a fishing village which Gustav Vasa had hoped would rival Reval (present Tallin) when he gave it a town charter in 1546. The great future never materialised and Ekenäs – 'the Island of Oaks' – has remained small; it retains a pleasant 18th- to 19th-century wooden quarter.

Eight kilometres (5 miles) further along road 53, a turning to the right leads to Snappertuna and the sturdy medieval **Raseborg Castle** on a rock over the river. Continue along the 53 to enter the old iron-ore districts, with a history of mining dating from the 16th century; the region grew prosperous on its deposits, a fact reflected in the number of manor houses. The area is similarly rich in churches, one of note being **St Lawrence's** (21km/13 miles from Mustio on road 53) with its fine 16th-century frescos.

Return to the coast via Siuntio and rejoin road 51 (27km/17 miles). Continue east for 28km (17.5 miles) to Espoo (Esbo), a smart residential district outside Helsinki which has more recently become a fast-growing dormitory town for the capital. Artist Akseli Gallen-Kallela

SPECIAL TO...

9 The long-distance runner, Paavo Nurmi (1887–1973), was born and bred in the town of Turku. Competing in three Olympic Games he won nine gold and three silver medals; he set 31 world records during his lifetime. The statue of Nurmi on the riverfront is by Wäinö Aaltosen (1894–1966), Finland's most celebrated sculptor whose works can be seen at the nearby museum which bears his name.

SCENIC ROUTE

9 One of Finland's greatest scenic sights is the archipelago off the southwest coast, stretching to Åland (and beyond – submerged – to link with the Stockholm archipelago). A ferry trip out to some of the islands – there are an estimated 41,000 in all – is a lovely way to spend a sunny day. There are services from Turku as well as from other harbours along the coast.

(1865–1931) – probably the most widely known Finnish artist – built his art nouveau villa studio on a hill between Espoo and Helsinki; it is now a **museum** about the man and his art. The distance from Espoo to downtown Helsinki is about 19km (12 miles).

🔲 Bulevardi 10, Hanko; Itatuulenkuja 11, Espoo

At this point in the tour, an optional extension can be taken east from Helsinki along the coast towards the Russian border.
From Helsinki take the E18/M7 for 50km (31 miles) to Porvoo.

Porvoo (Borgå)

11 Founded in 1346 by King Magnus Eriksson as a defensive site near the mouth of the Porvoonjoki (Borgå – its Swedish name – means 'Castle River'), Porvoo is Finland's second oldest town. To the south of the castle site is the town's old quarter, centred around the cathedral and leading down to the riverfront where there is a pretty row of boathouses. Although much of this district was rebuilt after a fire in the 18th century, the medieval street plan was adhered to and, with its many wooden houses, it is the most charming part of Porvoo.

South of Mannerheiminkatu is the Empire-style town built at the request of Tsar Nicholas I by Carl Ludvig Engel, the architect responsible for the buildings around Helsinki's Senate Square. National poet Johan Ludvig Runeberg lived on Aleksanterinkatu between 1852 and 1877.

🔲 Rauhankatu 20

From Porvoo continue on the E18 for 40km (25 miles) to Lovisa.

Lovisa (Loviisa)

12 The Swedes built Lovisa in 1745 as a garrison town and named it after their queen, Lovisa Ulrika. Briefly gaining popularity as a spa resort, it burnt down in the mid-19th century and was redesigned in the Empire style by George Chiewitz; the new, elegant Lovisa proved even more fashionable, and it is still attracting Helsinki folk today.

🔲 Aleksanterinkatu 1

From Lovisa continue on the E18 for 45km (28 miles) to Kotka.

Kotka

13 Built on an island in the estuary of the River Kymijoki, Kotka has long provided a link between the coast and the interior. The original 18th-century town was destroyed by the British during the Crimean War in 1855 and present-day Kotka is relatively modern, dating from 1878. The **Orthodox church**, consecrated in 1795, remains from that period and is Kotka's oldest building. In 1889 the Finnish state presented Tsar Alexander III of Russia with a simple fishing lodge at nearby Langinkoski and he and the Imperial family would holiday here; today, less prestigious vistors are welcome.

Modern Kotka is best known as an industrial town and a port for shipping Finland's timber.

🔲 Keskuskatu 17

From Kotka return to and continue on the E18 for 20km (12 miles) to Hamina.

Hamina (Fredrikshamn)

14 The old garrison of Hamina is the last town of note before the Russian border (43km/27 miles) and has a unique octagonal town plan. From the Old Town Hall (1798) in the centre, eight streets radiate to two outer circles. Founded in the 17th century on the site of the earlier town of Vehkalahti, Hamina is also noted for its 18th- and 19th-century buildings which dominate the inner circles. In 1809 the Swedes and Russians signed a treaty here that handed Finland to the Russians. Today Hamina – from *hamn*, meaning harbour in Swedish – is a major port.

🔲 The Flagtower (summer)

Helsinki – Riihimäki	67 (42)
Riihimäki – Hämeenlinna	33 (21)
Hämeenlinna – Iittala	22 (14)
Iittala – Pori	167 (104)
Pori – Rauma	47 (29)
Rauma – Uusikaupunki	47 (29)
Uusikaupunki – Luohisaari	65 (40)
Luohisaari – Naantali	22 (13)
Naantali – Turku (Åbo)	10 (6)
Turku (Åbo) – Hanko (Hangö)	132 (82)
Hanko (Hangö) – Porvoo	178 (110)
Porvoo – Lovisa	34 (21)
Lovisa – Kotka	45 (28)
Kotka – Hamina	20 (12)

The moat and rampart were the first lines of defence before Hämeenlinna Castle

4 days – 1,163km (723 miles)

Ice sculpting at Savonlinna

ℹ Verkatehtaankatu 2, Tampere

*Head northwest out of Tampere and then bear north on road **330** to Kuru (40km/25 miles). Continue on road **337** for 40km (25 miles) to Ruovesi. Finland's great artist, Akseli Gallen-Kallela, had his lakeside studio at nearby Kalela. From Kalela join road **66** and bear left and left again for road **344** to Vilppula (24km/15 miles). Continue on road **347** towards Mänttä, making a slight detour for Joenniemi and the Gosta Serlachius Art Museum, a legacy of the well-known industrialist and home of one of the finest private art collections in Finland. From Mänttä continue on road **58** for 37km (23 miles) to Keuruu, passing en route signs for the Nikolaintalo Liukko farmhouse with its traditional peasants' café. The small town capital of 400 lakes, Keuruu has a wooden church dating from 1758, and the Gosta Serlachius Museum, containing the Akseli Gallen-Kallela painting of* Girl *in Keuruu Church. From Keuruu drive east on road **23** for 28km (17 miles) to Petäjävesi, where the wooden church dating from 1763 is on the Unesco World Heritage List. From Petäjävesi continue on road **23** for 32km (20 miles) to Jyväskylä.*

Jyväskylä

1 Founded by Tsar Nicholas I in 1837, Jyväskylä is situated on a small lake which is joined to Lake Päijänne by a narrow strait. A university city and the provincial capital, it is best known for its unique collection of over 30 **Alvar Aalto buildings**, which include structures as diverse as an apartment block, a theatre, a university, a swimming pool and a museum with an exhibition devoted to the man himself. The most prominent structure, however, is the **water tower** (Vesilinna) from where there are extensive views.

From Jyväskylä there are boat trips on to **Lake Päijänne** and, since the opening of the Keitele-Päijänne Canal for leisure boats in 1994, it is possible to sail from Lahti, on the south shore of Päijänne, to Jyväskylä and then continue into Keitele and its northern shores, a journey of over 500km (311 miles) across beautiful lakes and waterways.

ℹ Vapaudenkatu 38

*From Jyväskylä drive northeast on road **9** (E63), picking up road **23** and continuing to Varkaus (130km/81 miles).*

Varkaus

2 Since the first saws ripped into action in the last century, Varkaus has developed into a major producer of wood pulp and paper. Finland is the most densely forested country in Europe, and this central and eastern region is the most heavily wooded area of all. Timber is Finland's source of revenue and busy, modern industrial towns like Varkaus are the

TAMPERE CIRCUIT

**Tampere • Jyväskylä • Varkaus • Savonlinna
Punkaharju • Lappeenranta • Lahti • Tampere**

With an area of about 7,000sq km (2,703sq miles), the Finnish Lakeland covers almost one-third of the country. It is a beautiful region of water, islands – nearly 200,000 of them – and forest. The tour encircles much of the central and eastern lakelands and touches the shores of Finland's two largest lakes, Saimaa (1,300sq km/502sq miles) and Päijänne (1,111sq km/429sq miles). But consider penetrating this circle – maybe even taking a boat trip or a cross-lake ferry to provide a break from the road.

cogs of the national economy.

The Varkaus curiosity – down at the **Museum of Mechanical Music** – is the Goljat orchestrion which weighs 4,000kg (8,800lbs) and sounds like a full symphony orchestra. From Varkaus there are boat services to Savonlinna to the southeast and Kuopio to the north. The nearby monastery of Valamo and convent of Lintula are described on page 111.

ℹ Kermanrannantie 10, Heinävesi

*Carry on along road **23**, turning right on to road **476** after about 31km (19 miles) for Heinävesi. Continue from this popular resort and bear right on the **471** through pretty Enonkoski and the Koloveden Kansallispuisto (Kolovesi national park), with its prehistoric rock carvings, to reach Savonlinna (136km/85 miles).*

Savonlinna

3 **Olavinlinna Castle** was built in the late 15th century by Erik Axelsson Tott, the Swedish governor of Vyborg, to protect Sweden's eastern frontier. Rising from its rocky island, it is the most spectacular medieval fort in Finland and today is a much

SPECIAL TO...

2 With an average of one for every four of the population, saunas are a way of life for Finns and in the past they were even born in them. The sauna is a place to rendezvous and maybe enjoy a meal of sausages cooked on the coals. It is an important culture among a normally introverted people; friends meet together naked, sweat with one another, gently hit each other with birch twigs to open the pores and then – in winter – jump in unison through a hole in the ice (*avanto*) to cool down. The **Museum of the Sauna** at Muurame, 10km (6 miles) south of Jyväskylä, recounts the history of this splendid invention; there are many saunas on show, some dating from the 18th and 19th centuries.

SPECIAL TO...

6 Sära is a delicious Karelian lamb dish which gains its name from the birch trough in which it is roasted. The hind leg of a lamb is salted down for five days and then put into the sära trough which is placed in an oven on pegs of alder. Here it is cooked for up to five hours. The meat should be turned periodically and the surplus fat poured away. Potatoes can also be roasted with the lamb and they should be placed under the meat for the final hour or so. For authentic sära, go to the village of Lemi, 22km (14 miles) west of Lappeenranta.

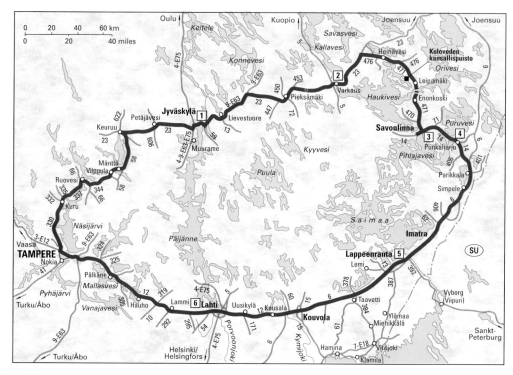

Top, far left: the strong fortifications of Olavinlinna rise from the lake at Savonlinna; today the castle is the venue for opera

Left: the Punkaharju ridge, the suggested path across the Saimaa waters

used venue for a variety of events ranging from the World Ice Sculpting Championships in winter to the Savonlinna Opera Festival (a highlight in the Scandinavian cultural calendar) in summer.

The town has long been a popular resort with the Russians and the most interesting of their villas is the carved wood **Rauhalinna** (a boat ride from town or a 16km/10-mile drive) which Nils Weckman – officer to the tsar – gave to his wife as an anniversary present in 1900.

ⓘ Puistokatu 1

From Savonlinna take road 14 southeast for 28km (17 miles) to Punkaharju.

Punkaharju

4 A relic of the last Ice Age, Punkaharju ridge forms a natural, narrow 7km (4 mile) barrier between two waters, and serves as a causeway between the regions of Puruvesi and Vaistonselka (make sure to follow the signs for the old road to the right). This very scenic stretch of the route is now a nature reserve; attractions of particular interest are the superb **Retretti Art Centre** (located on an island off the northern end of the ridge) and the **Lusto Finnish Forest Museum**, both of which are linked by ferry service to Savonlinna (2 hours).

From Punkaharju continue on road 14 (which joins road 6), via Parikkala and Imatra (with its rapids and border-crossing to Russia), to Lappeenranta (193km/116 miles).

FOR HISTORY BUFFS

6 Work on the Salpalinja (Salpa Line) commenced immediately after the conclusion of the Winter War in 1940. The line stretched from the Gulf of Finland north to Salla in Lappland and was to serve as a fortified trench along the eastern frontier in case of further Russian aggression. Gun bunkers, machine-gun nests, 200km (124 miles) of anti-tank stones and 130km (81 miles) of anti-tank ditches provided extra defence.

Work on the line continued into 1941 and, after a lapse, was resumed in 1944. At one stage 35,000 men were involved in the construction; the first to take up shovel and pick were a group of 900 Swedish volunteers who even paid for the building materials they used. The line never saw action, however; perhaps its very existence served as a deterrent. Today it can be seen in different states of repair, running parallel to the border. The strongest section of the wall is between the gulf and Lake Saimaa, and is best visited at the Korsukukkula Museum at Miehikkälä, between Lappeenranta and Virojoki.

SPECIAL TO...

6 About 4,000 years ago, a period of geological turbulence created a ridge which cut off Saimaa's access to the sea. Of the fauna left stranded in the new 'lake', some died out, while others, such as the ringed seal and Arctic char, adapted. Today there are an estimated 160 ringed seals in the lake, producing about 20 young a year.

FOR HISTORY BUFFS

6 Lappeenranta's history is integrally linked with its frontline position. With the conclusion of the Great Northern War in 1721, Sweden and Russia agreed to fix the frontier roughly along its present line. Lappeenranta thus became an important garrison town on Sweden's eastern border. A clash between the two super-powers in 1741, however, led to Swedish defeat and the burning down of Lappeenranta. The frontier subsequently moved further west to the Kymijoki (River Kymi) and the town became a border defence for the Russians. When Sweden lost the rest of Finland in 1809 – and the Russian Grand Duchy was born – Lappeenranta's strategic importance was temporarily ended.

Finland gained independence from Russia in 1917, but peace did not last long. With the Winter War of 1939–40 Lappeenranta once again found itself on the borderline. Russia demanded bases on Finnish soil and Finland was forced to cede Viipuri (1944) and parts of Karelia. Rather than be part of Russia, many thousands of Finns fled west as the frontier was redrawn along its present line. Karelia was split into east (Russian) and west (Finnish), causing the separation of many families; only now, with the fall of Communism, has it been possible for eastern Karelians to travel back to their old homes and visit the relations they left behind.

Lappeenranta

5 Merchants from Vyborg (Viipuri) travelled to the stage post of Lapvesi, on the southern shore of Lake Saimaa, to trade for tar. Business flourished and in 1649 Governor Per Brahe founded the town of Lappeenranta. Its proximity to the Russian border ensured that the settlement developed as a garrison town, until the discovery of mineral waters in 1824 transformed it into a spa resort favoured by Russian aristocrats. Attempts to build a canal between Lake Saimaa and Vyborg date from 1499, but it was in 1856, during the time of Tsar Alexander II, that the link between the lake (at Lappeenranta) and Vyborg was finally completed. Of its total length of 43km (27 miles), 23km (14 miles) are in Finland and 20km (12 miles) are in territory leased from Russia; the 76m (249 feet) drop in height between lake and gulf is levelled out by eight locks. A Russian entry permit is required for the one/two day canal trip to Vyborg; the paperwork can be arranged in four days by the tourist office in Lappeenranta.

In the heart of the downtown area is a cemetery with the graves of Karelians who died fighting the Soviet Union between 1941 and 1944. At the other end of the cemetery is the 18th-century **Lappee church** with its free-standing belfry. The fort, now the **Old Town**, became redundant after Finland became a Grand Duchy of Russia with the signing of the treaty of 1809. Known as Linnoitus, the whole complex dates from the 18th and 19th centuries, and the buildings have now been converted into museums – including the **Cavalry Museum**, the **South Karelian Museum** (which has a comprehensive exhibition on Vyborg, or Viipuri

The cavalry still guard Lappeenranta

as it was during Finnish times) and the **South Karelian Art Museum**.

Dating from 1785, the **Orthodox church** is the oldest in Finland; next to it are craft shops and the famous **Majurska's coffee house**, housed in the old officers' mess. The pleasant waterfront is below the fort. Every day two mounted soldiers make a round of this district to ensure there is peace in Lappeenranta, a symbolic gesture reminding us of the town's past as a pawn in the hands of greater powers.

i Bus Station

From Lappeenranta take road 6 west for 85km (53 miles) to Kouvola and then continue for 61km (38 miles) on road 12 to Lahti.

Lahti

6 The modern city of Lahti is famous in Finland as a centre for sport. Finns seem to excel at ski-jumping and the splendid facilities here are undoubtedly a contributing factor to their success. Lahti is also a 'port of entry' into the world of Finland's central lakeland. There is a ferry service north through lovely long (120km/75 miles) Lake Päijänne; it is a 10-hour ride to Jyväskylä.

i Torikatu 3B

From Lahti continue northwest for 126km (78 miles) to Tampere.

Tampere – Jyväskylä 204 (127)
Jyväskylä – Varkaus 130 (81)
Varkaus – Savonlinna 136 (84)
Savonlinna – Punkaharju 28 (17)
Punkaharju – Lappeenranta 126 (78)
Lappeenranta – Lahti 146 (91)
Lahti – Tampere 126 (78)

2 days – 424km (263 miles)

Vaasa, on the Gulf of Bothnia

[i] Hovioikeudenpuistikko 11

From Vaasa follow the signs for Old Vaasa (Gamla Vasa), about 6km (4 miles).

Old Vaasa

1 In 1606 Sweden's Karl IX founded Vaasa on the coast at the site of the 14th-century castle of Korsholm. Ironically its increasing success as a port led to its destruction during the 'rising of the resentful' in the Great Hate of 1715, and many a Swede fled back to the motherland. However, the city was reconstructed and prospered once again: a school, hospital and library were built and in 1794 the splendid Gustavian-style Court of Appeal was opened. By the mid-19th century the population had risen to 3,200 but during the fire of 1852 all except the Court of Appeal – now the Korsholm (Mustasaari) church – and Wasastjerna's manor (now a museum) were razed. The ruined stumps and shells of the old ramparts, the 14th-century St Mary's church and several other buildings give some idea of the size and status of the city. By now the sea had receded and the new Vaasa was built on the new coast 6km (4 miles) away; it was officially inaugurated in 1862. The church of Korsholm (Mustasaari) is now a venue for the Music Festival Korsholm which highlights Scandinavian chamber music.

From Old Vaasa cross the main E12 on to road 673 for Sulva (road 6741) and Stunders, 4km (2 miles).

Vaasa market

VAASA CIRCUIT

Vaasa • Old Vaasa • Stunders • Kristinestad (Kristiinankaupunki) • Seinäjoki • Jakobstad (Pietarsaari) • Vaasa

Vaasa is the closest point to Sweden across the Baltic and there are ferry services between here and Umeå (4 hours) and Sundsvall (8 hours). The Swedish influence has long been strong on this coast of Ostrobothnia – Vaasa was named after the Swedish royal family of Vasa who built the original city in the 17th century during their occupation of Finland. Place names are commonly written in both their Finnish and Swedish versions: while one can discern that Vaasa and Vasa (Swedish) are one and the same place, less obvious is the fact that Pietarsaari is Jakobstad. Of the ten municipalities in the Vaasa region, six are Swedish speaking and four are Finnish speaking, while one third of the city's population is Swedish speaking; further down the coast the villages of Korsnäs and Närpes are almost exclusively Swedish in tongue. The tour turns inland from the once thriving port of Kristinestad and in this farming hinterland the character is predominantly 'Finnish'. Seinäjoki – with its Alvar Aalto architecture – is the main town in this interior; the tour continues from here across flat farmlands to the seaport of Jakobstad, before returning along the coast to Vaasa.

SPECIAL TO...

The Swedish influence was strongest on the coast during their period of occupation and it is along here – all the way to the Russian border – that the Swedish town names are most commonly in use.

SPECIAL TO...

1 The lovely cluster of islands and skerries off the coast at Vaasa is a popular weekend retreat. Take road 724 to the north of the city and then cross by ferry (10 minutes) to Replot (Raippaluoto). For the best spots turn left to Sommarö sund at the end of road 7242, alternatively continue on the 724 to Björköby and the Fiskehamn. In a hard winter, when the ice is thick, they say you can drive from here across the Gulf of Bothnia to Umeå.

SPECIAL TO...

1 The Vaasa region is undergoing an extraordinary uplifting experience: the land is rising by 1 metre (3 feet) every 100 years. If the phenomena continues at this speed our descendants will be able to walk from Vaasa to Sweden on dry land in the year 5000.

SCENIC ROUTE

2 While the quickest way from Vaasa to Kristinestad is along road 8, the most scenic route follows the old coast road (673) via Malax and Korsnäs. This stretch of coast is the most 'Swedish' part of Finland; some of the locals speak old Swedish – in Korsnäs for example – which even the Swedes find difficult to understand! Much of the route is through forest and it is necessary to take turnings to the right to reach the small fishing villages. Places of note along the way include Malax-Åminne, Bergö Island, Korsnäs, Harrström, Nämpnäs and its harbour, Närpes (Närpiö) with its tomatoes and the parishioners' old stables and huts by the church – and Kaskinen (Kaskö).

Stunders

2 History lives on in Stunders. Throughout Scandinavia communities have· dug deep into their past and now present their roots: wherever you are you will find heritage-handicraft villages comprising old dwellings, with locals often dressed in folk costumes, working at traditional crafts and engaged in time-honoured pastimes. Gunnar Rosenholm created Stundars in 1938 and it has grown into a village of about 50 old buildings where traditional Östrobothnian culture is on display.

The old coast road (673) is the more scenic but longer way to Kristinestad. For the quickest route south rejoin the E12 and bear east, turning south on road 8 for Kristinestad, 94km (58 miles).

Exploring the waters around the town of Jyväskylä

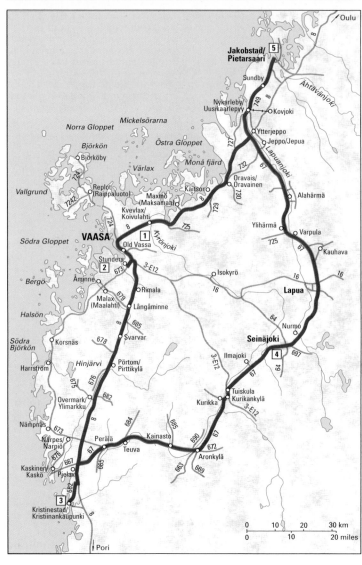

Kristinestad (Kristiinankaupunki)

3 In 1649 Per Brahe, the Swedish Governor of Finland, was granted permission by Queen Kristina to build on the Finnish coast. He called his town Kristinestad in honour of both his queen and his wife, who, by happy coincidence, shared the same name. During the glorious age of the sail ship in the mid-19th century, Kristinestad was one of the largest ship-building yards in Finland (300 barques were built between 1850 and 1890); it was also a significant port – tar was the main export – and had its own merchant fleet comprising 50 vessels. There was a bar in present Kattpiskargränden where the shipbuilders would drink, and brawls between the Finnish labourers and the Swedish workers,

The carefully preserved interior of the Lebell House, Kristinestad

who were from the nearby village of Skaftung, often ensued. During these skirmishes the Finns would boast their superiority, but they had a problem articulating 'Skaftung', which they pronounced 'Kattung' (Swedish for kitten), and henceforth the street became known as Kattpiskargränden, meaning the 'Katt beating street', with 'Katt' referring to the Swedish boys from Skaftung.

A delightful small **shipping museum** recounts Kristinestad's great maritime past which began to decline with the emergence of the steam vessels, and a large model of the sail ship *Alma* can be seen in the café by the waterfront. Unlike so many Swedish towns, Kristinestad did not suffer from a major fire and several interesting old wood buildings still stand on Brahe's original grid of straight streets. The

SPECIAL TO...

3 It is claimed that Kattpiskargränden is, with a width of 299cm (117inches), the third narrowest lane in Finland. Kitukränn in the old town of Rauma is said to be the narrowest at 213cm (84 inches).

4 The **Old Church of Isokyrö** – just off road 16, about halfway between Vaasa and Seinäjoki – dates from 1304. In the 1560s the dean, Jaakko Geet, paid out of his own pocket to have Biblical scenes painted on the walls. A hundred years later the prelate residing at the time found them distasteful and had the walls covered in whitewash. It was not until 1885 that the paintings were rediscovered.

4 In 1902 a 12km (7 mile) narrow-gauge (600mm/24 inches) rail track was opened from Kovjoki main line station to the port of Nykarleby. The rolling stock comprised two American Baldwin locomotives and passenger and freight cars. The line was closed in 1916, but 70 years later a group of train enthusiasts reopened 2km (1 mile) of the line and today you can catch a Baldwin loco at Kovjoki station (road 8, east of Nykarleby).

5 The beauty spots of this tour lie along the coast and out in the archipelago. Maxmö (Maksamaa) and its chain of skerries out to Ostero is a suggested stopping point *en route* between Jakobstad and Vaasa. Jean Sibelius was married here in Tottesund Manor in 1892.

1700 crooked wooden **church of Ulrika Eleonora** – which is slowly slipping on subsiding earth – is particularly charming. Also well worth a visit is the caringly preserved **Lebell house**, home of a middle-class family during the height of Kristinestad's prosperity in the 18th and 19th centuries. There are rooms in the rococo and Gustavian styles, plus the sofa where both Sweden's King Gustav IV Adolf and Russia's Tsar Alexander I sat (at different times, when their respective countries held sway over Finland).

Just north of town is the summer **villa of Carl Carlstrom**, built in 1896 and now a modest museum with a collection of children's toys in the old playroom.

ℹ Café Alma (summertime location)

From Kristinestad return to road 8, turn north, then branch off northeastwards on road 67 to Teuva (35km/22 miles), and then Seinäjoki, a further 70km (43 miles).

Seinäjoki

4 The main reason for stopping in Seinäjoki is to see the complex designed by Alvar Aalto – Finland's most celebrated architect – which includes the **Town Hall**, **Library** and **Cross of the Plains church**. Aalto (1898–1976) started his career in Jyväskylä – where there is a museum to the man – and one of his first works was **Kauppakatu 17** here in Seinäjoki; the building dates from 1920 and is now a rather interesting museum about the Voluntary Civil Guard; it includes an exhibition about the Lotta Svärd (Women's Guard).

ℹ Kirkkokatu 6

Sunsets in this part of the world are frequently dramatic

From Seinäjoki continue on road 67 north to Nykarleby (Uusikaarlepyy) to pick up road 749 to Jakobstad (Pietarsaari), 117km (73 miles).

Jakobstad (Pietarsaari)

5 An old trading town with links across the Gulf of Bothnia, Jakobstad is also a ferry port with a service to the Swedish city of Skellefteå. Most of Jakobstad burnt down in the mid-1800s, but the **Norrmalm quarter** – better known as Skata – survived reasonably intact and is now one of Finland's largest and best-preserved old wooden towns.

Finland's national poet, Johan Ludvig Runeberg – sometimes dubbed the peasant poet – came from Jakobstad (and was a schoolboy in Old Vaasa). A more recent son of the city, however, is Pentti Kronqvist whose **Nanoq** (the name for a polar bear in Greenland) **Museum** on the edge of town is, with its collection of Arctic paraphernalia, his tribute to the indigenous peoples of the far north. Jakobstad's 20,000 population is fairly evenly divided between Swedish and Finnish speakers.

ℹ Rådhusgatan 7, Jakobstad

From Jakobstad return via Nykarleby to join road 8 for Vaasa (98km/61 miles).

Vaasa – Old Vaasa 6 (4)
Old Vaasa – Stunders 4 (2)
Stunders – Kristinestad 94 (58)
Kristinestad – Seinäjoki 113 (70)
Seinäjoki – Jakobstad 117 (73)
Jakobstad – Vaasa 98 (61)

The green domes and golden crosses of the Orthodox church at Joensuu

From Kuopio travel north on road 5 to Siilinjarvi (22km/14 miles); turn right and follow road 75 northeast to Savikylä and continue to Nurmes (105km/65 miles).

Nurmes

1 On the northern shore of Pielinen, Finland's fifth largest lake and one of its most beautiful (if that is possible to gauge) – Nurmes was founded by Tsar Alexander II as a point on the waterway route from St Petersburg north into deep Finland. The spirit of Karelia can be found at **Bomba House**, a Karelian village and tourist complex dating from 1978. There are handicrafts for sale, but the best reason for coming here is the lunch buffet of traditional Karelian food.

From Nurmes take road 73 southeast to Lieksa (56km/35 miles).

Lieksa

2 The **Lutheran church**, completed in 1982, was designed by Raila and Reima Pietila (the architects of the Reider Sarestoniemi studio near Kittila in Lapland); 70 older buildings are on display at the **Pielinen Heritage Museum**. Savotaranta is Finland's largest forestry museum.

From Lieksa take road 73; soon after, bear left on road 522 via Pankakoski and continue on the eastbound road following its loop as it runs parallel to the Russian border through remote Finnish Karelia to Ilomantsi (134km/83 miles).

Ilomantsi

3 Ilomantsi, the country's most eastern town (further east than St Petersburg) is the spiritual and cultural centre for Karelians in Finland. This was where Elias Lönnrot met Mateli Kuivalatar, Karelian folk singer, shaman and provider of a substantial number of poems used in Lonrot's collection of *Kanteletar*.

In addition to the regular ferries there is always the option of private excursions

KUOPIO CIRCUIT

Kuopio • Nurmes • Lieksa • Ilomantsi • Joensuu Valamo • Kuopio

The tour encircles a lovely area of the northern central lakelands with the attractive 'lake town' of Kuopio in the west and the remote road along the Russian border to the west. The Karelian culture and the Orthodox church are evident throughout the region and most conspicuously at Ilomantsi, a centre for all things Karelian. Trees dominate the roadsides – as they do in most of Finland. As a pleasant break from driving, consider taking a boat trip across Lake Pielinen to Koli, from where there is a panorama across forests and lakes towards Russia.

The old customs are still practised – the celebrating of *prazdniks* (religious festivals), the playing of the stringed *kantele*, the wearing of traditional costumes, the cooking of favourite Karelian food. Things Karelian are currently fashionable in Finland and while some of what you see at Ilomantsi may seem contrived for tourists, there is, none the less, a genuine pride in displaying the culture. For heritage and handicrafts visit **Parppeinvaara Hill** on the south side of town; the famous Karelian songs and Kantele music is performed at the **Runonlaulajan Pirtii** (Bard's House).

SPECIAL TO...

2 It is possible to raft down the Ruunaankosket (**Ruuna Rapids**), which involves a drop of 15.7m (51.5 feet) over six rapids stretching along 31km (19 miles) of river. The journey starts 25km (16 miles) east of Lieksa. Go south along road 73, left on 522 and left again at Pankakoski. Boats – and boatmen are available; allow 3 to 4 hours for the ride.

SCENIC ROUTE

2 From Leiksa head south on road 73, bearing right on the 5071 which leads down to Lake Pielinen and Vuonislahti, about 30km (19 miles). From here follow the signs to the **studio and Forest Church of Eva Ryynanen** (Paateri). Ryynanen is a wood sculptor from Leiksa who lives and works up in these hills. Her sculptures are highly acclaimed and she is particularly well known for her Forest Church, the wood and glass church next to her studio. Continue with this scenic lake route, rejoining the main 73 near Eno from where it is 32km (20 miles) south to Joensuu.

SCENIC ROUTE

4 Twice a week the steamer M/S *Vinkeri II* departs from the wharf by Joensuu's Town Hall and sails up the Pielisjoki through a series of locks into Lake Pielinen, continuing northwards to Koli; it is a 7-hour one-way journey (shorter are the ferry services from Lieksa and Nurmes). Alternatively, drive to Koli along the Nurmes road (number 18), bearing right at Ahmovaara as indicated. Koli National Park covers 11sq km (4sq miles) of predominantly spruce-covered rocky hills with its summit at 347m (1,138 feet). From here you can drive to within a short walk of a high point – the view over Lake Pielinen, dotted with its many islands, is magnificent. Folklore has it that Sibelius was so overwhelmed by the scene that he had his piano carted to the top. In the distance, far beyond the lake, is Russia.

SPECIAL TO...

4 The large 1920s iron-ore mine at Outokumpu, on the Joensuu-Kuopio road 17, is now a museum. On display are parts of the mine, the works and mining gadgetry, including an Atlas-Copco Overhead Loader LM 100.

Right: Koli, overlooking Lake Pielinen, is an unusually high vantage in the flat lakelands

Up until the 15th/16th century all Christians in Karelia were Orthodox; today, here in Ilomantsi, they account for less than 20 per cent of the population. On the north side of town is the **Church of Elijah**, the largest Orthodox church, dating from 1891; the nearby **Lutheran church** is 100 years older. To the east, about 25km (16 miles) down road 500 to Russia, are the 18th-century iron-works of Möhkö. Ore used to be brought from the region's '57 lakes' to feed the foundry; the museum relates the history. On the way you pass Petkeljärvi National Park (Petkeljärven Kansallispuisto).

From Ilomantsi go west on road 74 to Joensuu (73km/45 miles).

Joensuu

4 Attractively situated with water on two sides, Joensuu has a young, modern feel to it. The university town, which is capital of the province of North Karelia, was founded in 1848 by Tsar Nicholas I, who was keen to use the network of natural waterways to probe far into the interior of the north. Joensuu's chief landmark is the huge red-brick towered **Town Hall** down on the River Pielisjoki which was built by Eliel Saarinen in 1914. Here a bridge crosses the river and

provides access to the island of **Ilosaari** (from which people bathe) with its **Museum of North Karelia**, devoted to the land, history and culture of the peoples of this torn region. Joensuu has a grid network of streets: a block inland from the Town Hall is the **Freedom Park**, behind this is the busy market square and two blocks further along is the **Art Museum** specialising in Finnish art from the mid-19th century to the present. Here hangs Albert Edelfelt's *Virginie, La Parisienne*, one of Finland's most famous paintings. Follow the main Koulukatu (Lieksa–Nurmes road) northwards: four blocks up and one to the right is the **church of St Nikolaos**, the town's late 19th-century Orthodox church which has an icon from the St Alexander monastery in St Petersburg. Ten per cent of the population are Orthodox Christians, and though this seems a small fraction, it constitutes 5,000 people, the second largest community of this faith outside Helsinki.

Take road 17 west from Joensuu and after 26km (16 miles) turn left on road 23 and continue for Valamo (45km/28 miles).

Valamo

5 Sergius, a Greek monk, arrived on the island of Valamo in Lake Ladoga in the 12th century. Here he

Brother Stefanus, a novice monk at Valamo monastery, is a recent member of the Orthodox sect founded by brothers Sergius and Herman

and his disciple Herman, a Karelian, established a highly reputable Orthodox monastic community. During the Winter War of 1940, however, the monastery was abandoned as Karelians fled Russia, and the monks settled in Heinavesi, where they founded the present Valamo, consecrated in 1977. Although this is a 'living' monastery, visitors are welcome. The **church** houses icons brought from old Valamo; an icon of special note is the Mother of God of Konevitsa, the greatest treasure of the Orthodox Church of Finland.

Accommodation is available. The canal boat *Sergei* ferries visitors to nearby **Lintula convent**.

Back on the main road (number 23) bear right to Karvio and right again, approaching Kuopio via Mustinlahti and Vehmersalmi.

Kuopio – Nurmes 127 (79)
Nurmes – Lieksa 56 (35)
Lieksa – Ilomantsi 134 (83)
Ilomantsi – Joensuu 73 (45)
Joensuu – Valamo 71 (44)
Valamo – Kuopio 113 (70)

SPECIAL TO...

Karelian pasties are famous and can be found at market stalls throughout east, central and south Finland. Among those to look out for are *supikka, sultsina, tsupukka, vatruska, piirakka* and *kukkonen*.

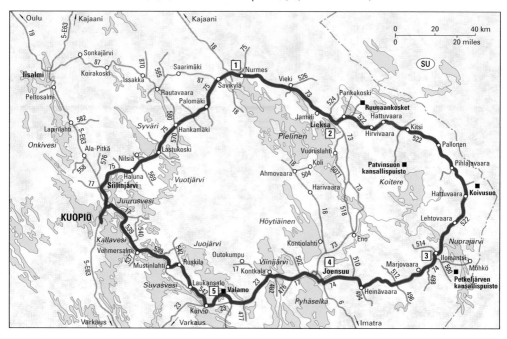

2 days – 345km (214 miles)

KAJAANI

**Kajaani • Suomussalmi • Kuhmo • Sotkamo
Kajaani**

A wilderness of forests, lakes and waterfalls runs along the borderlands with Russia. Tar was made in this deep interior during the 19th century and transported to the coast for export. It was here, to north Karelia, that Elias Lönnrot came in 1833 on his fourth and highly fruitful tour in search of ancient poems. With the emergence of 'Karelianism', these were among the lands which became known as 'Old Finland'. Fresher memories are the first battles of the Winter War of 1939–40 which were fought here on the frontier. Monuments on remote tracks remind us of the war that the rest of the world has forgotten.

SCENIC ROUTE

1 At Saarivaara bear left off the 912 to Kuivajärvi (20km/12 miles) where the **Domnan Pirtti**, a traditionally styled house, was built in memory of Domna Huovinen, a famous ballad singer of the region. This was one of the places Elias Lönnrot stayed while collecting poems on his fourth journey into Karelia. Double back a short distance and then bear south via Veihtivaara to Vartius – the region's only crossing into Russia. Continue parallel to the border, through Landenkylö and along the east side of Lake Anättijärvi to the junction with the 912 just south of Lentiira. Continue to Kuhmo.

i Kirkkokatu 24, Kajaani

*From Kajaani take road **5** (E63) northeast via Hyrynsalmi – with its church and heritage village – and, just before Ämmänsaari, bear right for the neighbouring Suomussalmi (108km/67 miles).*

Suomussalmi

1 The Winter War of 1939–40 was fought intensely along these borderlands and Suomussalmi, a pleasant village at a strategic road junction, was one of the first places to fall to the Russians. The successful counter attack launched by Colonel Hjalmar Siilasvuo is famous in local folklore. The museum at **Raatteen Portti** (Gateway to Raate), on road 912 about 24km (15 miles) east of Suomussalmi, recounts the history of the local battles. The Raate Museum Road (road 9125) continues eastwards to the border and alongside runs the Purasjoki Line. It was along here that the Russians made their offensive – and also their retreat.

i Jalonkatu 1

*From Suomussalmi join road **912** and travel south via Saarivaara to Kuhmo.*

The sound of music at Kuhmo

Kuhmo

2 In a vast forested wilderness miles away from anywhere, the one-time tar town of Kuhmo has arguably the finest concert hall in the country. The white and glass **Kuhmo Arts Centre**, with its splendid wood auditorium, was built as a worthy venue for the increasingly prestigious Kuhmo Chamber Music Festival which is held every summer. Other buildings of note are the **library** (1988), the 19th-century **church** designed by Jacob Rijf (Bell Tower by C L Engel) – which has been restored after bombing during the Winter War – and the nearby **Tuupala collection of traditional houses**. Elias Lönnrot made Kuhmo his base for his poem-searching ventures into remote Karelia. The *Kalevala*, the great Finnish epic poem he compiled, is now portrayed in the **Kalevala Village**; it provides an introduction to old customs and culture

The Winter War was fought along these quiet borderlands near Suomussalmi

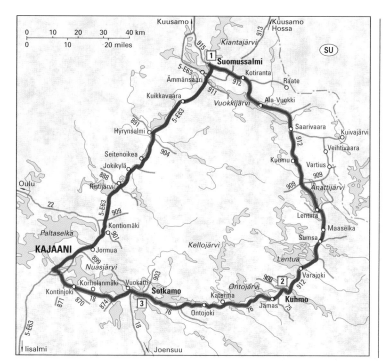

SCENIC ROUTE

1 From Suomussalmi take the road to Hossa (northbound road 913) which runs through the lovely remote countryside parallel to the Russian border; the side road from Juntusranta leading to Lehtovaara near the frontier was the site of early action during the Winter War. On the west side, after Hossa, is the **Julma Olkky canyon lake**. Continue on to Kuusamo, north of which is **Oulanka National Park**, famous for its waterfalls and rapids.

FOR HISTORY BUFFS

2 Some of the grimmest fighting of the Winter War took place between Kuhmo and the Russian border, at battlefields such as Kilpelänkangas and Löytövaara. Casualties were high: an estimated 1,350 Finnish and 10,000 Russian soldiers died in the battles of Kuhmo during that winter of 1939–40.

Above: dusk at eleven in mid-June on latitude 65 N; soon the sun will rise
Left: the port-town of Oulu on the Gulf of Bothnia

1800s the Kuhmo region alone was producing 10,000 barrels of tar a year. These were transported on barges – 22–26 barrels per vessel, 500 vessels each short summer – along the Sotkamo waterway to Kajaani and thereafter into Lake Oulu and down the River Oulu to the port of Oulu on the coast of the Gulf of Bothnia. From here the tar was exported to Sweden and then, very often, to Britain where it was known as 'Stockholm tar'. At one stage the Kuhmo-Sotkamo-Kajaani region was Europe's largest producer of wood tar.

Sotkamo was once voted the second most attractive village in Finland. It, along with nearby Vuokatti (to the west), are the main tourist centres on this stretch of the route.

From Sotkamo drive west to road 18 and continue to Kajaani.

Kajaani – Suomussalmi 108 (67)
Suomussalmi – Kuhmo 129 (80)
Kuhmo – Sotkamo 61 (38)
Sotkamo – Kajaani 36 (22)

BACK TO NATURE

People come to this region to canoe and trek; there is plenty of water and wilderness. The local tourist offices provide maps and information to help visitors find their way around.

which many Finns proudly call their heritage. Further information about the *Kalevala* and about trips into Russian Karelia can be had from the Cultural Chamber (in the fire station).

ⓘ Town Hall

From Kuhmo drive west on road 76 to Sotkamo.

Sotkamo

3 The endless forests in the region fed the tar industry and in the

3 days – 666km (414 miles)

Hopeful visitors panning for precious metal at the gold-mining settlement of Ludakirja

i Koskikatu 1, Rovaniemi

From Rovaniemi head north along the E75 (road 4) to the Arctic Circle and Santa's Workshop Village (8km/5 miles).

Santa's Village (Arctic Circle)

1 Santa is in residence throughout the year and will, for a small price, despatch 'Greetings' in time for Christmas to children of your choice. Lappish handicrafts and other souvenirs are on sale; certificates are awarded for crossing the Arctic Circle.

From Santa's Village continue on the E75 north to Sodankylä (120km/75 miles).

Sodankylä

2 In 1673 the Swedish King Karl XI – then ruler of Finland – initiated his programme to settle Lapland. Along with the pioneers who were encouraged to move north came the missionaries. The church at Sodankylä was built in 1689 – it is one of the oldest wooden churches in Finland – and had a parish which extended 80km (50 miles) to the east and to the west. With its rectangular nave, simple sacristy and high small windows, it is similar in plan to earlier medieval Finnish churches; the gabled roof, however, seems unusually steep. The interior was never painted and the silver sheen is part of the pine's ageing process. The picture of the *Last Supper*, painted by P Bergström, dates from the 17th century. During these times it was quite normal for prominent members of the community to be buried under the church floorboards. According to the parish newsletter, Abraham Cajander – a priest's son who died in the 18th century aged two weeks – is the best conserved of the bodies. In 1859 the nearby stone church was built; the old bell tower was dismantled and the bells taken to the new place of worship. The wood church, however, was left standing. The celebrated paintings of Andreas Alariesto, a Lapp from Sodankylä, depict Lappish life, and an exhibition of his work hangs at a gallery near the churches.

Visit the cluster of **traditional wooden buildings** assembled on the edge of town to gain a further insight into the old ways of the Lapps and the settlers who arrived from the south: the 100-year-old sauna was a place to clean the body as well as smoke the meat; shooting practice took place against the storehouse wall – hence the holes – because the embedded bullets could be salvaged and reused. Sodankylä, at the only east–west junction along this section of the north–south route, is the administrative centre and market town for the region.

i Jäämerentie 9, Sodankylä

From Sodankylä continue north on the E75 to Tankavaara (102km/63 miles).

FAR NORTH

**Rovaniemi • Santa's Village (Arctic Circle)
Sodankylä • Tankavaara • Urho Kekkosen
National Park (UK-Park) • Saariselkä and Ivalo
Inari • Lemmonjoen National Park • Kittilä
Reidar Sarestoniemi Art Gallery • Rovaniemi**

There is a world of vast untainted wilderness north of the Arctic Circle. It is the province of the Lapps, reindeers, gold, the midnight sun and Father Christmas. The tour leads north from Rovaniemi, the main city of Finnish Lappland, via Sodankylä to beautiful Inarijärvi (Lake Inari) and returns southwards on the more westerly route through Kittilä. This is a fairly flat landscape of forest, lake and river; the roads are straight and the settlements are small, few and functional.

Tankavaara

3 Lappland's gold was mentioned in *De Veteribus et Novis Metallis* by Georg Agricola in 1546. However it was not until 1836 that interest in gold really took hold and a team headed north beyond the Arctic Circle in search of the elusive metal. Others followed over the next decades, though the grains of gold discovered were too modest to warrant much excitement, let alone more intense prospecting. None the less the lure of gold persisted and in 1868 a government team led by Johan Lihr, a mining engineer, decided to push up one last river – the part frozen Ivalojoki – before abandoning the expedition. Lihr washed the first pan of earth near the Ritakoski Falls, as he had done a thousand times before on the journey, but this time gold glinted through the gravel. Nineteen panfuls yielded 200 milligrams (3 grains), including a 60 milligram (1 grain) nugget. The government established the first prospecting station at Kultala, just upstream of Ritakoski, and by 1871 500 diggers – as many people, apparently, as the entire population of the 17,000 sq km (6,564 sq mile) Inari district – had been drawn to this remote place in the hope of finding their fortune. According to the records 56kg (123lbs) of gold were collected that year (in fact an estimated three times that quantity was discovered and smuggled out of the country to avoid taxes). The amounts gradually declined, however, and by the end of the century nearly all the prospectors had left. But this was not the end of the story. In 1936 Sauva-Aslak Peltovuoma, an old and crippled

SPECIAL TO...

1 The E75 – the main route through Finnish Lappland and on to Nordkapp (North Cape) – is the path commonly taken by tourists. Lapp souvenirs – silver, the *noaidi* drum, knives, leather, antlers, textiles – can be bought at stalls and shops at places along the way.

SPECIAL TO...

6 North Lappland is the Land of the Midnight Sun. From the end of May to the end of July the sun never sets; there is no darkness, nor dusk. For over a month, starting in December, the sun never rises. This is the *kaamos* period; there is no light, save for the beautiful deep twilight blue of midday. Darkness is relieved only by the shimmering of the extraordinary aurora borealis, the Northern Lights. With spring and autumn – the lovely *ruska* with its golden colours – come skies deeper blue and more translucent than any to be found in lower latitudes.

BACK TO NATURE

6 'Language, customs, traditions, archaeology and literature are good means to get acquainted with Lappland and its people. Yet all in Lappland is influenced by Nature, in one way or another. Only he who has time, humility and maybe also a little love of adventure can come to know the simple beauty of its inmost heart.' Kirsi Kangas

BACK TO NATURE

Instead of wearing socks Lapps used to put hay in their shoes; it kept their feet warm in winter and cool in summer. Tufted sedge and bladder sedge, found on river banks and in wet willow thickets, were the most effective.

SPECIAL TO...

7 'Lapp' is not a native term, and increasingly these indigenous peoples of the north are being called Sami or Saami, the name they call themselves and the one they would prefer others to call them. Lappland, or Sampi, is Finland's northernmost region and about 5,000 of the country's 7,000 Lapps live here. Except for some places in the far north, they are now outnumbered by Finns in nearly all communities in Lappland.

Lapp man, dreamt about gold. He asked his friends to carry him to the site of his dream and there at Lauttaoja creek, at the foot of Tankavaara, they found gold. The rush was on and gold fever struck again. Today there is a **Gold Museum and Village** at Tankavaara and you can try your luck and pan in the nearby stream. Gold is still found here – the gold-panning competition is a popular annual event – and there are 'professional' prospectors who devote much of the time to scouring the surrounding rivers and forests for that big nugget. There is a home for retired prospectors in Inari where, in the cemetery, there are the graves of those who searched until their end.

Next to the Gold Village is the information centre of the Urho Kekkosen National Park.

Urho Kekkosen National Park (UK-Park)

4 UK-Park – covering 2,550sq km (985 sq miles) of Inari, Sodankylä and Savukoski districts between the E75 and the Russian border – came into being in 1983 after a successful campaign to protect this environment from the lumber industry. It was named after Urho Kaleva Kekkosen, president of the day and first to sign this 'Green' petition. In the south are *aapa* boglands, the habitat of a rich birdlife, while further north are the undulating fells of Saariselkä. There are around 750,000 reindeer in the whole of Scandinavian-Russian Lappland, of which about 20,000 – part of three large herds – graze the UK-Park. It is important not to disturb the reindeer, particularly in spring when the females are gestating. Hiking and fishing (permits required) are possible in the park, and for information about trekking routes, lodging in huts and all other relevant matters contact the Guide Hut; a slide show and display of flora and fauna provides an excellent introduction to the wildlife of the park.

From Tankavaara continue on the E75 via Saariselkä to Ivalo, 62km (39 miles).

Road 955 cuts through empty forest; there are few settlements and little traffic

Saariselkä and Ivalo

5 Saariselkä, a modern purpose-built tourist complex and ski resort 30km (18 miles) from Tankavaara, is below Kaunispaa, a 438m (1,437 feet) hill with panoramic views. The small town of Ivalo, the largest centre north of Sodankylä, is a further 32km (20 miles). Beyond, the way, which follows the southeastern shore of Inarijärvi (Lake Inari) to Inari, becomes more interesting and scenic; *en route* a signposted turning to the right leads up a hill to a café and a small museum about fishing in the Inari waters; from here there is a splendid view northwards over the lake.

From Ivalo continue on E75 to Inari, 39km (24 miles).

Inari

6 Situated on a bay overlooking Lake Inari, the town of Inari is a preferable stopping point to the slightly larger Ivalo. During World War II many Lapp settlements were destroyed but some of the wooden huts, houses, granaries, animal traps, an old *savusauna* (chimneyless sauna – air vents were in the wall) and other buildings which survived have been reassembled at the **Sami Museum** in Inari. About 3km (2 miles) along the side road from this Lapp village is a car park from where a delightful 4km (3 mile) walk can be taken through forest and beside lakes (all the more enchanting in the midnight light of summer) to the **Pielpajärvi Wilderness church**. Vicar Josef Wilhelm Durchman had the old church of 1646 restored and he cleared the surrounding land to provide a winter village for Lapps which comprised a cluster of cottages, a sauna and a barn. This small community shifted after a new church was built at Inari at the turn of the century and, once again, the Wilderness church was abandoned. It remains unattended but not neglected – services and weddings are sometimes held here; the door is never locked. The Inari church was destroyed by bombing in 1940; the present church dates from 1951.

A pleasant way to see the lovely Lake Inari – Finland's third largest lake with an area of 1,300sq km (502sq miles) – is by boat.

ⓘ Main street

Inari marks the northern point of this tour. For an extension to Nordkapp (North Cape), continue north from Inari on the E75 and bear left after 26km (16 miles) on to road 4 for Karigasniemi, 66km (41 miles), on the border with Norway. In a further 18km (11 miles) pick up the E6 at Karasjok and follow it north for 138km (86 miles). At Olderfjord continue along the coast on the E69 north to the ferry point, 71km (44 miles). Cross to Honningsvåg, from where it is 43km (27 miles) to North Cape.

Continuing on the tour, turn southwards on road 955 and bear right after about 35km (22 miles) for the final 8km (5 miles) to Lemmonjoki National Park's Guide Hut.

Lemmonjoen National Park

7 The park covers an area of 2,855sq km (1,102 sq miles) west of road 955 to the Norwegian border and is an immense area of beautiful wilderness. When gold was discovered here in the late 1940s Finland experienced its third and last Gold Rush (to date). People still come here every summer hoping for a lucky pan.

There is a reindeer round-up at a spot known as Sallivaara. Some 2,000 years ago the Lapps lived throughout Finland but over the succeeding centuries they gradually migrated northwards, following the herds of wild reindeer. A Chinese source of AD500 records that the people of the far north used 'deer' for transport and dairy products. The traditional fully nomadic lifestyle of the Lapps died out earlier this century. Today the reindeer herds are allowed to migrate within a large but limited area; the herdsman may have one or two permanent homes from where he can keep an eye on his animals. There are two annual round-ups of the reindeer; at midsummer when the calves – which were born in May – are earmarked, and autumn through to January when the slaughtering takes place. The Guide Hut at Lemmenjoen provides full information about the round-ups, trekking, hiring boats, fishing and accommodation.

Return to road 955 and continue south through the forests – there is little more than the occasional farmstead along the way – for the 125km (78 miles) to Kittilä.

Kittilä

8 Kittilä is the main town along this road between Inari and Rovaniemi. There is accommodation and services; the ski resort of Levi is 20km (12 miles) to the north at Sirkka, while 74km (46 miles) to the west is Sweden. Kittilä was home of the 'folk artist' Einar Junttila (1901–75), whose paintings of Lappish nature can be seen at his house.

ⓘ Main street, south end

From Kittilä take road 79 south to Kaukonen, 18km (11 miles), and follow the signs left into the forest for Sarestoniemen

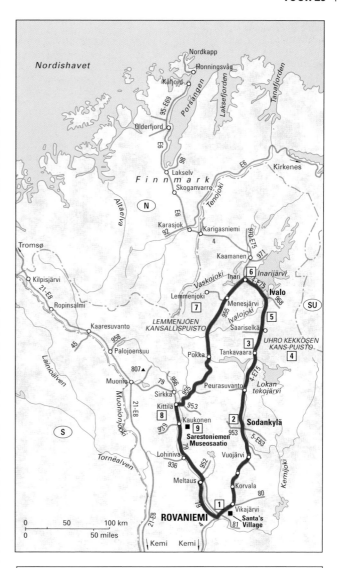

TO CROSS INTO NORWAY
Road 79 west from Kittilä leads to Norway. From Kittilä head for Muonio, 80km (50 miles); thereafter continue on road E8 **(road 21)** along the Finnish-Swedish border to the Finnish-Norwegian border near Kilpisjärvi, 205km (127 miles).

Museosaatio (the Reidar Sarestoniemi Art Gallery).

Reidar Sarestoniemi Art Gallery

9 Reidar Sarestoniemi (1925–81), one of Finland's foremost painters in recent times, spent most of his life here on the farm which bears his family name. However abstract his images, you can feel from the mood of the paintings that his is a very different world from countries further south. The stylish timber art gallery and centre were designed by Raili and Reima Pietila in the 1970s–80s.

Return to the main road 79, from where it is 141km (88 miles) south to Rovaniemi.

BACK TO NATURE

7 'The best season for slaughtering reindeer is late autumn. The reindeer is then fine-looking and sturdy after feasting on mushrooms and lichens. After the slaughtering we boiled the meat from the back of the reindeer and while waiting we roasted the liver and kidneys on a stick – sometimes we boiled them, too. The tongue was boiled in the first soup. The tip of the tongue was cut off, so that the eater would not become a liar. We used to make sausages with reindeer blood fresh from the slaughter. Headcheese was prepared from the head, and hoof brawn (another kind of headcheese) from the hoofs and the entire long shins with meat on them. Dried meat was prepared especially from the reindeer roast. But the best delicacy was the dried side of a fat reindeer, which was roasted on the camp fire, basted from time to time and roasted again.'
Native Lapplander

INDEX

ACKNOWLEDGEMENTS

The Automobile Association wishes to thank the following photographers, libraries and associations for their assistance with the preparation of this book.
BRENDA DRODGE 70/1, 90, 115a; FINNISH TOURIST BOARD, UK OFFICE 95c, 102/3, 105, 106, 109b, 112, 114b; PICTURES COLOUR LIBRARY 68/9; SPECTRUM COLOUR LIBRARY 5, 32a, 50/1, 76b, 79, 80, 84, 85a, 93a, 96, 102a, 108; SWEDISH TRAVEL AND TOURISM COUNCIL 64 (Mark Markefelt), 66a (Anders Ekholm), 66/7 (Tina Buckman), 69 (Bert Persson); ZEFA PICTURES LTD Cover, 66b. The remaining photographs are held in the Association's own library (AA PHOTO LIBRARY) and were taken by Kim Naylor with the exception of pages 9a, 9b, 10, 12, 13a, 22/3, 24a, 24b, 25, 26/7, 27a, 28 and 29 which were taken by Derek Forss and pages 7 and 17 taken by Jesper Westly Jørgensen.
The author would like to thank the following people and organisations for their help during the preparation of the book: the Dansk Kroferie group of Hotels in Denmark; the 71 Nyhavn Hotel in Copenhagen; Rasta Hotels in Sweden; Plaza Continental in Oslo; hotels in Finland operating with the Finncheque system; the Youth Hostel organisations of Scandinavia; Q8 Petroleum in Denmark and Sweden; the Scandinavian Seaways, Silja, Viking, Birka, Gotlandsline and Scandiline ferry companies; the Danish, Swedish, Norwegian and Finnish tourist offices in London and locally throughout their respective countries; and Anna Naylor.
The Automobile Association would also like to thank the following people and organisations for their help during the preparation of this book: the Danish, Swedish, Norwegian and Finnish tourist offices in London; Jane Steffensen, of Forenede Danske Motorejere; and Daina Johansson, of Motormännens Riksförbund.